THE

# RAY SOCIETY.

INSTITUTED MDCCCXLIV.

W. Bagg

LONDON:

MDCCCLVIII.

THE

# OCEANIC HYDROZOA;

A DESCRIPTION OF THE

## CALYCOPHORIDÆ AND PHYSOPHORIDÆ

OBSERVED DURING THE VOYAGE OF H.M.S. "RATTLESNAKE,"

IN THE YEARS 1846-1850

WITH A GENERAL INTRODUCTION

BY

## THOMAS HENRY HUXLEY, F.R.S., F.L.S., SEC. G.S.;

ACAD. IMP. LEOP. CAR. NAT. CUR.; PROFESSOR OF NATURAL HISTORY, GOVERNMENT SCHOOL OF MINES.

EDWARD BOWDITCH LTD

The Oceanic Hydrozoa; A description of the calycophoridæ and physophoridæ observed during the voyage of H.M.S "Rattlesnake," in the years 1846-1850 with a general introduction.

Published by Edward Bowditch Ltd. 2008.
Binding: Paperback

ISBN 13: 978-0-9555528-1-6
ISBN 10: 0955552818

## PUBLISHER'S PREFACE

The Oceanic Hydrozoa is a seminal piece of marked distinction by Huxley, the eminent biologist, nicknamed 'Darwin's bulldog' for his advocacy of Charles Darwin's theory of evolution. This monograph, first published by the Ray Society in 1859, is a description of the Calycophoridae and Physophoridae observed whilst Huxley served as Assistant- Surgeon on the survey vessel HMS "Rattlesnake" in the years 1846-50. The twelve plates at the back of the book have become an invaluable record of the study of the Oceanic Hydrozoa. These plates are also available to download in high resolution colour from our website. Please visit:

www.langtoninfo.co.uk/plates

About the author:

Thomas Henry Huxley (1825 – 1895), the eminent English biologist, was born in Ealing, Middlesex on the 4th of May 1825. Remarkably, Huxley had only two years of formal schooling and therefore taught himself almost everything he knew. At 16, Huxley entered Sydenham College and a year later, he was admitted to study at Charing Cross Hospital, where he obtained a small scholarship. In 1845, Huxley published his first scientific paper demonstrating the existence of a previously unrecognized layer in the inner sheath of hairs, which has subsequently been known as Huxley's layer. On entering the Royal Navy, Huxley was made Assistant Surgeon to HMS Rattlesnake, and joined its voyage of discovery to New Guinea and Australia, devoting his time to the study of marine invertebrates. Later Huxley was able to summarise this work in The Oceanic Hydrozoa.

Huxley's work over his lifetime included researching the relationships between groups of invertebrates and later working on vertebrates, especially on the relationship between man and the apes. Another of his important conclusions was that birds evolved from dinosaurs, a view which is widely held today. He produced a number of important papers on such groups as the Ascidians, the morphology of the Cephalous Mollusca and on brachiopods and rotifers.

Huxley was known as "Darwin's Bulldog" for his advocacy of Charles Darwin's theory of evolution. Huxley's famous 1860 debate with the Lord Bishop of Oxford, Samuel Wilberforce, was a key moment in the wider acceptance of evolution, and in his own career. He was also instrumental in developing scientific education in Britain, and fought against the more extreme versions of religious tradition.

The value of Huxley's work was recognized and, on returning to England in 1850, he was elected a Fellow of the Royal Society. In the following year, at the age of twenty-six, he not only received the Royal Society Medal but was also elected to the Council. In July 1854, having resigned from the Royal Navy he became Professor of Natural History at the Royal School of Mines and naturalist to the Geological Survey in the following year. In addition, he was Fullerian Professor at the Royal Institution 1855–58 and 1865–67; Hunterian Professor at the Royal College of Surgeons 1863–69; President of the British Association for the Advancement of Science 1869–1870; and, later, President of the Royal Society 1883-85; and Inspector of Fisheries 1881-85.

In 1855, he married Henrietta Anne Heathorn (1825–1915), an English emigrée whom he had met in Sydney. They had five daughters and three sons. Huxley died on the 29th June 1895 in Eastbourne, Sussex.

Jenny Shimell BSc

# PREFACE.

"It is the opinion of the Lords Commissioners of the Admiralty that it would be to the honour and advantage of the Navy and conduce to the general interests of Science, if new facilities and encouragement were given to the collection of information upon scientific subjects by the officers, and more particularly by the medical officers, of Her Majesty's Navy, when upon foreign service. . . . . . . . And it will be for their Lordships to consider whether some pecuniary reward or promotion may not be given to those who succeed in producing eminently useful results."[1]

In the autumn of the year 1846, Her Majesty's Ship "Rattlesnake" was commissioned by the late Captain Owen Stanley, who had been charged by the Admiralty with the duty of surveying the intricate passage within the Barrier Reef which skirts the eastern shores of Australia, and of exploring the sea which lies between the northern end of this reef and New Guinea and the Louisiade Archipelago. A very competent naturalist, Mr. J. Macgillivray, was appointed to the vessel, but Captain Stanley, justly appreciating the largeness of the field likely to be opened to students of Natural History by the cruise, desired to increase the strength of his expedition in this department of science. To this end, he applied to Sir John Richardson, at that time the Medical Inspector of Haslar Hospital, to recommend him an assistant-surgeon who should possess some knowledge of Natural History, or who, at any rate, had sufficient zeal and love for it to be likely to convert opportunity into knowledge.

Since the spring of 1846, when I joined the medical service of the Navy, I had been doing duty at Haslar, under the orders of Sir John Richardson, who, always thoughtful and kindly in act, though sparing of words, to his subordinates, had, I suppose, noticed my bent; for, in the summer, I found that, without any solicitation on my part, he had endeavoured to obtain for me an appointment to the Haslar Museum. Failing in this,

[1] Extract from a Memorandum by the Lords Commissioners of the Admiralty prefixed to the first edition of the 'Manual of Scientific Inquiry prepared for the use of Her Majesty's Navy,' edited by Sir J. F. W. Herschel, and published in 1849.

my chief still kept me in mind, and I shall not easily forget the day when, with Captain Stanley's letter in his hand, he came to offer me that share in an exploring expedition which had been one of my childish ambitions, and which afforded the largest scope for the faculties, or, at any rate, the tastes, which had grown up with my manhood.   I need not say how gladly I accepted the proffered appointment.

The "Rattlesnake" sailed in the winter of 1846; and as a full history of her voyage has been given to the world by Mr. Macgillivray, it is needful only to state that, after safely effecting her circumnavigatory voyage and successfully surveying the regions she was sent to explore, the ship returned to England, and was paid off on the 9th of November of the year 1850.

Although occasionally in circumstances which might give rise to anxiety, no serious evil befel the "Rattlesnake," or her crew, until her last return to Sydney, in the spring of 1850, when her Commander, whose health had been shattered by the trying climate of New Guinea, and by the still more wearing responsibilities of his office, sank with lamentable suddenness.

I will not allude to the private circumstances which intensified the sadness of this sudden blow to all who were witnesses of it, but I can truly say that nothing could have been more unfortunate for the scientific interests of the expedition or for the personal welfare of the officers who had performed its duties and shared its fatigues.

Captain Stanley possessed large means of influence, and as it was an eminent virtue of his to stand by his officers, there can be no doubt that, had he lived, his lieutenants, already men of standing and experience, would not have been left for years without promotion; nor would his and their hydrographic labours have been indistinguishably merged in those of other persons; nor would the official naturalist of the expedition have been refused the means of publishing the narrative of the voyage; nor, in all probability, would the present work be making its appearance so many years after date.

In truth it is to the explanation of the circumstance that all the original illustrations in my plates were drawn between the years 1847 and 1850 inclusively, and that all my observations, with the exception of those on *Porpita*, were made so long ago, that I feel it necessary to devote these prefatory remarks.

The facts are these.   I made a good many observations during our cruise, and sent home several papers to the Linnean and Royal Societies; but of these doves, or rather ravens, which left my ark, I had heard absolutely nothing up to the time of my return; and, save for the always kind and hearty encouragement of the celebrated William MacLeay, whenever our return to Sydney took me within reach of his hospitality, I know not whether I should have had the courage to continue labours which might, so far as I knew, be valueless.

On reaching England, however, I found not only that the Royal Society had thought my Memoir on the Medusæ worthy of publication, but helping hands were stretched out to me on all sides; and among the men of science, I met with many generous friends whose sympathy and appreciation were bestowed in a measure far beyond my deserts. Among these, the genial and noble-minded Edward Forbes supported me with all that energy which he was wont to throw into his advocacy of the cause of a young man; and now that I have succeeded (though, alas! not replaced) him in the professorial chair he then held, and have some personal experience of an analogous variety of occupations and weight of responsibilities, I cannot reflect without emotion on the patient attention which he bestowed upon me, and the self-sacrificing zeal with which he exerted all his " power, amity, and authority " in my favour.

On reviewing the materials which I had collected with this experienced friend, it seemed that some of my work might fitly be sent in the form of papers to the learned societies; while, on the other hand, the more copious observations upon the *Medusidæ*, *Calycophoridæ*, and *Physophoridæ*, might better be published in a separate form; and Forbes and other friends of weight were of opinion that the work had sufficient value to justify the Government in aiding its publication.

We were the more readily led to hope for this aid, as, in the year 1849, the Lords of the Admiralty had caused a Manual of Scientific Inquiry to be published, and had prefixed to it a Memorandum containing the enlightened and liberal expressions and promises quoted at the head of these pages. And it will be observed that their Lordships' distinct promise of encouragement to naval officers who should do good work was wholly irrespective and independent of any other aid given by the Government to Science.

Clearly, therefore, supposing my work to have any value—and in favour of this supposition I had all sorts of high testimony—I had a claim upon the Admiralty for aid in bringing it out, and a simple person might have imagined that that claim would be strengthened by being the first that had been made (to my knowledge) since the publication of the Minute.

I do not know that I can accuse their Lordships of refusing my application, for they took the simpler course of rendering it impossible I should make one. Before my ship was paid off, I applied in due form, through my commanding officer, for a simple permission to publish; and, when one thinks of the Memorandum, there is a touch of humour about the reply which he received: " I have been commanded to convey to you their Lordships' full sanction to his (my) so doing (*i. e.* publishing). . . . . . But I have to add that their Lordships will not allow any charge to be made upon the public towards the expense." Nevertheless, the writer hopes that " he will produce a work alike creditable to himself, to his late Captain by whom he was selected for it, and to Her Majesty's Service."

Even could I have flattered myself that I had succeeded in producing "eminently useful results," I fear this letter would have effectually damped any hopes of "pecuniary reward or promotion," or other aid, which I might have formed; but my friends were not content that I should make bricks without straw, and, by dint of considerable exertion, they got me a nominal appointment, so that my assistant-surgeon's pay ran on, while they endeavoured to obtain the £300, required for the publication of my book, from the Government.

It would be wearisome were I to narrate the history of their other efforts at length.   In vain the Presidents of the Royal Society and of the British Association, separately and conjointly, officially and unofficially, solicited the Treasury; in vain did I visit and write to, and I fear, bore, numerous persons in authority about this unfortunate grant.   It must be confessed the business was troublesome enough while it lasted; but, in looking back, I would fain only remember with gratitude the zeal of the friends who aided me, and the long-suffering courtesy of the various Government officials, who listened so attentively to the claims of that Natural Science about which, unless I am greatly mistaken, they neither knew nor cared very much.

During the three years the contest lasted, I reckon that the Admiralty was good enough to give me, in the form of pay, rather more than fifty pounds over the sum required, although, with steady consistency, their Lordships from the first refused to enable me to publish the work which they paid me for publishing.   I by no means quarrel with an arrangement, which, although very annoying at the time, has been of the utmost service to me; for when, in 1854, their Lordships, as I suppose, weary of our pertinacity, cut the knot by calling upon me to serve afloat, new prospects had presented themselves, and, in giving up my commission, I obtained the long-sought funds for publication—the administrators of the Government Grant no longer objecting, that the Admiralty was pledged to supply its officers with funds for the publication of work done in its service.

I offer my hearty thanks to the Government Grant Committee for this aid, and, in conclusion, I must apologise to them and to the Ray Society—who two years ago undertook to publish my book—for the delay which has occurred in bringing it out.   I can only plead the pressure of new and heavy official duties in palliation of my seeming dilatoriness; and I may add that, since 1850, so much has been done by the eminent German observers, whose works are incessantly quoted in the following pages, that the literature of the subject, slight enough when my observations were made, has attained considerable dimensions; and its study has retarded the progress of my book, as much as it has increased my knowledge of the organization of the Oceanic Hydrozoa.   As it is, I have been obliged to omit the *Medusidæ*, which were included in my original plan, and the illustrations of whose organization are already engraved.   I trust that they may yet some day see the light.

# THE OCEANIC HYDROZOA.

## SECT. I. MORPHOLOGY OF THE HYDROZOA.

THE body of every Hydrozoon is essentially a sac, composed of two membranes, an external and an internal, which have been conveniently denominated by the terms *ectoderm* and *endoderm*. The cavity of the sac, which will be called the *somatic cavity*, contains a fluid, charged with nutritive matter in solution, and sometimes, if not always, with suspended solid particles, which performs the functions of the blood in animals of higher organization, and may be termed the *somatic fluid*. The ectoderm is commonly ciliated, at any rate while young; the endoderm is also very generally ciliated, though not always, nor in all parts. The cilia of the endoderm, aided by the contractions of the walls of the body, are the sole means provided by nature for the circulation of the nutritive fluid in the *Hydrozoa;* the cilia of the ectoderm, similarly aided by contractility, constitute the only respiratory mechanism.

Notwithstanding the extreme variety of form exhibited by the *Hydrozoa*, and the multiplicity and complexity of the organs which some of them possess, they never lose the traces of this primitive simplicity of organization; and it is but rarely that it is even disguised to any considerable extent. I know of no Hydrozoon in which the two primary membranes, but little altered, cannot be at once detected in the walls of almost every part of the organism.

This important and obvious structural peculiarity could hardly escape notice, and I find it to have been observed by Trembley, Baker, Laurent, Corda, and Ecker, in *Hydra;* by Rathke, in *Coryne;* by Frey and Leuckart, in *Lucernaria;* and it is given as a character of the Hydroid polypes in general (*Hydræ, Corynidæ,* and *Sertulariadæ*) in the second edition of Cuvier's 'Leçons.' I pointed it out as the general law of structure of the Hydroid polypes, *Diphydæ,* and *Physophoridæ,* in a paper[1] sent to the Linnean Society, from Australia, in 1847, but not read before that body until January, 1849; and I extended the generalization to the whole of the *Hydrozoa* in a 'Memoir on the Anatomy and Affinities of the *Medusæ,*' read before the Royal Society in June, 1849.

---

[1] 'Observations upon the Anatomy of the *Diphydæ,* and the Unity of Organization of the *Diphydæ* and *Physophoridæ.*' An abstract of this essay was published in the 'Proceedings of the Linnean Society' for 1849.

Professor Allman, in his valuable 'Memoir on Cordylophora' ('Philos. Trans.,' 1853), has adopted and confirmed this morphological law, introducing the convenient terms "ectoderm and endoderm," to denote the inner and outer membranes; and Gegenbaur ('Beiträge zur näheren Kenntniss der Schwimmpolypen,' 1854, p. 42), has partially noticed its exemplification in *Apolemia* and *Rhizophysa*; but it seems, singularly enough, to have failed to attract the attention of the other excellent German observers, to whose late important investigations I shall so often have occasion to advert.

The peculiarity in the structure of the body-walls of the *Hydrozoa*, to which I have just referred, possesses a singular interest in its bearing upon the truth (for, with due limitation, it is a great truth) that there is a certain similarity between the adult states of the lower animals and the embryonic conditions of those of higher organization.

For it is well known that, in a very early state, the germ, even of the highest animals, is a more or less complete sac, whose thin wall is divisible into two membranes, an inner and an outer; the latter, turned towards the external world; the former, in relation with the nutritive liquid—the yelk. The inner layer, as Remak has more particularly shown, undergoes but little histological change, and, throughout life, remains more particularly devoted to the function of alimentation, while the outer gives rise, by manifold differentiations of its tissue, to those complex structures which we know as integument, bones, muscles, nerves, and sensory apparatus, and which especially subserve the functions of relation. At the same time the various organs are produced by a process of budding from one, or other, or both, of these primary layers of the germ.

Just so in the Hydrozoon: the ectoderm gives rise to the hard tegumentary tissues, to the more important masses of muscular fibre, and to those organs which we have every reason to believe are sensory, while the endoderm undergoes but very little modification. And every organ of a Hydrozoon is produced by budding from one, or other, or both, of these primitive membranes; the ordinary case being, that the new part commences its existence as a papillary process of both membranes, including, of course, a cæcal diverticulum of the somatic cavity.

Thus there is a very real and genuine analogy between the adult Hydrozoon and the embryonic vertebrate animal; but I need hardly say that it by no means justifies the assumption that the *Hydrozoa* are in any sense "arrested developments" of higher organisms. All that can justly be affirmed is, that the Hydrozoon travels for a certain distance along the same great highway of development as the higher animal, before it turns off to follow the road which leads to its special destination.

The entire double-walled body of the Hydrozoon, whether it be a minute, simple, oval sac, as in the embryonic condition, or such a vast and complex mass as a tree of *Plumularia*, an *Agalma* three feet long, or a *Rhizostoma* of still more massive proportions, will be termed, in the course of the ensuing pages, a *hydrosoma*.

The simplest condition of this hydrosoma is that observable in the common fresh-water *Hydra*, one end of whose body is expanded into a kind of disc, whereby the creature adheres to its support, while the opposite extremity presents a widely-open mouth, opening into a cavity which extends through the whole length of the animal, and surrounded by a circle of long tentacular organs. Here, then, the body exhibits only three distinct morphological constituents: a disc of attachment—which, with its homologous organs in other *Hydrozoa*, may be termed the *hydrorhiza*; a sac for the digestion and (as there is, in this case, no distinct somatic cavity) for the distribution of nutriment—the *polypite;* and, lastly, organs for prehension—the *tentacula.* Furthermore, at particular seasons, tubercular elevations are developed, which contain either an ovum or spermatozoa, and are the reproductive organs.

A polypite and reproductive organs are, in fact, the sole essential constituents of any Hydrozoon, but, so far as I know, no member of this group has yet been discovered of so simple a composition. Organs of prehension and of fixation, or of flotation at least, are always superadded, and, in the majority, there is more than one polypite. But when this is the case it becomes necessary to distinguish between the polypites and the common trunk on which they are supported. To the latter, Professor Allman's term of *cœnosarc* is very usefully applicable; and it will be found convenient, in treating of these more complex forms, to speak of the hydrosoma as composed of a cœnosarc and *appendages,* the latter being those specially modified parts of the hydrosoma which subserve the functions of support, locomotion, alimentation, and so forth.

I will now proceed to point out the principal modifications which are undergone, first by the cœnosarc, and next by the appendages, throughout the *Hydrozoa.*

## The Cœnosarc.

The cœnosarc of the *Corynidæ* and *Sertulariadæ* has the form of a branching stem, resembling that of a plant, and presenting almost as many diversities in form and habit. It may be slender and creeping, or twining; or it may simulate a tree, with stout, erect trunk, and multitudinous branches, arranged according to a definite pattern; or its ramifications may run into a sort of fleshy expansion, as in *Hydractinia.*

In these orders, especially in those forms which possess an erect and branching stem, the cœnosarc is usually strengthened by the development of a strong cuticular layer upon the exterior of its ectoderm. This structureless, or at most laminated, cuticular substance, may remain in close contiguity with the rest of the ectoderm, or, as in the *Campanulariæ,* may become separated by a greater or less interval. In the latter case, it seems at first sight as if the wall of the cœnosarc were composed of three membranes instead of two; but the examination of young organs will clearly show that the outermost or cuticular layer is nothing but an excretion from, or metamorphosis of the outermost substance of, the ectoderm.

In the *Calycophoridæ, Physophoridæ, Lucernariadæ,* and *Medusidæ,* no such thick and hard cuticular layer is developed, and, consequently, the cœnosarc remains, throughout life, soft and flexible. In the two former orders it is never tree-like, and when it gives off branches they are exceedingly short. In some few of the *Lucernariadæ,* on the other hand (*Rhizostomidæ*), the cœnosarc is regularly branched, but, nevertheless, is extremely different from that of the *Sertulariadæ.*

The cœnosarc of the *Calycophoridæ* is slender and filiform; that of the *Physophoridæ* varies from extreme slenderness and elongation to a spheroidal or discoidal shape.

In both these orders it is excessively contractile, a property which it owes to the abundant muscular fibres developed in its walls, principally in the ectoderm. So far as I have observed, these fibres are always disposed longitudinally (except perhaps in *Stephanomia*); but other investigators describe transverse fibres.

The transverse section of the filiform and tree-like cœnosarcs is usually nearly circular, but in some *Physophoridæ* (*Forskalia, e. g.*) it is said to be reniform, from the presence of a deep longitudinal groove on one side.

The cœnosarc, as has been stated, always contains a cavity filled with nutritive fluid—the somatic cavity. The endoderm lining this cavity is in many, if not in all, *Corynidæ* and *Sertulariadæ*, provided with cilia, whose motions are, in many cases, so directed as to give rise to currents in opposite directions on opposite sides of the cavity. The like phenomenon has been observed in his "*Agalma rubra*" (*Halistemma, mihi*) by Vogt (p. 64); and cilia have been noticed on the endoderm of the cœnosarc of many *Physophoridæ*. I have observed them in *Physalia, Velella,* and *Rhizophysa*. Gegenbaur (p. 42) saw them in *Rhizophysa* and *Apolemia*. Kölliker, however, denies the existence of cilia on the endoderm of the cœnosarc in *Forskalia, Agalma,* and *Halistemma* and is silent with respect to the other species of *Physophoridæ* which he describes, except *Velella* and *Porpita,* in which the ciliation is distinctly mentioned. Leuckart (Z. U., p. 4) agrees with Kölliker in denying cilia to the first-named genera.

Will ('Horæ,' p. 78) expressly affirms that the inner wall of the cœnosarc of *Diphyes* exhibits as lively ciliary motion as that of the polypites; but I could never verify this state-ment, nor find cilia on the endoderm of the cœnosarc (except at its proximal end) in any of the *Calycophoridæ*. On the contrary, I have distinctly observed and noted the fact, that solid particles, which, so long as they are in the cavity of the polypite, exhibit a lively rotatory motion, impressed upon them by its cilia, lose that rotation the moment they pass through the pyloric valve into the somatic cavity, and then either remain stationary, or are forced sud-denly along it, backwards or forwards, by the contractions of its walls or of the attached organs. Leuckart and Kölliker have been equally unable to find cilia in any part of the somatic cavity of the *Calycophoridæ*, except its proximal dilated end; but Gegenbaur affirms that it is ciliated throughout in his *Diphyes gracilis* (= *D. Sieboldii* of Kölliker, in which, however, that observer distinctly states no cilia exist), and in *Praya maxima* ('Beiträge,' p. 21).

In the *Lucernariadæ* and *Medusidæ,* the inner surface of the endoderm is, so far as I have seen, everywhere ciliated.

### *The Appendages.*

Before attempting to describe the structure and relations of the manifold appendages of the *Hydrozoa,* it will be necessary to determine the corresponding ends of the hydrosoma throughout the series of forms, a task which is not quite so easy as it may at first appear to be. The *Hydra* is fixed by one end, which is ordinarily lower than the other, and may be regarded as the base; and the end which answers to this is inferior, or basal, in all the *Corynidæ* and *Sertulariadæ*. But the *Calycophoridæ* swim with the corresponding end upwards or forwards. The *Physophoridæ* float with it upwards. The *Lucernariadæ* have it sometimes upwards and sometimes downwards. It would be impossible, therefore, to designate the corresponding ends by the terms " upper and lower" throughout the series without great risk of confusion. Under these circumstances I think it will be best to discard such phraseology, and to employ the terms " proximal" and " distal" for the same object.

In fact, the growth of every hydrosoma is, absolutely or relatively, stationary towards one end of its axis, while it takes place with rapidity towards the other.  This growing extremity, therefore, is, as it were, constantly moving away from the opposite end, and the open mouths of all the polypites are turned more or less in its direction.  Hence, I shall call this the distal end, while the other, comparatively fixed, extremity may be regarded as proximal.  The latter is the basal or lower end in *Hydridæ*, *Corynidæ*, and *Sertulariadæ*.  It is the anterior end, in the actively swimming *Diphyes*, the upper end, in *Hippopodius* and the *Physophoridæ*.  It is the upper side of a *Medusa*, *Cyanæa*, or *Rhizostoma ;* the lower, or attached, end of a *Lucernaria*, and of a larval *Cyanæa* or *Rhizostoma*.

The distal extremity of the hydrosoma is always, so far as I am aware, either cæcal, or ends in a polypite, but is never modified into any other appendage.  The proximal end is variously metamorphosed in the *Hydridæ*, *Corynidæ*, and *Sertulariadæ ;* and becomes a *hydrorhiza*, either expanding into a disc, or sending out many radicles, by which it attaches itself to other bodies.

In the *Calycophoridæ* (Pl. V, figs. 3 and 4), the proximal end of the cœnosarc dilates a little, and becomes ciliated internally, forming a small chamber, which gives off the ducts, by whose intermediation the systems of canals, which embrace the cavities of the organs of loco-motion, are brought into communication with the somatic cavity.  At its upper end, this chamber is a little constricted, and so passes, by a more or less narrowed channel, into a variously shaped sac, whose walls are directly continuous with its own, and which will hence-forward be termed the *somatocyst*.  The endoderm of this sac is ciliated, and it is generally so immensely vacuolated as almost to obliterate the internal cavity and give the organ the appearance of a cellular mass.

The somatocyst very commonly contains large, strongly refracting globules of an apparently albuminous matter, of precisely the same character as those which may be observed occasionally to pass through the pyloric valves of the polypites, into the somatic cavity ; and I do not doubt that the globules result from the accidental accumulation of such products of digestion.  Not unfrequently an air-bubble may be seen in the somatocyst, whither it has travelled, there can be but little question, by the same channel, being either swallowed with the prey or accidentally sucked in by a polypite, whose mouth has been raised above the surface of the water.  Such a chance bubble has of course no relation whatever with the air contained within the float of a Physophorid ; and it is somewhat surprising that any one acquainted with both structures should have imagined the existence of even an analogy, still less of a homology, between them.

The float or *pneumatophore* characteristic and diagnostic of the *Physophoridæ* is, indeed, a most remarkable and well-defined structure (Pls. VI, VIII, &c.)

In these *Hydrozoa* the proximal end of the cœnosarc expands into a variously shaped enlargement, whose walls consist of both the ectoderm and endoderm, and which encloses a wide cavity in free communication with that of the cœnosarc, and, like it, full of the nutritive fluid.  From the distal end or apex of this cavity depends a sac, variously shaped, but always with tough, strong, and elastic walls, composed of a substance which is stated to be similar to chitin in composition,[1] and more or less completely filled with air.

---

[1] At least in *Velella*.  See Leuckart, Z. N. K., p. 114.

In the adult, this sac, which I shall term the *pneumatocyst*, is sometimes open at the apex (*Physalia, Rhizophysa*), and can communicate with the exterior by a pore which traverses the ectoderm of the pneumatophore. In other cases its apex is shut, but the pneumatocyst has other external openings (*Velella, Porpita*); and, lastly, in *Physophora, Forskalia, Agalma, Halistemma*, and *Athorybia*, no external opening at all has hitherto been discovered.

In certain of these genera (*Forskalia, Agalma, Halistemma*), the pneumatocyst appears to be widely open below. I suspect that more careful examination would show that it only becomes very thin ; but however this may be, it is a mistake to suppose that there is any communication between the interior of the pneumatocyst and that of the cœnosarc.[1]

In fact, as I have particularly noted,[2] in *Physalia, Velella, Rhizophysa, Physophora*, and *Agalma*, the endoderm of the pneumatophore is reflected on to the pneumatocyst, where the latter is in contact with the walls of the pneumatophore, and completely invests it, forming a loose bag over the apparent inferior aperture, in those genera which possess one.

The pneumatocyst is thus firmly held in its position by the reflected endoderm, and in some genera (*Forskalia* and *Agalma*) additional support is afforded by septiform processes, which pass from the lateral walls of the pneumatocyst to those of the pneumatophore. These were first described by Milne Edwards in his admirable Memoir on *Stephanomia* (*Forskalia*) *contorta*,[3] in which he says, that "the air-vesicle is open below, and retained in a central position by membranous partitions disposed in a radiating manner, and stretched between its parietes and those of the great pyriform cavity (of the upper end of the stem), nearly in the same way as the mesenteries by which the alimentary canal is surrounded in the Alcyonian polypes."

I find no notice of these suspensoria in the works of either Vogt, Gegenbaur, or Kölliker, and Leuckart expressly states (Z. U., p. 6) that he has "sought in vain for the suspensoria described by Milne Edwards in *Stephanomia*." I observed them, however, very distinctly in *Agalma*. (See the description of that genus *infrà*.)

A very peculiar structure is attached to the distal surface of the pneumatocyst of *Rhizophysa* (Pl. VIII). A great number of elongated, and more or less branched, processes, in fact, project freely from it into the cavity of the pneumatophore. Each process consists of a cellular axis, invested by the ciliated endoderm. The cells of the axis are clear and very large, measuring as much as $\frac{1}{50}$th of an inch in length, and have an opaque, oval "nucleus" $\frac{1}{100}$th of an inch in diameter, with an oval or circular nucleolus of $\frac{1}{1250}$th of an inch in diameter. Quoy and Gaimard would seem to have originally observed these appendages, and they have since been carefully described by Gegenbaur. Nothing of the kind appears to have been seen in other *Physophoridæ*, but in *Velella* and *Porpita*, the hepatic organ occupies the same position, and hence one is led to suspect a relation between the two structures. It does not appear to me that these ramified processes have any real resemblance to the *pneumatic filaments* attached to the distal surface of the pneumatocyst in the last-named genera.

[1] See Leuckart, Z. U., p. 6, and Z. N. K., p. 67, who states of the pneumatocyst of *Apolemia* : "Die untere Oeffnung derselben die in den Reproductionskanal hineinführt."

[2] Gegenbaur describes the same structure in *Rhizophysa*, and Leuckart in *Apolemia* and *Forskalia*, so that the rule doubtless holds good for all *Physophoridæ*.

[3] 'Annales des Sciences Naturelles,' t. xvi, 1841.

In form, the pneumatocyst (and the pneumatophore which contains it) varies from that of a spheroid (*Rhizophysa, Athorybia*) or of an elongated oval (*Physophora*) to that of a cylinder with a narrow inferior neck (*Agalma*), or an irregular, pear-shape (*Physalia*), or the figure of a flattened disc (*Velella, Porpita*). No less does one genus differ from another in the proportional size of this apparatus. In *Physalia, Velella,* and *Porpita*, it occupies almost the whole of the hydrosoma, and constitutes the largest and most conspicuous part of the body, while in such genera as *Agalma* and *Forskalia* it attains to only such insignificant proportions as to be readily overlooked.

Its functional importance, of course, depends very nearly on its relative size. When it is large it must necessarily play a very considerable part in determining the habits of its possessor, though we have at present no information as to whether it acts as a permanent buoy or whether it can be voluntarily emptied and filled again.[1] When the pneumatic apparatus is so small in proportion to the rest of the organism, as in many *Physophoridæ*, on the other hand, its office in the economy ceases to be easily comprehensible, and can hardly be very important.

The last modification of the proximal end of the hydrosoma of which I have to speak is an organ—I mean the disc or *umbrella* of *Lucernariadæ*—which is commonly confounded under one head, with others—the nectocalyces—of quite distinct structure; apparently, because, like the latter, it acts as an organ of propulsion. Nevertheless, in development, in structure, and in even in mode of action, the umbrella is altogether distinct from any other organ possessed by the *Hydrozoa*.

I am inclined to think that the rudiments of this structure are visible in the *Hydridæ*, and in some *Corynidæ* and *Sertulariadæ*. In examining a *Hydra* carefully, it is seen that the tentacles do not immediately surround the oral aperture; but they arise in a circle at some distance below it, so that the oral aperture is supported on a kind of conical crater, from whose base they take their origin.

In some *Campanulariadæ*, this separation of the polypite into a distal and a proximal portion is still more marked. The latter ends distally in a truncated disc, from whose edges the tentacula spring, while the oral division of the polypite is longer than the basal, and arise from the truncated face of the latter by a narrow neck. The like structure is observable in the " Hydra tuba," the larval form of the Lucernarian *Medusæ*, and from hence to the structure of *Lucernaria*, there is but a step. In the latter genus, in fact, the discoid, proximal portion of the polypite, or proximal end of the hydrosoma, is greatly enlarged, and produced into eight obtuse lobes, each of which gives rise to a few short tentacles; while the short distal division of the animal lies in the middle of the disc.

In *Tubularia*, the buds which give rise to the reproductive organs are developed from the surface of the polypite within the margins of the proximal disc and internal to its

---

[1] There is very little good evidence to be met with on this much disputed question. I have seen part of the contained air to all appearance voluntarily expelled from the pneumatocyst of *Rhizophysa*, and Forskäl appears to have witnessed something of the same kind, for he says of his *Physophora filiformis* : " Vivæ, vesica aere plena, tamen subsidere possunt ; dum corpus arctando, se reddunt specifice graviores." Eschscholz found, on irritating a young *Physalia* five lines long, that it " suddenly expelled all the air from the bladder, and sank to the bottom of the glass" (p. 159).

series of tentacula. In *Lucernaria*, the reproductive organs are developed in the same way from the surface of the body on the distal side and within the margins of the disc, into which the proximal division of the body is expanded.

The mode of origin of the Lucernarian *Medusæ* from their larvæ is such, that their umbrella is clearly, like that of *Lucernaria* itself, nothing more than a lobed expansion of the body-walls, and as in *Lucernaria*, the reproductive organs are developed on the distal surface of this expansion. The peculiar lithocysts of these *Lucernariadæ* are developed in the deep notches which mark the ends of the lobes of their umbrella.

It will be seen presently, that in the mode of development just described, in its lobed margins, and in the absence of any muscular membranous valve attached to its circumference, the umbrella is wholly different from all other organs of natation.

Such is the general structure of the axis of the hydrosoma, and of its anterior and posterior terminations, throughout the *Hydrozoa*. The different orders exhibit many remarkable variations in their number, kind, and mode of attachment. To begin with the last-mentioned point, it is to be observed that no regularity is traceable in the arrangement of the appendages in many *Corynidæ*; while in others, and in the *Sertulariadæ* in general, the branchings of the cœnosarc and the disposition of the appendages upon it, follow a very definite law, to which the regular and symmetrical forms of the organisms are due. The appendages may be developed on one or on both sides of the cœnosarc.

In such *Physophoridæ* as possess a filiform cœnosarc (*e. g.*, *Agalma*, *Forskalia*, *Stephanomia*), the appendages appear to be always fixed to only one side of it. And even the strikingly radiate disposition of some of the appendages in *Forskalia* and *Stephanomia*, for example, does not result from their forming exceptions to this rule—for their appendages are all really attached to one side of the stem only—but is due partly, perhaps, to a spiral twisting of the cœnosarc, but in a much more important degree, to the manner in which these appendages are forced by their peculiar form, to adapt themselves to one another.

Whether the appendages in *Physophora*, *Velella*, *Porpita*, and *Physalia* follow the same law is not certainly made out.

In the *Calycophoridæ* I am inclined to believe that all the appendages are primarily attached to one side of the cœnosarc, and that the subsequent opposition of the nectocalyces to one another, and of the hydrophyllia to the polypites is a secondary modification.

The following distinct kinds of appendages exist in the *Hydrozoa*, and will now be successively described. 1. *Polypites;* 2. *Tentacula;* 3. *Hydrocysts;* 4. *Hydrothecæ;* 5. *Hydrophyllia;* 6. *Nectocalyces;* 7. *Reproductive organs*, consisting of *Gonoblastidea* and *Gonophores;* 8. *Lithocysts*.

### 1. *Polypites.*

By this term I understand the principal organ of alimentation of a Hydrozoon. It would be wrong to call it merely a stomach, for it is much more; and the word "polype" has been, and is, used in so many senses that it is better avoided.

Every polypite is essentially a sac, open at one end, which serves as a mouth, while at the other it communicates with the somatic cavity. The oral end is usually produced into a thin, flexible, and very distensible lip, whose edges are either quite simple (*Hydridæ*,

*Corynidæ, Sertulariadæ* [all?], *Calycophoridæ, Physophoridæ*), or are produced into longer or shorter folds or processes (many *Medusidæ*, Lucernarian and other).

I have above referred to the division of the polypite into a distal and a proximal portion in many *Hydrozoa*. In the *Calycophoridæ* and *Physophoridæ*, the polypite presents, in many cases, a further division into a proximal ("basal-stück" of the Germans), a median, and a distal division. There is no distinct line of demarcation between the two latter, but in many cases the median and basal divisions are very sharply separated, not only by their texture, but by a distinct valve (Pl. V).

This, in the *Calycophoridæ*, is a very well marked structure, though I do not find it noted by any of those writers whose works I have consulted. It is a strong, circular fold of the endoderm, whose lips, when the valve is shut, project into the cavity of the gastric, or median, division of the polypite. As the oily or albuminous globules which result from the digestive process are formed, they usually accumulate close to the valve, and are kept constantly rotating by the cilia which line the gastric chamber. After remaining for a while in this position, the fundus of the gastric chamber contracts, and forces the globule through the valve, which appears to dilate at the same moment. The position and functions of this apparatus, therefore, fully justify the appellation of a *pyloric valve*.

The proximal division of the polypite usually takes on the form of a peduncle, which is sometimes very long, and gives origin to various appendages. Its walls are ordinarily thin and muscular, but the endoderm is sometimes much vacuolated, and partially obliterates its cavity.

The median division of the polypite is the widest of the three, and has the thickest walls. In it the process of digestion goes on, and hence it may with propriety be termed the gastric division. The inner surface of the endoderm is richly ciliated, and not only is its general thickness considerable, but in many *Calycophoridæ* and *Physophoridæ* it is developed into larger or smaller, slender, conical, villous elevations. These villi are larger and more distinct in *Physalia* (where they attain the length of $\frac{1}{100}$th of an inch or more) than in any other Hydrozoon I have examined (see the description of that genus, *infrà*); but they are very well developed in *Athorybia*. In both genera they exhibit in their interior one or more clear spaces or vacuoles, sometimes obscured by a quantity of dark pigment, and they contain numerous thread-cells (Pls. IX, X).

In *Rhizophysa, Physophora, Diphyes, Abyla*, and other *Calycophoridæ*, the villi are represented by shorter processes of the endoderm, which are sometimes obsolete, all that remains of the villus being the characteristic clear vacuoles, imbedded in the endoderm, and the production of the endoderm into ragged-looking filaments over them.

Kölliker and Vogt describe similar organs in *Hippopodius* and *Praya*, so that such short villi would seem to obtain universally among the *Calycophoridæ*.

In the *Agalmopsis* of Sars, in *Agalma, Forskalia*, and *Apolemia*, the villi take on the form of longitudinal ridges, which usually contain much pigment, and thus give a very marked character to the gastric division of the polypite. They have been confounded with reproductive organs.

Gegenbaur (p. 23) describes the vacuoles in the villi of *Praya maxima* as cells. "The contents of these cells differed greatly, sometimes appearing perfectly clear, at others yellowish or brownish, and, in this case, frequently consisting of minute particles. The colour then shines through the walls of the polypite. I consider these to be hepatic cells, analogous to those cellular elements which coat the gastric cavity and the intestines of so many of the lower animals." In his *Diphyes gracilis*, Gegenbaur states that the " cells " possess a distinct double contour and a nucleus, neither of which have I ever observed. "There can be no question," he adds, " that these elements must be regarded as glandular cells; and their ultimate fate is in favour of this view. For we find between them empty depressions, with sharply defined edges, which correspond exactly in form and size with those in which the cells in question are imbedded. These depressions can be hardly anything else than the spaces formerly occupied by such glandular cells, which have burst and emptied their secretion."

Kölliker (p. 26) gives a still more definite account and figure of the structure of the villi and vacuoles in *Athorybia*. He considers them to be " glandular sacs of the simplest kind," also that they are " open sacs, lined with cells," and inclines to the opinion that their function is hepatic.

Leuckart takes the same view of the cavities in the villi of the *Physophoridæ* as myself, regarding them not as cells, but as vacuoles (Z. N. K., p. 68).

Vogt (p. 102) appears also to consider the cavities of the villi in *Praya* to be vacuoles and not cells; and he gives an account of an experiment, which would be well worth repeating. " Having mixed indigo in the water of a vessel containing a lively *Praya*, I saw after some time that the digestive cavities were streaked with blue, the colouring matter being detained by the villi (*bourrelets*); and I convinced myself by microscopic examination that the colouring granules existed only in the cellœform spaces, which are nothing else than shallow depressions or widely open glandular sacs."

Without by any means denying the possibility that the vacuoles (for such mere excavations full of fluid I must confess they always appeared to me to be) contain a special secretion, I am inclined to think that the villous eminences in which they are imbedded have other functions. I once observed a half-digested mass in the stomach of an *Athorybia*, all the villi in the neighbourhood of which were much elongated, and thrust into it. The ends of these villi contained fewer thread-cells than usual, while many thread-cells were scattered through the mass of food. Is it not possible that when the living prey is introduced into the gastric cavity, its struggles may be restrained and cut short, not only by the mechanical application of the elongated villi, but by the shooting out of the threads of the numerous thread-cells with which they are provided?

Allman[1] has described structures corresponding very closely with these vacuolated villi in *Cordylophora*, and it is therefore probable that something of the same kind will be found in other *Hydrozoa*. But, so far as I know at present, the only structures in the *Lucernariadæ* to be compared with the villi are those solid tentacular filaments, with vacuolated axes, which project from the endoderm into the stomach or into the somatic cavity. They are, like the villi, covered at their extremities with abundant thread-cells.

The villi and vacuoles are confined to the gastric division of the polypite. The walls of the distal or buccal division are thin and smooth, but richly ciliated internally.

[1] "Anat. et Phys. of Cordylophora," 'Phil. Trans.,' 1853.

## 2. *Tentacula.*

All the *Hydrozoa* possess more or less numerous filiform appendages, abundantly provided with thread-cells, and subserving purposes of offence or defence, which receive the general name of tentacula, though they differ very widely in structure and place of attachment.

In the *Hydridæ, Corynidæ,* and *Sertulariadæ,* numerous tentacula are always attached to the body of the polypite itself, and they usually form a circle not very far below the mouth, though sometimes they are scattered irregularly (*Coryne, Cordylophora*), and sometimes form a double circlet (*Tubularia*). The *Calycophoridæ* and most *Physophoridæ* have single tentacula springing from the base of the gastric division of the polypite, or from the peduncle just on the proximal side of that base. But in the *Physaliadæ* and *Velellidæ,* the tentacles are wholly distinct from the polypite, arising by themselves from the cœnosarc. In the *Lucernariadæ* and *Medusidæ,* finally, the tentacles are developed from the margins of the umbrella and from its under surface.

The tentacles of the *Hydridæ, Corynidæ, Sertulariadæ, Lucernariadæ,* and *Medusidæ,* are always extremely simple in structure, consisting, at any rate primarily, of tubular processes of the endoderm and ectoderm, enclosing a diverticulum of the somatic cavity, and sometimes clavate at the ends, or presenting little papillary elevations, but hardly ever branched. The internal cavity is sometimes persistent, but it very commonly becomes almost obliterated by the vacuolar thickening of the endoderm; and when this has occurred, the tentacles usually appear as if they had a solid cellular axis.

Besides these ordinary tentacles, certain *Sertulariadæ* possess organs which must be ranged in the same category, though they differ greatly from them in position and in external appearance. These *nematophores,* as they have been termed by Mr. Busk, are cæcal processes of the cœnosarc, invested by a continuation of its hard cuticular layer, so as to be quite firm and inflexible. The cuticular investment, however, is open at the end, and in the soft substance beneath the opening lie a number of large thread-cells. These bodies are particularly characteristic of the *Plumulariadæ.*

The tentacles of the various genera of the *Physophoridæ* and *Calycophoridæ* differ very widely in structure, gradually increasing in complexity as we advance along a series, the lowest term of which is *Velella,* and the highest *Physophora.*

The tentacles of *Velella,* in fact, differ in no essential respect from those of the *Hydridæ* and *Sertulariadæ;* they are simple cæcal processes of the wall of the cœnosarc, with a greatly vacuolated endoderm (Pl. XI). Those of *Porpita* have the same fundamental structure, but they are branched at the ends.

The tentacles of *Apolemia* are described by Leuckart and Gegenbaur[1] as simple, tapering, unbranched filaments, which are beset with large thread-cells on one side, and are traversed by a narrow, ciliated canal. One of these tentacles is said to arise from the base of each polypite.

The tentacles of *Physalia* (Pl. X) exhibit an advance on this structure. They arise independently from the cœnosarc, and each is provided at its base with a large, pyriform, saccular

[1] Z. N. K., p. 69; Gegenbaur, p. 40.

dilatation—the basal sac.    The tentacle itself is a filament which in a large specimen attains the length of many feet when fully extended.  It has no lateral branches, but it is beset along one side, at regular intervals, with reniform enlargements, full of large thread-cells, which are disposed transversely to the axis of the tentacle, and look like so many beads threaded upon it.    On the opposite side, the tentacle widens out into a ribbon-like muscular band, which, attached above to one edge of the basal sac, is the agent of its rapid and extensive contractions.  A canal traverses the whole length of the tentacle, and sends cæcal diverticula into the reniform enlargements, while above, it communicates with the cavity of the basal sac.   It has been supposed that the latter organ, by its contraction, drives the liquid which it contains into the canal of the tentacle, and thus effects its elongation.   Without denying that such may be its office, I would remark, that the tentacles of other species which are not provided with basal sacs are just as capable of rapid elongation.

The reniform enlargements to which I have referred may be regarded as rudimentary lateral branches.  If they be supposed to elongate and become filamentary, the result will be a tentacle very similar to that possessed by *Rhizophysa*, except that in this genus there is no basal sac, nor muscular band, and that each tentacle is attached to a polypite.  The lateral branches of the tentacles of *Rhizophysa* have one wall much thicker than the other, but it contains only spheroidal thread-cells, and the branches are not divided into distinctly characterised regions.

In *Forskalia*, however, while the tentacles have essentially the same structure, each lateral branch is divided into three distinct portions: a proximal slender part; a median division, with one wall much thicker than the other, containing numerous elongated thread-cells, arranged in transverse rows perpendicularly to the wall, and flanked on each side by a longitudinal series of larger oval thread-cells; and, finally, a terminal cylindrical thread, full of small, rounded thread-cells.  I shall term the first of these regions the *pedicle*, the second the *sacculus*, and the third the *filament*.    The muscular band of *Physalia* is partially represented by two pairs of muscular cords, which, according to Leuckart (Z. N. K., p. 99), lie in the thin wall of the sacculus.  In the contracted state, the sacculus and the filaments are thrown into spiral coils.

The structure of the tentacles of *Halistemma* is essentially the same, except that they are provided with a more complex muscular apparatus, for a description of which I must refer to the works of Vogt and Leuckart.

The tentacula of the *Calycophoridæ* (Pl. V) resemble those just described, and arise either from the base of the gastric division of the polypite, close to the pedicle, or from the latter itself. The larger, oval thread-cells are confined to the distal end of the sacculus, which is usually bent so as to have a half-moon shape, the thick wall forming the convexity.   The filament is coiled up into a close spire, folded against the straight, thin wall; and, where it joins the sacculus, the points of five or six oval thread-cells commonly project, like those of the rowel of a spur.    Where the peduncle joins the sacculus it exhibits a small dilatation, which I conceive to be a rudiment of a part to be described presently as the involucrum.

Leuckart has particularly described a structure in the sacculus of the *Calycophoridæ*, where it has also been noticed by Vogt and Kölliker, which he terms the "angelband." It is "a simple, but strong and sharply defined, muscular cord, which is folded in zigzags, and lies in the posterior (thin) wall of the canal of the sacculus, partly covers it at the sides, and then appears to be coiled almost spirally around it. The upper end passes gradually into the pedicle, while the lower extends as far as the beginning of the filament. In *Praya* and *Hippopodius*, this cord has a diameter of about $\frac{1}{3000}$th of an inch, and differs in no essential respect from the muscles in other parts of the body, especially in the stem, although at times a slight transverse striation can be detected in it. In *Diphyes*, and still more in *Abyla*, however, this muscular cord becomes gradually thicker during its course, so as even to attain as much as $\frac{1}{400}$th of an inch in *Abyla*, and therewith assumes a very distinct transverse striation, so that, especially in *Abyla*, it might be compared to the most beautiful transversely striped muscular fibres. No nuclei can be observed in this cord, nor can its sheath be distinguished from its contents. It appears as if the transverse striation were caused by a regular jointing, for the edges of the cord are completely incurved at intervals, corresponding with the constrictions between the joints. In *Abyla*, furthermore, this muscular filament is but little flattened, and becomes triangular in many places by the mutual pressure of the superimposed folds. If one of the thin edges be accidentally turned directly towards the microscope, the transverse striation readily leads one to suppose that two series of transverse rods are imbedded in the cord, as I indeed previously supposed to be the case." (Z. N. K., p. 19.)

I confess I entertain great doubts as to the real nature of this structure, which is particularly worthy of the attention of future observers.

In the tentacles of *Stephanomia* (Pl. VII), which, in many respects, resemble those of *Halistemma*, a new part makes its appearance, in the shape of a sort of hood, which is developed at the junction of the pedicle with the sacculus, and encloses the latter like a cup. I term this the *involucrum*. It is a solid, lamellar process of the ectoderm, containing no internal cavity. The sacculus is very long and spirally coiled, terminates in a single filament, and has a well-developed muscular band in its thin wall.

In the genera *Agalma* and *Athorybia*, the involucrum has become much larger in proportion to the sacculus, and the latter is terminated, not by a single filament, but by two filaments, between which the sacculus ends in a clear, thin-walled, median lobe, devoid of thread-cells, and said to be contractile by Leuckart and Kölliker, though in the species I observed it exhibited no such faculty (Pls. VI, IX).

Finally, the tentacular branches attain their utmost complexity in *Physophora*, the spheroidal involucrum here completely investing the sacculus, which lies coiled up within it, and having undergone other changes, which will be particularly described under the head of that genus (Pl. VIII).

### 3. *Hydrocysts.*

I apply this name to certain singular organs which are found more particularly in the *Physophoridæ*, and which resemble nothing so much as the imperfectly developed polypites of the species to which they belong. As such, indeed, I always considered them, until the perusal of the works of Philippi, Leuckart, and Kölliker, led me to modify my opinion.

These investigators term the organs in question "fühler" and "taster," and are inclined, not without a great show of reason,[1] to regard them as organs of prehension and touch, to which may perhaps be added excretory and respiratory functions.

The hydrocysts are always pyriform sacs, composed of the ectoderm and endoderm, shut at their apical or distal ends, where they are commonly provided with large thread-cells, but, at their proximal ends, in free communication with the somatic cavity. Like the polypites, they usually give origin to a tentacular appendage. But this is always simple and filiform, and the hydrocysts further differ from the mere polypites in their closed apices and in the general absence of villi. The latter, however, exist in a rudimentary state in the hydrocysts of *Apolemia*, according to Leuckart (Z. N. K., 70), and I have seen them in the closed sacs, which appear to be hydrocysts, of *Physalia* (Pl. X). These bodies are not found in *Velella* or *Porpita*, and I must confess I am very doubtful, whether the structures to which I have just referred in *Physalia* are other than young polypites. In the *Stephanomiadæ* they are attached to the cœnosarc, between the polypites, and are usually in more or less close relation with the reproductive organs. In *Physophora* (Pl. VIII) a circlet of large hydrocysts is interposed between the nectocalyces and the polypites, and in *Apolemia*, according to Kölliker, Gegenbaur, and Leuckart, a group of them surrounds the base of each polypite, while solitary ones are, in addition, interspersed between the nectocalyces.

### 4. *Hydrothecæ*, and 5. *Hydrophyllia*.

Many *Hydrozoa* possess appendages whose only function would appear to be to serve as a protection to other parts of the organism, more especially the polypites. Of these organs there are two very distinct kinds, the one peculiarly characteristic of the *Sertulariadæ*, the other found only among the *Diphydæ* and *Physophoridæ*. The former, or *hydrothecæ*, are what are commonly termed "polype cells." They are cup-like receptacles, entirely composed of the cuticular layer of the ectoderm, and consequently contain no diverticulum of the somatic cavity at any period of their existence. They are primarily developed from the whole outer coat of a budding polypite.

For the second class of protective organs, or *hydrophyllia*, there is no generally accepted English name. I have termed them "bracts" in my earlier memoirs, and the Germans call them "deck-stücke."

The hydrophyllia differ entirely from the hydrothecæ, for they always contain a diverticulum of the somatic cavity, or *phyllocyst*, and are consequently composed of both ectoderm and endoderm, though their principal mass is furnished by the ectoderm. Again, they always commence their existence by budding from a limited segment of the cœnosarc, or of the pedicle of a polypite. In the *Calycophoridæ*, they are attached to the pedicles of the polypites, which they eventually surround more or less completely (Pl. V). They are either thin and foliaceous, as in *Diphyes*, or thick and facetted externally, as in *Abyla*. Their form and arrangement vary greatly in the *Physophoridæ*. In *Forskalia*, numbers of them are developed from the pedicles of the polypites, as well as from the cœnosarc, while in *Agalma* (Pl. VI) they

---

[1] See Kölliker, p. 21; Leuckart, Z. U., p. 17; and, again, Z. N. K., p. 69, where the strong resemblance of these bodies to polypites is fully admitted.

are confined to the latter. Where nectocalyces are present, the series of hydrophyllia always ends on their distal side, these organs being never found intermixed with the nectocalyces, or on their proximal side. The *Velellidæ*, *Physaliadæ*, *Rhizophysidæ*, and *Physophoriadæ* have no hydrophyllia.

## 6. *Nectocalyces.*

Nothing is more peculiarly characteristic of those orders of the *Hydrozoa* to which the following pages are particularly devoted, than the structure of their locomotive organs, which, whatever the modifications they undergo, may be reduced to a very simple type —that of a cup lined by a muscular membrane, by whose contractions the water is expelled, the animal being consequently urged, by its reaction, in the opposite direction. Nor is the essential internal structure of this cup less uniform. Its summit contains a cavity, which is connected with the somatic cavity on the one hand, and, on the other, sends off at least four canals, which traverse the walls of the cup in a radiating manner, and eventually open into a circular canal, which surrounds its mouth. These *nectocalycine canals* are lined by a continuation of the endoderm. The cavity of the cup, which, with its muscular wall, may be termed the *nectosac*, does not communicate with this system of canals, but is freely open externally, and, opposite the circular canal, its wall is always produced into a contractile, valve-like membrane, which, when at rest, projects inwards all round the aperture, and narrows it to a greater or less extent (Pls. I, VI, VIII).

The presence of the valvular membrane at once distinguishes a nectocalyx from an umbrella.

These organs of propulsion[1] are only known to exist among the *Calycophoridæ*, where they are universal, and the *Physophoridæ*, which only partially possess them.

In the typical *Calycophoridæ* (*Diphyes*, *Abyla*, *Galeolaria*), there are normally only two nectocalyces, which are attached upon opposite sides of the proximal end of the hydrosoma, but in *Vogtia* they are numerous, and in *Hippopodius*, according to Leuckart, amount to as many as twelve or more. In the *Physophoridæ* they are often extremely numerous, and (though all originally developed on one side of the cœnosarc) are, in the adult state, either arranged in two opposite series, or in several series, which are disposed in a radiating manner around the proximal end of the cœnosarc.

In the *Physophoridæ* the inner faces of the nectocalyces are usually excavated to enclose the cœnosarc, and those of opposite sides simply alternate with, and fit in between, one another. Each nectocalyx is connected with the cœnosarc by a pedicle, traversed by a tubular duct, which opens on the one hand into its apical cavity, and on the other into the somatic canal, and is, in truth, nothing but the original base of the organ elongated.

In all the *Physophoridæ*, and in most of the *Calycophoridæ*, that portion of the cœnosarc which supports the nectocalyces lies in the same straight line with the rest; but in *Hippopodius*, Leuckart has pointed out that it is bent down, and, as it were, folded upon the remainder of the cœnosarc, whence the distal end of the series of nectocalyces may be readily mistaken for the proximal, and *vice versâ*.

---

[1] It is necessary to distinguish carefully between these simply locomotive organs and those similar structures which are subordinated to reproduction, and contain a central gastric or genital sac.

In *Praya*, the two nectocalyces are attached, nearly on the same level, to the proximal end of the cœnosarc. The inner surface of each is marked by a deep groove, and the smaller is received within the bounding folds of the groove of the larger, so that the two form, by their application, a sort of chamber or *hydrœcium*, into which the cœnosarc can be retracted, as into a house.

In the typical *Calycophoridæ*—*Diphyes*, and *Abyla*—a still further change has taken place (Pl. V). As in *Praya*, there are but two perfect nectocalyces, but of these, one is altogether on the distal side of the other, its pointed apex being received into a peculiar cavity of the proximal nectocalyx, which takes the place of the internal groove in the *Physophoridæ* and *Praya*. It is to the summit of this cavity that the proximal, slightly dilated end of the cœnosarc, described above, is attached, its continuation, the somatocyst, being imbedded in the substance of the nectocalyx. Proximally, therefore, the hydrœcium in these *Calycophoridæ* is entirely formed by the conical chamber of this nectocalyx; distally, it is continued by a groove, converted more or less completely into a covered way, on the inner surface of the distal nectocalyx. The cœnosarc, with its appendages, travels up and down the complex hydrœcium thus formed, and can sometimes be completely retracted into it.

The ducts which connect the nectocalycine canals with the somatic cavity come off, as I have stated above, from the somewhat dilated, ciliated chamber in which the cœnosarc ends. The duct which goes to the canals of the proximal nectocalyx in *Diphyes*, runs along that side of the hydrœcium which is nearest to the nectosac, and divides into the longitudinal nectocalycine canals close to the mouth of the latter. In *Abyla*, on the contrary, it is extremely short, and divides directly opposite the middle of the nectosac.

The duct which supplies the canals of the distal nectocalyx almost immediately enters that beak-like process of the latter, which fits into the hydrœcium of the proximal nectocalyx, and traversing it, divides into its four longitudinal nectocalycine canals, either opposite the apex of the nectosac or close to it.

I have described above the general arrangement of the four canals in the nectocalyces, which radiate from the end of the communicating duct. Whatever the form of the nectocalyx, that pair of these canals which occupies the median plane remains straight, or as nearly so as the form of the organ will permit; but the two lateral ones not uncommonly undergo a curious flexure, of which a marked example may be seen in *Physophora*[1] (see the description of that genus, *infrà*). Leuckart describes. in the nectocalyces of *Hippopodius, Praya, Halistemma*, and *Agalma* (and I can testify to their existence in the last-named genus), what he terms "mantelgefasse." These are two slender, curved, cæcal diverticula, which are given off on opposite sides of the duct, shortly after it enters the substance of the calyx, and lie in the same plane as the median nectocalycine canals.

#### 7. *Reproductive Organs.*

These consist, throughout the *Hydrozoa*, of *spermaria* and *ovaria,* portions of the tissue of the wall of the hydrosoma, and, I believe, more particularly of the ectoderm, metamorphosed

---

[1] Also, according to Leuckart, in *Agalma, Halistemma,* and *Apolemia.*

into spermatozoa or ova. As an invariable rule, while the reproductive organ is in contact, on the one side, with the nutritive somatic fluid, it is, on the other, directly exposed to the water in which the animal lives. The genital apparatus is therefore always external, and is never contained within the cavity of the body, a character which at once distinguishes the *Hydrozoa* from the *Actinozoa*.

These organs are found in their simplest state in *Hydra*, in *Lucernaria*, and in many *Medusæ*, where they are distinguishable from other parts of the body only by their contents; but more usually they assume the form of pouches or sacs, termed *gonophores* by Allman,[1] containing a diverticulum of the somatic cavity. Such is their form in *Hydractinia*, in *Coryne pusilla*, and in some *Plumulariæ*.

The reproductive organs of both sexes in *Cordylophora*, the female organs of *Stephanomia*, *Agalma*, *Athorybia*, *Forskalia*, *Apolemia*, and the male organs of *Physalia*, exhibit an interesting series of transitions from the simplest to the most complex condition of the genital apparatus in the *Hydrozoa*. For we find in all these cases that the reproductive organ is no longer simple, but that its investment has acquired more or less the structure of a nectocalyx, from whose walls those of the actual genital sac, the *manubrium* of Allman, tend to become independent. To this investing part I apply the name of *gonocalyx*.

In *Tubularia indivisa* both the male and the female reproductive organs are included within a gonocalyx, in which the four longitudinal canals are distinguishable while the organ is yet young, though they appear to become obliterated with age. But the organs remain attached, and their calyces, so far as I have observed, never exhibit contractions. A similar condition of the reproductive organs has been observed in some *Campanulariæ*.

*Hippopodius* and *Voglia* have, according to Kölliker, long manubria (sperm-sacs and ovisacs), surrounded at their bases by short and shallow hemispherical gonocalyces, which have the four longitudinal canals united by a circular canal, characteristic of a complete nectocalyx.

The reproductive organs of both sexes of other *Calycophoridæ*, and the male organs, of *Athorybia*, *Agalma*, *Apolemia*, *Stephanomia*, *Halistemma*, and *Forskalia*, have a still more complete, contractile gonocalyx, provided with its membranous valve, and the manubrium or reproductive sac suspended from its roof either projects but very little beyond its aperture, or is much shorter. In many of the *Calycophoridæ* these organs become detached, and swim about for a long time, propelled by the contractions of their calyces.

From these conditions of the reproductive apparatus, the transition is easy to that presented by those of both sexes in *Laomedea geniculata*, many *Corynidæ*, and *Velella*, and by the female organs of *Physalia*; in which the reproductive organ is detached before the development of the generative products within the manubrial sac suspended from the roof of the gonocalyx, and swims away as a medusiform zöoid. Not unfrequently, this "Medusa" has to undergo great changes in size and form before attaining its sexually perfect state; and it is, consequently, necessary that it should feed and support itself for a considerable period. To this end, the central sac or manubrium no longer remains a mere short receptacle, but

---

[1] "On the Structure of the Reproductive Organs in certain Hydroid Polypes," 'Proceedings of the Royal Society of Edinburgh,' Session 1857-8; and "Additional Observations on the Morphology of the Reproductive Organs in the Hydroid Polypes," *Ibid*. December 6th, 1858.

opens at its extremity, acquires the structure, and takes on all the functions of a polypite. At the same time, tentacular organs and lithocysts may be developed from the margins of the calyx. Eventually, the ova or spermatozoa appear either in the walls of the polypite, or in special spermaria or ovaria developed in the parietes of the canals of the calyx of this independent medusiform zöoid, which is occasionally a more complex organism than that from which it sprang.

This is still more remarkably the case in most of the *Lucernariadæ*, whose reproductive zöoids surpass the "Hydræ tubæ," whence they proceed, many thousandfold in size and mass, and no less remarkably, in complexity of organization. Known under the same general title of "Medusæ" as the foregoing, and in many ways analogous to them, they are, nevertheless, widely different in structure and origin. Their swimming apparatus is an umbrella, and neither in structure nor in mode of development a gonocalyx, and they are developed, not by budding from a limited area of one side of a cœnosarc or its polypite, but by the transverse constriction of a polypite into superimposed segments, each of which becomes lobed at its margins, and assumes the form of an umbrella with a central polypite.

The arrangement of the tentacles, again, is quite different from that which obtains in the other *Medusæ*, and the lithocysts differ in being covered by a hood, and in not having each mineral particles which they contain, spheroidal and enveloped in a distinct vesicle.

In *Cyanæa*, the polypite is simple and single, and the spermaria or ovaria are sacculated portions of the distal (or under) wall of the umbrella, inclosed in a peculiar chamber formed by the outgrowth, into a thick ridge, of the ectoderm round each reproductive organ, so as to leave only a small, circular aperture, leading into a chamber, from whose roof the plaited membrane containing the reproductive elements depends.

In this genus, moreover, the edges of the produced angles of the lips of the polypite, which hang down like four great arms, are so folded as to form little cups, into which the fertilised ova are received, there to undergo their first changes.

In the *Rhizostomidæ*, a complex, tree-like mass, whose branches, the *stomatodendra*, end in, and are covered with, minute polypites interspersed with clavate tentacula, is suspended from the middle of the umbrella in a very singular way. The main trunks of the dependent polypiferous tree, in fact, unite above into a thick, flat, quadrate disc, the *syndendrium*, which is suspended by four stout pillars, the *dendrostyles*, one springing from each angle, to four corresponding points on the under surface of the umbrella, equidistant from its centre. Under the middle of the umbrella, therefore, there is a chamber whose floor is formed by the quadrate disc, while its roof is constituted by the under wall of the central cavity of the umbrella, and its sides are open. The reproductive elements are developed within radiating, folded diverticula of the roof of this genital cavity.[1]

In passing from *Hydra* to *Rhizostoma*, we thus see the reproductive organs acquiring a greater and greater relative mass, when compared with the organism from which they spring, and, as it were, grouping round themselves and subordinating to their own perfection a greater and greater number of morphological elements. First, they are parts of the body wall, indistinguishable in form from the rest; then they are distinct sacs; then they are

[1] I have described at length and figured, the structure here indicated, in my "Memoir on the Anatomy of the Medusæ," 'Phil. Trans.' 1849.

sacs with a gonocalyx; then that gonocalyx becomes a well-developed contractile organ; next the reproductive apparatus is detached, and swims about independently by means of its gonocalyx or umbrella; and, finally, it acquires total independence, feeding and nourishing itself, and attaining the most complex organization exhibited by the class to which its originator belongs.

Even this, however, is not the whole extent of specialization attained by the reproductive system in the *Hydrozoa*, for, in certain members of the class, the reproductive organs, or zöoids, themselves are developed from, or in, organs especially devoted to that object.

Thus, among the *Corynidæ*, the gonophores of *Hydractinia echinata* are developed neither from the ordinary polypites nor directly from their connecting cœnosarc; but the latter gives rise here and there to cylindrical processes (*blastostyles*), each of which is about as long as a polypite, but is terminated distally, not by a mouth, but by a pyriform enlargement, which gradually diminishes to a point, and is covered with small, irregular lobes or tubercles. The circumference of the widest part of the enlargement is produced into ten or twelve such particularly well-marked conical enlargements, which are thickly beset with thread-cells. From the stem of the process below these, the gonophores are developed, and from its base there arises a short, cylindrical body, dilated at its extremity into a globular head, full of minute, dark reddish orange granules. At first sight this body looks very like the lithocyst of a *Cyanæa*, but I have been unable to find evidence of its possessing a similar structure.

Some *Sertulariadæ* exhibit organs similar in principle to these, though differing in the details of their structure. Thus, pedunculated, urn-shaped bodies rise from the cœnosarc of *Laomedea gelatinosa*. The peduncle has the same structure as the cœnosarc, containing a central canal, and having the cuticular layer of its ectoderm more or less distinct from the deeper substance. Where the peduncle enlarges into its urn-like dilatation, the walls of the latter may be clearly seen to be continuous with this cuticular layer of the ectoderm only; at the distal end of the urn its walls turn abruptly inwards on all sides, thus forming a concave face, the middle of which is produced into a short, spout-like, open mouth. The continuation of the rest of the substance of the peduncle (consisting of the inner moiety of the ectoderm, with the whole endoderm, and their contained cavity) traverses the axis of the urn nearly to its end as a sort of columella—the blastostyle of Allman—but its termination is hidden by the mass of buds in advanced stages of development which are clustered round it. These buds may be traced down the sides of the blastostyle, until, at the base of the urn, they are to be detected in their primary condition of cæcal processes of its wall. Each eventually acquires the form of a "Medusa," with marginal tentacles and lithocysts, and leaves the theca by its superior aperture to swim about by itself, and eventually develope the reproductive elements.

The relation of the reproductive organs of many *Physophoridæ* to the peduncles of those peculiar cæcal polypiform bodies described above under the name of hydrocysts, or, as in *Velella*, to true polypites, is very similar to that between the reproductive organs of *Hydractinia*[1] and their support, or between the budding medusiform zöoids of *Laomedea* and

---

[1] Vogt (p. 133) and Leuckart (Z. U., p. 16, and Z. N. K., p. 71) have already drawn attention to this resemblance, and have included, under the common term of "proliferous individuals," not only these bodies, but the small polypites of the *Velellidæ*.

the columella of the urn; and it will be so convenient to have a special name for these organs set apart for the production of generative buds, that I will term them *gonoblastidia*.

Among the *Medusidæ, Willsia* (itself possibly only a zöoid) possesses stem-like gonoblastidia terminated, as in *Hydractinia*, by an enlarged end, abounding in thread-cells.

I have already spoken of the detachment of the medusiform gonophores of many *Hydrozoa*. But in many *Calycophoridæ*, and, perhaps, in some *Physophoridæ*, the organism undergoes a still further subdivision in the natural course of its development.

This process will be found described in detail below, as it occurs in *Abyla*. It will be seen that each segment of the cœnosarc, provided with a polypite, its tentacle, reproductive organ, and hydrophyllium, as it acquires a certain size, becomes detached, and leads an independent life—the calyx of its reproductive organ serving it as a propulsive apparatus. In this condition it may acquire two or three times the dimensions it had when detached, and some of its parts may become wonderfully altered in form.

It is by no means improbable that some of the *Physophoridæ* may undergo a similar disruption, whole groups of organs, as in *Apolemia*, or at any rate the gonoblastidia, becoming detached.[1] Eschscholz (p. 159), who observed the ready separation of the latter in *Physalia*, imagined that they developed directly into young *Physaliæ*.

The preceding section was written before Professor Allman's valuable papers, cited at p. 17, came into my hands. I have adopted his terminology as far as possible; but I have been compelled to make certain modifications in it, for reasons which will be stated in a note at the end of this general introduction to the study of the *Hydrozoa*.

## SECT. II. SPECIAL MORPHOLOGY OF THE HYDROZOA.

I have now briefly described all the organs[2] of the *Hydrozoa* and their leading modifications, or, in other words, I have given some account of the general morphology of the class. The various modes in which these organs are grouped together is the subject matter of the present section on the special morphology of the group. Of these modes there are, at most, six or seven, and each, when clearly expressed, defines the plan of structure common to the members of one of the several groups or orders into which the zoologist divides the class—for a scientific classification is, after all, nothing more than a convenient mode of expressing the facts and laws established by the morphologist.

The first type, or plan of structure, is that exhibited by the order of the *Hydridæ*, containing the single genus *Hydra*, whose hydrosoma consists of only a single polypite, surrounded towards the distal end by a circlet of simple filiform tentacula, and expanded at the proximal end into a discoid hydrorhiza. The reproductive organs are simple spermaria or ovaria developed in the walls of the polypite, and the ectoderm developes no hard cuticular layer.

[1] See Leuckart, Z. U., pp. 69, 70.
[2] I have reserved the consideration of the Lithocysts for a future occasion, when the *Medusidæ* observed during my voyage will be described.

The second order, or the *Corynidæ*, have the hydrosoma developed into a cœnosarc of very various forms, supporting many polypites without thecæ, upon which are arranged in circlets, or irregularly, many filiform tentacula. The ectoderm of the cœnosarc (always?) developes a strong cuticle. The reproductive organs are produced by budding from the bases of the polypites, or from the cœnosarc, or from special *gonoblastidia*, but they present every variety in structure. The hydrosoma is fixed by a hydrorhiza.

The *Sertulariadæ*, which form the third order, have a cœnosarc, with a strong, chitinous cuticular layer, which is usually branched, and supports polypites enveloped in thecæ. Each polypite supports a subapical circlet of filiform tentacula. The reproductive organs vary in structure, but are always developed either from the cœnosarc or from gonoblastidia. The hydrosoma is fixed by a hydrorhiza.

The fourth order, or the *Calycophoridæ*, have an unbranched cœnosarc, which is flexible and contractile, and has no hard, chitinous cuticular layer. The hydrosoma is free, and is propelled by nectocalyces attached to its proximal end. The polypites have only one tentacle, developed near their basal or proximal ends, and provided with lateral branches ending in saccular enlargements. They have no thecæ, but are sometimes enveloped in hydrophyllia. The reproductive organs are always medusiform gonophores, produced by budding from the peduncles of the polypites.

The fifth order contains the *Physophoridæ*, which have an unbranched or very slightly branched, flexible, and contractile cœnosarc, which has no hard, chitinous outer layer. The hydrosoma is free, and its proximal end is modified into a pneumatocyst. It may be propelled by nectocalyces or not. The polypites have either a single basal tentacle, or the tentacles, whose structure varies greatly, arise directly from the cœnosarc. There are no thecæ. Hydrophyllia are commonly, but not always, developed from the peduncles of the polypites, or from the cœnosarc. The reproductive organs vary, but are never simple sacs. They are developed upon gonoblastidia.

The *Lucernariadæ*, which constitute the sixth order, have the base of their hydrosoma developed either primitively, or in the medusiform zöoids to which they may, by a process of fission, give rise, into an umbrella. The cœnosarc has no chitinous cuticle. The tentacles are simple, and are developed from the umbrella or its representative. There are no nectocalyces or hydrophyllia. The reproductive organs are developed in the wall of the umbrella of the primitive polypite, or in that of the medusiform zöoids produced from it.

Finally, I have retained the term *Medusidæ* as, at any rate, a temporary denomination for all those members of the group termed *Cryptocarpæ* by Eschscholz, *Gymnophthalmata* by Forbes, *Craspedota* by Gegenbaur, with whose origin we are unacquainted. It is not yet proved[1] that any of them are developed directly from the eggs of similar organisms, and until this is the case the order can be regarded only as a provisional one.

Using the term in this sense, the *Medusidæ* have a hydrosoma consisting of a single

---

[1] In using this expression, I by no means wish to question the great probability of the supposition that those ciliated embryos, which were observed by Müller ('Müller's Archiv,' 1851) and Gegenbaur ('Zur Lehre vom Generations-wechsel,' 1854) to pass directly in the "Medusæ" *Œginopsis mediterranea* and *Trachynema ciliatum*, proceeded from the eggs of similar Medusæ. But, I repeat, there is no proof of the fact.

polypite, with or without tentacles, suspended from the roof of a bell-shaped body, having the structure of a nectocalyx, and like it, provided with a marginal valve, and with radiating and circular nectocalycine canals. The reproductive organs are usually simple spermaria or ovaria, developed in the walls of the canals or in those of the polypite.

## SECT. III.  GENERATION AND DEVELOPMENT OF THE HYDROZOA.

The substance of the spermarium in all the *Hydrozoa* in which I have traced its development (and I have studied to this end members of each of the orders) becomes differentiated into minute, clear, spherical vesicles, of about $\frac{1}{4000}$th to $\frac{1}{3000}$th part of an inch in diameter, in which I have been able to observe no further structure. The vesicle gradually becomes pointed at one end, while at the other it developes a slender cilium, and, eventually, the vesicle assumes the characters of the head of the spermatozoon, while the cilium becomes its tail. The head of the spermatozoon is always broader at that end to which the cilium is attached.

The ovarium, in like manner, breaks up into a number of spheroidal, or originally, polygonal masses, each of which contains a clear space, with or without a distinct wall—the germinal vesicle, and in its centre a smaller, thick-walled vesicle—the germinal spot. I have never observed any vitelline membrane around these ova. Allman describes none in *Cordylophora*, and Gegenbaur (p. 49) distinctly denies the existence of any in the ripe ova of those *Calycophoridæ* and *Physophoridæ* which he examined.

Gegenbaur (p. 49) has observed the direct contact of the spermatozoa with the ova in the *Calycophoridæ* and *Physophoridæ*. The spermatozoa never entered the ovisacs, but as soon as the ova were detached they were surrounded by the spermatozoa, which fixed themselves by their heads to the yelk, their vibrating tails radiating in all directions. Gegenbaur, however, does not appear to have witnessed the direct penetration of any of them into the substance of the yelk. Complete yelk-division takes place in the ordinary way in all *Hydrozoa*, and Gegenbaur has made the important observation that, in certain *Corynidæ*,[1] *Calycophoridæ* and *Physophoridæ*, the germinal vesicle does not disappear, but that its division immediately precedes that of the yelk—so that its progeny must eventually become the " embryo cells " of the division masses.

Towards the end of the process of yelk-division, cilia appear upon the surface of the embryo.

Thus far all the *Hydrozoa* appear to follow a like course, but from what is at present known it would seem that the different orders diverge somewhat in their further progress.

In *Tubularia* and *Cordylophora*, in *Campanularia* (?) in *Cyanæa* (and hence, probably, in all *Corynidæ*, *Sertulariadæ*, and *Lucernariadæ*), a cavity rapidly makes its appearance in the centre of the germ-mass, which thus becomes a blastodermic vesicle, and then the walls of this vesicle are differentiated into ectoderm and endoderm.

From Gegenbaur's observations it would appear that in the *Calycophoridæ* and *Physo-*

---

[1] See the account of the development of the ova of the Corynidan medusiform zöoid, *Oceania armata*, in Gegenbaur's instructive Essay, ' Zur Lehre vom Generations-wechsel,' 1854.

*phoridæ*, on the other hand, the blastoderm, whence the organs are developed, is, at first, confined to a comparatively small portion of the divided yelk, where it appears as a thickened elevation. What becomes of the rest of the germinal mass, and what organ is first formed in the *Physophoridæ*, is not known, but in the *Calycophoridæ*, at least in *Diphyes*, Gegenbaur states that the first-formed protuberant blastoderm gives rise to a nectocalyx. The short and broad peduncle of this body is traversed by a canal, which expands within the remainder of the germinal mass into a ciliated cavity, which would appear to correspond with the internal cavity of the germ in the other orders. The nectocalyx attains a considerable relative size, and carries about the germinal mass with its contained cavity as an appendage at its proximal end. The first rudiments of the polypites bud out between this appendage and the nectocalyx (See Pl. V).

Thus far, Gegenbaur's direct observations go. He concludes from them that the nectocalyx which is first formed is the distal one of the two possessed by the adult, and that the mass of the yelk with its central cavity is converted into the somatocyst, which lies within the substance of the proximal nectocalyx of the adult.

The first conclusion is grounded on the fact that the nectocalycine duct divides into its canals close to the apex of the nectosac, which, as Gegenbaur justly points out, is an arrangement characteristic of the distal nectocalyx. But I confess this argument loses much of its apparent weight in my mind, when I reflect on the immense changes the minute nectosac must undergo before it can attain its adult form, and on the readiness with which, during this metamorphosis, the relations of the point of division of the duct to the sac might be changed.

Again, without by any means denying the possible or probable validity of the second conclusion, I must remark that mere similarity of tissue is hardly a sufficient ground for assuming the identity of an embryonic with an adult structure.

Of the mode of formation of the body of the embryo and of the pneumatocyst in the *Physophoridæ* nothing is at present known. The youngest forms hitherto observed are those described by Gegenbaur (in *Physophora*, *Forskalia*, and *Agalma*) and myself (in *Physali infrà*), and they were already provided with a pneumatocyst of large proportional size, and were terminated by a single large polypite, with a rudimentary tentacle.

In the *Corynidæ*, *Sertulariadæ*, and *Lucernariadæ* the ciliated embryo, after swimming about for awhile, fixes itself by one end, which is modified into the hydrorhiza, and then, elongating, becomes the cœnosarc, whence all the appendages are developed.

A wonderful uniformity pervades the first stages of the development of all the appendages of the *Hydrozoa*, notwithstanding their striking ultimate differences; but before passing to this part of the subject I must direct attention to the laws which govern the development of appendages in general upon the cœnosarc.

In the *Corynidæ*, *Sertulariadæ*, and *Lucernariadæ* new polypites are very generally, if not always, developed at, or near, the distal end or surface of the cœnosarc, so that the distal polypites are the youngest. Whether this law also holds good with regard to the reproductive organs of the first-named groups is perhaps doubtful.

Among the *Physophoridæ*, on the other hand, a precisely opposite general law obtains; not only the new polypites, but the new nectocalyces and reproductive organs, and even the branches of the tentacles, being developed on the proximal side of the old ones;

so that the distal appendages are the oldest.[1]   Where the organs are arranged in distinct groups, as in *Apolemia*, the same rule holds good, and the young groups are formed on the proximal side of the old ones.

The like is true for the distinct groups of organs (polypites, tentacles, hydrophyllia, &c.) which are arranged upon the cœnosarc of the *Calycophoridæ*, the young buds being continually developed on the proximal side of the old ones ; so that close to the proximal end of the cœnosarc there is a point which may be regarded as a sort of centre of growth, whence new parts are continually being thrust out towards the distal end.

The nectocalyces of the *Calycophoridæ*, however, do not appear to follow the same law as the other appendages.   For if the deflexed axis which supports the nectocalyces of *Hippopodius* is simply the bent-down proximal end of the cœnosarc, as the study of its development (Leuckart, Z. N. K., p. 68) would seem to prove, the young nectocalyces certainly originate upon the distal side of the old ones, or, in other words, they diverge from the same centre of growth as the other appendages of the cœnosarc, and, consequently, they must be successively pushed out in the opposite direction.

If, again, Gegenbaur is right in considering the first-formed nectocalyx of *Diphyes* to be the distal one, then the locomotive appendages of this genus would follow yet another law, the second being developed on the proximal side of the first formed, while the third bud, destined to replace the first or distal nectocalyx, is certainly produced from the hydrosoma on the distal side of the first, and the successor of the third again arises on its distal side, and so onwards.   If, on the other hand, the first-formed nectocalyx of *Diphyes* is really the proximal one of the adult, this genus follows the same law as *Hippopodius*, the young nectocalyces being developed on the distal side of the old ones, while all the other appendages are developed on the proximal side of the old ones, and the two sets thus diverge from a common centre of growth.

However this may be, the knowledge of the fact that new appendages and parts of appendages are constantly being formed in definite localities is of great importance to the student of the *Hydrozoa ;* for he is thereby enabled to study their development as easily on adults as on embryos, and to find in almost every specimen a complete series of stages of every organ.   The result is that this part of our knowledge of the *Hydrozoa* is tolerably complete.

Every appendage (except the hydrothecæ and lithocysts) commences its existence as a cæcal process of the ectoderm and endoderm, the latter being very generally, if not always, ciliated upon its surface, and containing, of course, a diverticulum of the somatic cavity.

If the appendage be a polypite, it gradually elongates, assumes its characteristic form, and eventually opens at its extremity.   The villi, where they exist, are developed as outgrowths of the endoderm.   The polypite is at first a perfectly simple sac, and the ultimate division into peduncular, gastric, and buccal portions is the result of the different form assumed, and histological differentiation undergone, by its corresponding regions.`

The pyloric valve of the *Calycophoridæ* is formed by the inward growth of the walls of the polypite at the junction between its peduncular and gastric divisions.

---

[1] Whether the hydrophyllia invariably follow this law may be doubted, and it is not certain that it obtains even for the other organs in such *Physophoridæ* as *Velella* and *Porpita*.

The tentacula originate in cæcal diverticula either of the wall of the polypite or of some part of the cœnosarc, and, in their simpler forms, merely elongate and acquire thread-cells in their ectoderm, while their endoderm may or may not undergo that process of vacuolation which, in some cases, obliterates the central canal.

In all the *Calycophoridæ* and *Physophoridæ* which I have examined, except *Velella* and *Porpita*, the canal of the tentacle remains freely pervious, its endoderm being thin and not vacuolated. When the tentacle is branched, its branches appear successively as close-set buds on one side of the proximal end of the tentacle, the younger buds being always, as I have stated above, developed on the proximal side of the older ones. The buds are, at first, simple, short cæca, and such, with a slight change in form, they remain in *Physalia*; while in *Rhizophysa* they elongate and become filiform.

The complex tentacular appendages of the *Calycophoridæ* (Pl. V), of *Athorybia* (Pl. IX), or *Physophora* (Pl. VIII), arise in the same way, but, as the bud elongates, it becomes divided into three portions : a proximal, slender division (the peduncle), with walls of the same thickness all round ; a median, thickened, cylindrical sac, whose walls are much thicker on one side than on the other ; and a distal, more slender, cylindrical portion. Shortly after this has taken place, the rudiments of the large, oval, and small palisade-like, thread-cells appear in the thick wall of the median division, which gradually acquires the characters of the sacculus. In the *Calycophoridæ* as in *Halistemma* and *Stephanomia*, the distal division elongates very greatly, and becomes the single filament. In *Athorybia* and those other *Physophoridæ* which have a median lobe and two filaments, it divides at a very early period into three lobes ; the lateral ones elongate into the filaments, and acquire numerous thread-cells in their thick walls, while the walls of the median process or lobe, which undergoes far less elongation, remain thin and free from thread-cells.

The involucrum is formed as a process of the ectoderm of the distal end of the peduncle. In *Physophora*, as will be more particularly described below, the distal end of the peduncle itself undergoes a singular dilatation, and helps to form the envelope for the sacculus.

The rudiments of the hydrocysts are at first indistinguishable from those of the polypites ; and, indeed, as I have already remarked, they are in their perfect condition like nothing so much as polypites which, having reached a certain stage of development, have subsequently merely increased in size.

A hydrotheca is simply the cuticular investment of its polypite, and, in the young bud, is represented merely by the outer layer of the ectoderm. But, as growth proceeds, this becomes more and more widely separated from the body of the polypite, assumes its characteristic shape, and eventually opens at its distal end so as to allow of the protrusion of the distal moiety of the polypite. This process of development may be very easily traced in the *Campanulariæ*.

Hydrophyllia, on the contrary, are always developed as buds precisely similar in composition to those which give rise to polypites or tentacles, and are therefore composed of both ectoderm and endoderm. As they grow they assume their characteristic form, the ectoderm enlarging out of all proportion to the endoderm and its contained diverticulum of the somatic cavity. Consequently, when they have attained their full growth, they appear like masses of a solid and glassy substance, traversed by an apparently insignificant and narrow cavity, which assumes very various shapes, and in whose wall the endoderm is often hardly distinguishable.

All nectocalyces, whatever their ultimate form, are developed in the same way. The bud from one side of the cœnosarc, in which they originate, becomes somewhat rounded and enlarged distally, so that its proximal end takes on the form of a narrow peduncle, and the diverticulum of the somatic cavity becomes pyriform. The distal wall of this cavity now thickens, so as to form a prominent, hemispherical boss, whose convexity is turned inwards— and which thus alters the form of the cavity from that of a pear to that of a cup. The nectocalyx gradually enlarges, and at the same time the cup-shaped cavity is so modified as to appear prolonged at its circumference into four equidistant cornua or cæca, which embrace the hemispherical thickening, running along its sides parallel with the axis of the organ (Pls. VII, VIII, X).

I have elsewhere described the production of these canals to be the result of the union of the sides of the boss with the walls of the cup-shaped cavity, but I by no means deny the possibility of its being partly due also, to the extension of cæcal processes of the cavity into the solid substance itself. Whatever be the minuter steps of the process, however, the final result is that the primitive central cavity becomes proportionally very small, and that it is continued by four longitudinal canals to near the distal end of the young organ. The cæcal ends of these nectocalycine canals now send out a lateral process on each side, and the adjacent lateral processes eventually unite so as to form a circular canal, so that the cavities of the four longitudinal canals are now in free communication distally as well as proximally, while the canal of the peduncle (the nectocalycine duct) connects the whole system with the general somatic cavity.

During these changes the central prominence or boss, which has become very large, does not remain solid. An irregular cavity appears within it, and gradually pushes aside its substance until the latter is reduced to a thin coat, which acquires a muscular structure. The cavity is at first closed, but it does not remain so; for an aperture appears at the distal end of the organ, and puts the nectosac in free communication with the surrounding medium. The membranous valve is a process developed from the muscular wall round this aperture.

The multifarious accessory ridges and ornaments, all the peculiarities of form, all the singular contortions of the lateral canals, and the curious processes of the nectocalycine duct, which Leuckart terms "mantel-gefässe," are superinduced in the course of growth upon the primitive model whose formation has just been traced.

The gonophores are always, when they are distinct from the rest of the walls of the hydrosoma, originally developed as cæcal processes of the ectoderm and endoderm, between which, and as I believe, by a histological modification of the deeper layer of the ectoderm, the generative elements make their appearance. They differ from one another throughout the series of the *Hydrozoa*, simply according to the progress which they make towards the development of a gonocalyx around this sac; or, in other words, towards acquiring a medusiform structure. In *Hydra* and in *Plumularia* I can find no trace of such a structure at any period of development. In *Cordylophora*, in the androphores of *Physalia*, in the gynophores of *Athorybia* and other *Physophoridæ*, the system of canals is more or less irregularly developed; but it is only in the *Calycophoridæ*, in the *Velellidæ*,[1] and in some *Corynidæ* and *Sertulariadæ*, that the development of the medusiform generative zöoids is to be observed in full perfection.

The first stages in the development of these bodies precisely resemble those exhibited by the ordinary nectocalyces; but when the longitudinal canals are making their appearance, the central boss does not remain convex at its apex. On the contrary, it becomes excavated at this point, and the excavation gradually extending distally, eventually takes the form of a saccular diverticulum of the cavity of the organ, occupying the axis of the boss, and extending for a greater or less distance towards the distal end of the organ. It, therefore, lies in the middle, between the four longitudinal canals, and nearly takes the place of, though it by no means represents, the central cavity of the nectocalyx. The latter is, in fact, in consequence of the appropriation of the greater part of the substance of the boss to form the walls of this central cavity, reduced to a mere fissure, which gradually separates that part of the organ which contains the system of canals (as the calyx) from a free central sac (the manubrium), connected with the calyx only opposite the peduncle. An opening is formed at the distal end of the calyx, and becomes surrounded by a valvular membrane in the same way as has been described above for the nectocalyx: finally, as the fissure widens, that wall of it which belongs to the calyx becomes more and more widely separated from the central sac, and acquires a muscular structure.

The calyx is thus exactly comparable to a bell, and the manubrial sac to its clapper, while the peduncle is its handle. The future fate of the body thus formed varies. In some cases it remains attached by its peduncle, and the ova or spermatozoa making their appearance at a very early period in the walls of the sac, which never opens at its apex, are detached, apparently by the dehiscence of its outer wall; or the manubrium, having the same structure and being nothing but a genital sac, does not get rid of it products until the whole body has been detached from its peduncle, and swims about independently; or the reproductive elements may not have appeared in the walls of the manubrium when the organ is detached, and then the sac opens at its end and becomes functionally and structurally a polypite. The reproductive elements are ultimately developed either in its walls or in those of its system of canals; or it may be that such bodies are in some cases (*Willsia, Lizzia?*) mere gonoblastidia, whence the true reproductive apparatus is eventually developed.

[1] Sars ('Fauna,' p. 38) has however shown that the androphores are detached as free medusiform bodies in his '*Agalmopsis elegans.*'

The note upon the nomenclature of the parts of the reproductive organs of the *Hydrozoa* which should have been inserted here (see p. 20) will, I find, take so much more space than I anticipated, that it must be deferred to the end of the work.

## SECT. IV.—THE GENERA AND SPECIES OF THE CALYCOPHORIDÆ.

The generic term *Diphyes* was proposed by Cuvier to designate the singular animal originally described by Bory de St. Vincent under the name of "Biphore biparti." Cuvier imagined that the nectocalyces—the two most obvious organs of the *Diphyes*—were distinct animals, temporarily united, and possibly in copulation. It was not until 1827 that Quoy and Gaimard established the family of "Diphides," or *Diphydæ*, to include this genus, together with their *Calpe, Abyla, Nacella, Cuboides,* and *Enneagonum.*

Two years later, Eschscholz formed the group of *Siphonophoræ*, to include these and other "Acalephæ," with the definition, "No central digestive cavity, but separate suckers. Swimming organs either special cavities or vesicles filled with air, or both combined." The assemblage is very natural, though its definition requires some rectification. Its author divides it into three families: "1. The *Diphyidæ*, having a soft body coalescent at one end with a cartilaginous part, and possessing a second swimming organ with a swimming cavity. 2. The *Physophoridæ*, having a soft body provided at one end with a vesicle filled with air. 3. The *Velellidæ*, whose body contains a cartilaginous or calcareous shell, in whose many cells air is contained."

Eschscholz's family of *Diphyidæ* contains the genera *Eudoxia* (including the *Pyramis* of Otto), *Ersœa, Aglaisma, Abyla* (including *Calpe, Abyla,* and *Rosacea* of Quoy and Gaimard), *Cymba* (including *Enneagonum* and *Cuboides,* Q. and G.), and *Diphyes.* *Hippopodius* is arranged with the *Physophoridæ.*

Quoy and Gaimard subsequently added the genera *Cucubalus* and *Cucullus;* and De Blainville, *Amphiroa, Praia, Galeolaria* (*Sulculeolaria*), and *Tetragonum.* Unfortunately, the author of the 'Actinologie' winds up the list with *Noctiluca!* and *Doliolum!!*

Kölliker made a substantial addition to our knowledge of this group by his account of the structure and determination of the affinities of *Hippopodius*, and by his description of a new genus, *Vogtia;* while his researches, conjoined with those of Vogt, Leuckart, and Gegenbaur, added largely to our acquaintance with the general organization of the order;— and finally Leuckart, in his excellent general account of what has been done of late years towards the elucidation of the relations of these animals, proposed the term *Calycophoridæ* instead of *Diphydæ*, which is inapplicable to such genera as *Hippopodius* and *Vogtia.*

These *Calycophoridæ* he divides into two families: 1. *Diphyidæ*, including *Abyla, Diphyes, Galeolaria,* and *Praya.* 2. *Hippopodiidæ*, containing *Hippopodius* and *Vogtia.*

The "monogastric" *Calycophoridæ*, such as *Eudoxia* and *Ersœa*, which were erected by Lesson into a distinct group, are considered to be only derivative forms.

I agree with Leuckart in adopting the ordinal name *Calycophoridæ*, instead of *Diphydæ;* and with Sars, Vogt, and Leuckart in regarding the monogastric genera as derivative forms, properly classed under the genera whose zöoids they are.

Nevertheless, in the present imperfect state of our knowledge, it will be more convenient

*Genus* IV. PRAYA.

*P. cymbiformis.*

(**P.** *diphyes,* **P.** *maxima.*)

IV. *Fam.* HIPPOPODIIDÆ.

Calycophoridæ with many nectocalyces, whose hydrœcia are incomplete. No hydrophyllia.

*a.* The nectocalyces horseshoe-shaped, smooth.

*Genus* V. HIPPOPODIUS.

1. *H. gleba.*

*b.* The nectocalyces produced into several pointed processes.

*Genus* VI. VOGTIA.

1. *V. pentacantha.*

*Fam.* DIPHYDÆ.

*Genus* DIPHYES (*Cuvier*).

Both the nectocalyces have a mitrate form, with five more or less convex faces, and hence, a pentagonal transverse section. The proximal nectocalyx is as large as, or larger than, the distal one. The hydrophyllia are folded round like the spathe of an arum, and have their outer surfaces not facetted or irregular, but smoothly convex.

1. DIPHYES DISPAR (*Chamisso* and *Eysenhardt,* 1821). Pl. I, fig. 1.

*Biphore biparti,* Bory de St. Vincent, 1804.

*Diphyes,* Cuvier, 1817.

*Diphyes dispar,* Chamisso and Eysenhardt, 1821.

—— *Bory,* Quoy and Gaimard, 1824.

*Diphyes,* Quoy and Gaimard, 1827.

—— *angustata,* Eschscholz, 1829.

—— *dispar,* Idem.

—— *campanulifera,* Idem.

—— *Boryi,* De Blainville, 1830.

—— *dispar,* Lesson, 1830.

—— *Bory,* Quoy and Gaimard, 1833.

—— *regularis,* Meyen, 1834.

—— *turgida?* Gegenbaur, 1854.

The proximal and distal nectocalyces are of the same length; but the **proximal is the** thicker.

The latter (fig. 1) is compressed from side to side, and ends superiorly[1] in a point whose obtuseness or acuteness varies much in different individuals. The anterior contour presents a slight, the posterior, a very marked, convexity. The ridges of the anterior face are more or less strongly serrated, and end below in three inflexed points. The hydrœcial aperture is quadrilateral, and very large in full-grown individuals; occupying more than two thirds of the antero-posterior diameter of the lower end. Its lateral edges are cut off very obliquely from behind downwards and forwards, and its anterior boundary (1 a) is formed by two very broad, quadrate, overlapping septal plates.

The hydrœcium extends for about half the length of the organ.[2] The somatocyst is narrow and subcylindrical, and does not extend so far as the upper cœcal extremity of the nectosac.

The latter is long and narrow; it widens superiorly, and then narrows suddenly into a tubular cæcum. The superior third of the distal nectocalyx (fig. 1 b, 1 c) is elongated into a pointed process, which is completely received within the hydrœcium of the proximal nec-tocalyx. The anterior margin of this process forms an obtuse angle with the anterior margin of the main body of the organ; but the posterior margin passes at a right angle into the truncated inferior half of the anterior end, so as to form a sort of step. The anterior and posterior sides of the inferior two thirds of the organ are nearly parallel; the anterior contour being nearly straight, while the posterior is a little convex.

The nectosac is subcylindrical and rounded superiorly, the nectocalycine duct abutting anteriorly a little below its apex. Of the five pointed processes which surround its mouth, three are the ends of the serrated ridges which extend along the posterior face of the organ. The other two correspond with the terminations of the antero-lateral longitudinal ridges, and when viewed from above are seen also to form the margins of a broad, transverse septal plate, which continues backwards the floor of the hydrœcial canal (fig. 1 c).

The latter is bounded laterally and in front by two thin plates, which commence about the middle of the superior process, opposite whose lower part their anterior margins bend inwards, and finally overlap for a short distance.[3] The inflexed edges next separate for a brief space, so as to leave an oval interval, and then the left again overlaps the right, by a broad inflected process. Inferiorly the latter ends suddenly, and the two plates run parallel for a short distance, to terminate by abruptly truncated inferior edges.

The hydrophyllium (fig. 1 e) is a delicate and transparent glassy plate—its edges over-lapping both above and below its point of attachment. Its truncated distal margin is produced and acuminated at its angles.

| Length of the superior nectocalyx | . | . | 1 inch. |
|---|---|---|---|
| Depth ,, ,, | . | . | $\frac{11}{14}$ ,, |
| Thickness ,, ,, | . | . | $\frac{1}{4}$ ,, |

---

[1] In this and all the following descriptions of the species of *Calycophoridæ* it is supposed that the apex of the proximal nectocalyx is directed upwards, and that the side on which the hydrœcium lies is posterior.

[2] Eschscholz indeed says, " Cavitate ductus nutritorii ante medium corporis desinente," which is in strictness true; but the difference between the length of the hydrœcium and half the length of the organ is very slight indeed.

[3] This overlapping is well figured by Chamisso and Eysenhardt, loc. cit., tab. xxxii H.

| | | | | |
|---|---|---|---|---|
| Length of the inferior nectocalyx | . | . | 1 | inch. |
| Depth          „          „ | . | . | $\frac{1}{3}$ | „ |
| Thickness      „          „ | . | . | $\frac{5}{44}$ | „ |

Cœnosarc, between two and three inches long.

Polypite, $\frac{1}{8}$ inch.

Sacculus of the tentacle, $\frac{1}{125}$ inch.

The three specimens on which this description is founded were taken on the 15th of July, 1847, in the Southern Pacific Ocean, in lat. 36° 31′ south, and about fourteen miles from the eastern coast of Australia. One was quite colourless, except the sacculi of the tentacles, which had the usual reddish hue. In the other two the nectosacs were irregularly stained with red.

I took several specimens of what I believe to be this species once again, on the eastern coast of Australia (December 21st, 1848). At least, the only difference I could detect was the absence of the median division of the transverse plate which forms the anterior boundary of the hydrœcium in the superior nectocalyx. In the largest of these specimens the superior nectocalyx was even thicker and blunter than in the figured specimen; while the smaller forms showed insensible gradations to such a figure as that represented in 1 *d*. It will be observed, however, that this young specimen has the characteristic somatocyst and tubular cæcum of the nectosac. The detached superior nectocalyces of young specimens of the same species were taken in the South Atlantic and in the Indian Ocean.

MM. Quoy and Gaimard, took *D. dispar* in the Straits of Gibraltar, but it is not noted by the German investigators of the Mediterranean *Calycophoridæ*, unless, as I am inclined to think, it is identical with Gegenbaur's *D. turgida*.

I have taken some pains to unravel the history of this, the first discovered of the *Calycophoridæ*, and to trace its identity through the manifold changes of name which it has undergone. It is described in the following words by its original observer, Bory de St. Vincent :

"*Salpa* (bipartita) *lanceolata bipartita*.—Le Biphore biparti est si transparent qu'on ne le distingue pas dans l'eau ; lorsqu'on l'en tire, il a l'air d'une lame de cristal, et ne présente aucune sorte d'organisation. Son corps est oblong, et comprimé latéralement. La partie antérieure présente cinq angles saillans ; le côté dorsal étant caréné, l'inférieur est au contraire sillonné. On reconnaît dans cette partie deux cavités longitudinales ; de la supérieure sort un filet, souvent très-long et rarement entier ; il supporte, quand il existe, une foule de petits corps qui ressemblent aux glandes pedicellées de plusieurs végétaux. La partie postérieure est amincie à son extrémité, et a quelques rapports avec la forme du fer d'une lancette ; le côté supérieur, qui est plat, est épais d'une ligne et demie. Dans cette épaisseur se trouve une cavité interne, dans laquelle entre une sorte d'éperon qui termine la partie antérieure ; et c'est là toute l'union apparente de deux parties de l'animal. Il y a aussi une autre cavité inférieure dans la moitié de derrière, dont l'ouverture échancrée au point de jonction des deux parties, forme un cran à leur union."[1]

[1] Bory de St. Vincent, 'Voyage dans les quatre principales Iles des Mers d'Afrique,' 1804, t. i, pp. 134, 135, note ; and 'Collection de Planches,' pl. vi, fig. 3 A, B, C.

It is clear from this description that Bory de St. Vincent regarded the proximal nectocalyx as the posterior, the distal as the anterior, which is not their relation in swimming. In his figure A, the cœnosarc is represented as issuing from the nectosac of the distal nectocalyx, and the minuter details of structure are not given. Nevertheless, its identity with the species under description is unmistakeable. It was taken about midway between Tristan da Cunha and the Cape of Good Hope.

Cuvier (as has been stated above) gave the generic name of *Diphyes* to this species in the 'Regne Animal' (1817), but conferred no specific denomination upon it.

Chamisso and Eysenhardt (De Animalibus quibusdam, 'Nova Acta,' x, 1821, p. 365) describe and figure a *D. dispar*, which they justly consider to be the same as Bory's species, and which is certainly identical with mine. They took it in the equinoctial Pacific.

In the ('Zoology of Freycinet's Voyage,' 1849), Quoy and Gaimard say (under the head of "Diphyes Bory")—"Only a single species of this genus is known: it was discovered by M. Bory de St. Vincent, who has figured it under the name of *Biphore biparti*. It is the same as that which we reproduce here, and which we dedicate to this naturalist. After him, MM. Tilesius and Chamisso have also given figures of it" (p. 577). I am inclined to judge from the figure (tab. lxxxvi, fig. 2), which, however, is not so good as that of Bory or that of Chamisso and Eysenhardt, that the "Diphyes Bory" is really the same as Bory's species. At any rate, Quoy and Gaimard admit that it is so, and therefore one does not see how they were justified in suppressing the name *D. dispar*, given by Chamisso and Eysenhardt three years before, and creating a new one.

The French voyagers and naturalists give the Atlantic, the Indian Ocean, the coasts of New Holland and of Timor, as the geographical range of their *Diphyes*.

Curiously enough, Quoy and Gaimard confer no specific name at all on the *Diphyes* which they figure and describe in the 'Annales des Sciences,' 1827, and leave one in doubt whether they consider it identical with that previously described by Bory de St. Vincent and themselves or not.

Eschscholz (1829), not recognising its identity with Chamisso and Eysenhardt's *D. dispar*, and with Quoy and Gaimard's *D. Boryi*, with both of which he was acquainted only by figures and descriptions, calls it *D. campanulifera;* while he establishes a new species (*D. angustata*) upon a form which he observed himself. I can find in his figures and descriptions, however, nothing to justify the separation of *angustata* from *dispar, campanulifera,* or *Boryi.*

Lesson did good service in his 'Centurie Zoologique' (1830), by rehabilitating the name *Diphyes dispar*, and by reproducing side by side with his own drawing the various figures of this *Diphyes* already given, so as to show the identity of the forms described by Bory, Chamisso, and Quoy and Gaimard. He took the species frequently in the Indian Ocean and about the Moluccas.

In the 'Zoology of the Voyage of the Astrolabe' (t. iv, 1833, p. 83) Quoy and Gaimard, still ignoring the name given by Chamisso and Eysenhardt altogether, and not even referring to these able naturalists, describe and figure anew the *Diphyes Boryi*. In its general outline the new figure perfectly resembles that given by Lesson and others, but while in all the preceding figures, in which the hydrœcium and the nectosac of the proximal nectocalyx are depicted, the hydrœcium hardly extends beyond the middle of the nectosac, it is made to be as long, or even longer, in this. Nevertheless, in the 'Annales' (1827), a figure of a species, which is supposed by the French voyagers themselves to be the same, is given with the two parts in the ordinary proportion.[1] I make no question that there is some error here, and that *D. dispar* was the only *Diphyes* seen by Quoy and Gaimard.

The 'Beiträge zur Zoologie' of Meyen ('Nov. Acta,' t. xvi, Supp. 1, 1834) contains a long and in some respects valuable description of a species of *Diphyes*, which he considers to be new, and calls *D. regularis;* without, however, entering into any comparison with the species already described by Eschscholz and Quoy and Gaimard, or in any proper way defining the characters of the supposed new species. In fact, *D. regularis* is nothing but *D. dispar*, as an attentive examination of the figures and description at once shows. Meyen has fallen into an error in describing four cavities in the proximal nectocalyx instead of three, and he regards the canals of the gonocalyx as muscles " intended by their contraction to facilitate the birth of the ova." However, his account is the best that had been up to that time given of the anatomy of a *Diphyes*. As I have hinted above, I have a strong suspicion that the *Diphyes turgida* of Gegenbaur ('Beiträge,' p. 62) is no other than this species; but it is not figured, and the description is very brief.

## DIPHYES APPENDICULATA. Pl. I, fig. 2.

*Diphyes appendiculata*, Eschscholz, 1829.
—— *elongata*, Hyndman, 1841.
—— *Sieboldii*, Kölliker, 1853.
—— *gracilis*, Gegenbaur, 1854.
—— *acuminata*, Leuckart, 1854.
—— *Kochii* (?), Will, 1844.
—— —— (?), Busch, 1851.
*Muggiœa pyramidalis* (?), idem.
*Eudoxia Lessonii* (Diphyozooid).

The proximal nectocalyx is larger than the distal; and is acuminated at its apex. The posterior contour is slightly and evenly curved; the anterior is a little concave below the apex, then strongly convex, and finally retreats a little at its inferior boundary. The anterior face presents three serrated ridges, which end below in but very slight points around the aperture of the nectosac, which therefore appears to be placed in the midst of a truncated inferior facet, occupying the anterior half of the inferior extremity of the organ. The posterior half is produced for some distance beyond this, so that the hydrœcium opens far below the nectosac. The aperture of the hydrœcium is as usual quadrate, and its anterior boundary is formed by two overlapping quadrate plates. The inferior edges of its lateral walls are cut

---

[1] De Blainville improves on this ('Manuel d'Actinologie,' tab. v) by making the hydrœcium and nectosac of equal size in the unmagnified figure of the " Diphye de Bory," and very unequal (or in their true relations, as I conceive) in the magnified one !

off obliquely from behind downwards and forwards. The hydrœcium is very short, not equalling more than a fourth the length of the whole organ, and its apex is curved backwards, so that its contour resembles that of a Phrygian cap. The somatocyst is connected with its anterior face, below its apex, by a narrow duct, and then expands into a wide subcylindrical sac, which terminates superiorly at about the junction of the inferior and middle fourths of the length of the organ. The nectosac gradually widens from its mouth, and having attained about two thirds of its entire length, gradually narrows again to end in a rounded apex, close to the superior extremity of the organ.

The distal nectocalyx is hardly more than two thirds as large as the proximal. The nectosac occupies not more than two thirds of its length. It is elongated, wider in the middle than at the ends, and is rounded superiorly. The inferior aperture is situated in the middle of a truncated facet, with almost obsolete ridge points, as in the proximal nectocalyx.

The distal portion of the organ, which contains the nectosac, is obliquely truncated proximally, passing into a slender beak-like process of the proximal moiety, which is inserted into the hydrœcium of the proximal nectocalyx, and carries the nectocalycine duct.

Two perpendicular plates rise from this process, and run down parallel with one another, to end below in free, pointed and serrated processes, which extend far beyond the aperture of the nectosac, and whose posterior edges are united for about half their length by a transverse plate (fig. 2 *b*). This continues downwards the floor of the hydrœcial canal, which is bounded at the sides by the two perpendicular plates, and in part by a transverse lamina, which stretches from one plate to the other for the greater part of their length.

The hydrophyllia are like those of *Diphyes dispar*, but are without the inferior truncated edge and acuminated angles.[1]

| | | | |
|---|---|---|---|
| Length of the proximal nectocalyx | . | . | $\frac{15}{24}$ inch. |
| Depth   ,,   ,, | . | . | $\frac{5}{24}$ ,, |
| Length of the distal nectocalyx | . | . | $\frac{11}{24}$ ,, |
| Depth   ,,   ,,  . | . | . | $\frac{7}{48}$ ,, |

This species was particularly abundant in Bass's Straits, in February, 1848. Several specimens were also taken in the southern part of the Indian Ocean. It has been taken[2] on the Irish Coast, and it seems to abound in the Mediterranean. Leuckart says he has seen it with a hydrosoma many inches long when fully extended, and with as many as fifty completely-developed polypites.

I entertain no doubt that the species which I have here described is identical not only with the *D. appendiculata* of Eschscholz, but with the *D. Sieboldii* of Kölliker. Leuckart admits that the *D. gracilis* of Gegenbaur is the same as Kölliker's *D. Sieboldii*. And in this I fully agree with him, though Gegenbaur says that the hydrœcium of the distal nectocalyx

[1] Compare Leuckart's account of their structure, Z. U., p. 67.

[2] See a 'Note on the occurrence of the genus *Diphya* on the Coast of Ireland,' by Mr. G. C. Hyndman ('Annals of Natural History,' vii, 1841.) Mr. Hyndman names the species *D. elongata*, but from his sketches I entertain no doubt that it is *D. appendiculata*.

in his species is open.  I believe, however, he has overlooked the anterior wall of its hydrœcial canal.  If he has not, then *D. acuminata* is not *D. Sieboldii*, in which Kölliker has not only described (p. 38), but has figured (tab. xi, fig. 8), the wall in question.  Leuckart also admits the great similarity of his *D. acuminata* with *D. Sieboldii*, but says that his species is "distinguished by the presence of a closed canal for the passage of the cœnosarc (Durchlass-kanal) in the posterior swimming organ."  However, this is contrary, as we see, to Kölliker's express statement.

Under the head of *Eudoxia Lessonii* (*infrà*) will be found my reasons for believing that form to be the free Diphyozooid of *D. appendiculata*.


DIPHYES CHAMISSONIS (n. sp.)  Pl. I, fig. 3.

The proximal nectocalyx is very wide above, where it ends in an obtuse point.  The anterior and posterior contours are nearly parallel; the posterior is straight; the anterior, a little convex.  The anterior ridges are serrated, and produced below into three strong incurved points.  The nectosac is wider superiorly than at the mouth, and ends above, close to the apex of the organ, in an obtusely pointed dome.

The hydrœcium has about half the length of the nectocalyx, and is straight, conical, and widely open below; its anterior wall is a single plate, deeply emarginate below, and somewhat convex forwards; the posterior wall is also emarginate; and the inferior edges of the lateral walls are but very slightly oblique.

The somatocyst is subcylindrical, and not so long as the hydrœcium.

The hydrophyllia resemble those of *Diphyes dispar*.

I took the detached proximal nectocalyces, with the cœnosarc attached, of this species, repeatedly, on the east coast of Australia and in the Louisiade Archipelago, during the years 1847, 1848, and 1849; but I was never able to obtain the inferior nectocalyx.

The specimen figured was about half an inch long; the fully formed hydrophyllia measured one twelfth of an inch.

I am unable to identify this with any of the described species of *Diphyes*.


DIPHYES MITRA, n. sp. (? APPENDICULATA).  Pl. I, fig. 4.

The proximal nectocalyx is considerably wider above than below; and is obtusely pointed at its apex.  The ridges of the anterior face are serrated, and end below in almost obsolete points.  The hydrœcium attains hardly more than one fourth of the length of the organ; it is obtusely conical, with a slightly recurved apex, beneath and in front of which arises the narrow neck of the somatocyst; the latter hardly extends beyond the middle of the length of the nectosac, and its walls are not vacuolated.  The anterior wall of the hydrœcium is formed below by two triangular plates, which extend inwards from its lateral walls, and overlap one another throughout their superior halves.

Hydrophyllium a very thin plate, whose edges are bent upon themselves, but do not completely overlap; the middle part of the inferior margin produced into a lobe.

Nectocalyx not more than one quarter of an inch long.

This obviously young and imperfect *Diphyes* was taken only once in the Indian Ocean, to the south-east of Mauritius, May 27th, 1847.

## DIPHYES KOCHII.

> *Diphyes Kochii*, Will, 1844.
>
> *Muggiæa pyramidalis*, Busch, 1851.

Will, in his 'Horæ Tergestinæ,' 1844, describes and figures a *Diphyes Kochii*, which he found in the Adriatic, and which appears to resemble the form just described in many respects. However, it differs from *D. mitra* in the gradual widening of the nectosac towards its lower end, so that the nectocalyx does not exhibit the peculiar inferior narrowing characteristic of *D. mitra*. All the specimens of *D. Kochii* examined by Will were devoid of a distal nectocalyx, and the proximal nectocalyx was not more than a line and a half long.

I am inclined to suspect that both *D. Kochii* and my *D. mitra* may be the young of *D. appendiculata*.[1] The *Muggiæa pyramidalis* of Busch ('Beobachtungen ueber Anatomie und Entwickelung einiger wirbelloser Seethiere,' 1851) is identical with *Diphyes Kochii*.

---

[1] Gegenbaur's account of the development of *D. appendiculata*, to which I have referred at p. 23 (see also Pl. V), shows that the nectocalyces of this species must undergo a very considerable change of form in the course of their development.

Sub-genus GALEOLARIA (*Lesueur* and *De Blainville*).

Distinguished from the other species of the genus *Diphyes* by the obsoleteness of the hydrœcium of the proximal nectocalyx.

GALEOLARIA FILIFORMIS.　Pl. III, fig. 5 ; and Pl. XII.

> *Physophora filiformis*, Delle Chiaje.
> *Galeolaria*, Lesueur, De Blainville, 1830.
> *Sulculeolaria quadrivalvis*, idem.
> *Beroides*, Quoy and Gaimard.　MSS. cited in Lesson's ' Acalèphes,' 1843.
> *Epibulia aurantiaca*, Vogt, 1851.
> —— *filiformis*, Leuckart, 1853.
> *Galeolaria aurantiaca*, Vogt, 1854.
> —— *filiformis*, Leuckart, 1854.
> *Diphyes quadrivalvis*, Gegenbaur, 1854.

I have only obtained a single detached distal nectocalyx of this species, and I must therefore borrow a brief description of its most important characters from other observers, more especially Leuckart and Gegenbaur.

Originally described by Delle Chiaje (' Descriz. et Notom.,' t. v, p. 135), and confounded by him with Forskäl's *Physophora filiformis*, subsequently termed by Quoy and Gaimard " Beroides," one or more species of this genus formed the basis of two genera, *Sulculeolaria* and *Galeolaria*, founded by Lesueur, and adopted and published by De Blainville in his manual.　De Blainville arranges both genera among his *Diphydæ*, and rightly suspects that *Sulculeolaria* may be only an organ ; but with respect to the *Galeolaria*, he hazards the unaccountable suggestion that " these animals differ essentially from the *Diphydæ*, approaching the *Beroidæ*."

The *Diphyes truncata*, so well described by Sars (' Fauna litt. Norv.,' 1846), is clearly a *Galeolaria*, but the Norwegian naturalist appears to have been unacquainted with De Blainville's manual, and hence has not referred to that genus or to *Sulculeolaria*.

Vogt observed the *Galeolaria* and *Sulculeolaria* forming one animal, which he described, at first, under the title of *Epibulia*, the name which Eschscholz had mistakenly conferred upon the Lamarckian *Rhizophysa* (*Physophora filiformis*, Forskäl).　Subsequently, Vogt adopted the name of *Galeolaria*, and Leuckart follows his example.　Gegenbaur is inclined to suppress both *Galeolaria* and *Sulculeolaria*, and calls his *Galeolaria* a *Diphyes*.　But the difference appears to me amply sufficient to warrant at least a subgeneric distinction.

For although the proximal and distal nectocalyces closely resemble those of *Diphyes* in their general structure and arrangement, the hydrœcium of the former is reduced to a mere depression, and, according to Leuckart, the anterior rounded ends of the lateral walls of the hydrœcial canal of the distal nectocalyx embrace the adjacent end of the proximal one.

The septal wall, which bounds the hydrœcial canal of the distal nectocalyx anteriorly, again, is divided by a median emargination into two wide lobes, with rounded margins (Pl. III, fig. 5 *a*); and the pointed processes which surround the lower apertures of the nectocalyces are large and strongly incurved. One, or even two, additional nectocalyces, smaller than the others, and apparently destined to replace them, are commonly attached to the proximal end of the cœnosarc.

The somatocyst is short, and of even diameter throughout. The course of the necto-calycine canals in the proximal nectocalyx is the same as in *Diphyes*; but, according to Leuckart, the lateral and posterior median canals are united by peculiar anastomosing trunks. The arrangement of the canals in the distal nectocalyx differs in the great loop, directed forwards, which the lateral canals make.

The polypites have the same structure as in *Diphyes*. The hydrophyllia are spathe-like, expanded, and deeply excavated on one edge.

The distal nectocalyx figured in Pl. III, fig. 5, was about five eighths of an inch long, and was obtained in the Indian Ocean, near Timor. The species has been taken in other parts of the Indian Ocean, and it appears to abound in the Mediterranean. Leuckart (Z. N. K., p. 33) records the same, or a very similar species, from Greenland; and Sars took it and another species of the same genus (*G. biloba*) on the coast of Norway.

### Genus ABYLA (*Quoy* and *Gaimard*).

The proximal nectocalyx differs widely from the distal one in form and size, the latter having an elongated, more or less mitrate shape, while the former presents many straight-sided, plane, tetragonal, pentagonal, or hexagonal facets.

The proximal nectocalyx is shorter than the distal. The hydrophyllia are thick and facetted, or produced into points on their outer surface, and their edges do not overlap spathe-wise.

ABYLA PENTAGONA. Pl. II, fig. 2.

> *Pyramis tetragona* (?) Otto, 1823.
> *Calpe pentagona*, Quoy and Gaimard, 1827.
> *Abyla pentagona*, Eschscholz, 1829.
> —— —— Delle Chiaje.
> —— —— Kölliker, 1853.
> —— —— Leuckart, 1853.
> —— *trigona*, Vogt, 1854.
> *Aglaisma Baeri*, Eschscholz, 1825.
> —— —— Busch, 1851.
> —— *pentagonum* (?), Leuckart, 1853.
> *Eudoxia cuboides*, idem, 1853.
> *Aglaismoides* (?), Huxley (*infrà*).

The proximal nectocalyx has not more than one third the length of the distal. If it be placed with the axis of its nectosac vertical and its hydrœcium backwards, it will be found to be four-sided and to have two parallel, flat, pentagonal faces, one of which is anterior and the other posterior. Each pentagon has one of its angles superior, and one side consequently inferior. The lateral faces are divided into two portions, one supero-lateral, four-sided, looks upwards and outwards, and meets its fellow of the opposite side in a ridge which joins the superior angles of the anterior and posterior faces. The other, infero-lateral, also four-sided, looks downwards and outwards, and is produced posteriorly and inferiorly into the lateral wall of the hydrœcium, as the posterior face is produced into its posterior wall. Anteriorly, the lateral plates are united by an undivided, anterior septum, which, like the posterior, has its lower edge deeply emarginated and serrated.

The nectosac opens upon the truncated anterior moiety of the inferior face of the organ. It is subcylindrical, and ends above before reaching the superior edge of the nectocalyx. The hydrœcium is a conical, wide-mouthed cavity, extending through less than half of the length of the organ. The somatocyst arises from it by a short and narrow duct, which opens into a large oval sac as wide as the nectosac, opposite whose extremity it suddenly contracts, and sends off from its anterior wall a narrow, cæcal process, which extends very nearly to the upper edge of the nectocalyx. The walls of this organ are greatly vacuolated.

The nectocalycine duct passes off at right angles from the base of the cœnosarc, and divides opposite the middle of the nectosac. The distal nectocalyx is wider distally than proximally. Its distal extremity is pentagonal, and of the five angles the four lateral are prolonged into strong, serrated points (of which the left hand and anterior is the largest); while the posterior is not at all produced, and as its ridge is correspondingly obsolete, while those from the others are tolerably well marked, the organ appears to be only quadrilateral. The posterior part of the proximal extremity is truncated, but anteriorly it sends off a short triangular process, through which the nectocalycine duct passes. From the edges of the anterior face two plates arise, which inclose the hydrœcial canal (fig. 2 *a*). The wider, right-hand, plate bends over, to end by a free, convex, serrated edge posteriorly, while its left, free edge is smooth. It overlaps the other, which is narrower, rises perpendicularly from the anterior surface of the organ, and ends in a number of very strong, distant, curved teeth.

The hydrophyllia are subcubical, sending off a process from behind the middle of their inferior surface. The phyllocyst has the form of a cross, with short, lateral arms.

| | | | | |
|---|---|---|---|---|
| Length of the proximal nectocalyx | . | . | $\frac{3}{16}$ | inch. |
| „ distal „ | . | . | $\frac{9}{16}$ | „ |
| „ hydrophyllium | . | . | $\frac{1}{60}$ | „ |

The history of my acquaintance with this species is somewhat instructive. On the 15th of April, 1847, while in the South Atlantic (lat. 38° 9′ south, long. 52° 31′ east), I first made acquaintance with a detached proximal nectocalyx, with which only a single polypite was connected, and which exhibited no trace of a distal nectocalyx. In the Indian Ocean, off Timor, and in the South Pacific,[1] I found other specimens in precisely the same condition ; and it was not until the 22d of December, 1848, that I met with one having the small inferior nectocalyx represented in fig. 2 *c*. The lower part of this organ had the form of a pentagonal prism, with three strong posterior longitudinal crests, and two anterior ones. All these terminated in strong incurved points below, and a strong plate projected backwards internal to the right anterior ridge. The proximal moiety was an irregular pyramid, traversed by the nectocalycine duct, which connected its extremity with the cœnosarc. This organ was so small as not to project beyond the hydrœcium.

This specimen, like the others, had only one polypite, and on subsequent occasions I repeatedly took the animal in the same state, and without any sign of a distal nectocalyx ; until, at last, on the 21st of July, 1849, while off the south-east coast of New Guinea, I obtained the entire individual represented in fig. 2. Even in this, however, the cœnosarc

---

[1] Leuckart (Z. U., p. 41) remarks on the wide geographical distribution of *Abyla pentagona*. Quoy and Gaimard took it at Gibraltar, and "in different seas" ('Zool. de l'Astrolabe,' iv, p. 90) ; Delle Chiaje and Costa at Naples ; Kölliker at Messina.

was incomplete, both the hydrophyllium and the reproductive organ of the terminal zöoid being imperfectly developed.

The two genera *Abyla* and *Calpe* were established by Messrs. Quoy and Gaimard[1] to include certain species of *Calycophoridæ* which they met with in the Straits of Gibraltar, in Bass's Straits, and elsewhere, and which were distinguished from *Diphyes* by the irregularly cuboidal form and small proportional size of the anterior nectocalyx.

Eschscholz, justly perceiving that no difference of generic importance existed between *Abyla* and *Calpe*, suppressed the latter name in the 'System der Akalephen,' and united all the species into the one genus *Abyla*,[2] which he characterised thus: "Ductus nutritorius tubulis pluribus obsitus; pars corporis natatoria cavitate parva natatoria interna, extrorsum se aperiente, instructa."

The genus thus defined contained the two species *A. pentagona* and *A. trigona* (neither of which was observed by Eschscholz himself); and Eschscholz adds, as a doubtful appendix to the genus, the two *Rosaceæ* of Quoy and Gaimard, which, however, are nothing but detached nectocalyces of *Praya*.

In a previous work ('Isis,' 1825) Eschscholz had established another genus of *Diphydæ*, *Aglaisma*, having the following diagnosis: "Tubulus suctorius unicus; pars corporis nutritoria cavitate parva natatoria interna instructa." And this genus he retains in the 'System.'

Leuckart, during his investigations at Nice, met with some individuals of the *Aglaisma* of Eschscholz, which he considers distinct from the *A. Baeri* of the latter writer, and terms *A. pentagonum*. His description of the nectocalyx agrees down to the smallest particulars with the structure of the corresponding part in the species of *Abyla* at present under description; and he shows that this so-called *Aglaisma* is essentially nothing but the detached anterior nectocalyx of *Abyla pentagona*, the precise result to which I was led in a different way in 1849.

Leuckart considers that this "*Aglaisma*-form" of *Abyla* is not a regular stage in the development of the animal; but that an adult *Abyla* has undergone mutilation—that it has lost its cœnosarc and inferior nectocalyx—and while in the act of reproducing them, necessarily takes on the *Aglaisma* form. In one "*Aglaisma*" he found a second polypite, with its tentacle, budding from the neck of the ordinary one; and he states that a more or less developed rudiment of the inferior nectocalyx is always present.

This was certainly not the case in my specimens, and I suspect Leuckart has fallen into error in describing the rudimentary inferior nectocalyx as a "four-sided" pyramid. (Z. U., p. 52.) Gegenbaur appears to have made similar observations to those of Leuckart and myself. He says ('Beiträge,' p. 14): "I have often seen young, entire *Abylæ pentagonæ* with only one polypite; and young *Diphyes* in the same condition." So that he regards these "Aglaisma-forms" as young, and not as mutilated adults.

Leuckart's careful investigations enable me to add some other particulars of interest to my account of the structure of *Abyla pentagona*. I did not trace the four canals which are given off from the short nectocalycine duct of the superior nectocalyx. But, according to

[1] 'Annales des Sciences Naturelles,' t. x, 1827.

[2] Eschscholz retained *Abyla* because he considered the form so named to have been more completely observed. But there is another reason for suppressing the name *Calpe*, in the fact that it had been applied by Treitschke to a genus of Lepidoptera in 1825 (Agassiz, Index, p. 176).

Leuckart, one descends directly from the end of the nectocalycine duct along the posterior wall of the nectosac to its mouth. Another passes upwards to the blind end of the nectosac, over which it runs, and down the middle line of its anterior face. The two other canals form an arch, convex upwards, on the lateral faces of the sac, and descend to its aperture, round which all four canals are united by a circular canal.

The inferior nectocalyx of the Mediterranean *Abyla pentagona* occasionally attains an inch in length. It has four longitudinal canals (*conf.* Kölliker, p. 46). To the upper end of the cœnosarc a rudimentary accessory nectocalyx is almost always attached, and the basal part of the cœnosarc, as far as the first rudiments of polypites, is ciliated internally.

Those groups of organs or zöoids which are provided with perfectly formed tentacles (and which occur at about the junction of the upper with the middle third of the cœnosarc), exhibit two other appendages; one, the rudiment of the hydrophyllium, and the other that of the reproductive organ. The latter becomes larger and larger, and finally its calyx assumes the form of a four-sided pyramid, while the generative elements are developed within its manubrium.

The rudiment of the hydrophyllium assumes at first the form of a trefoil leaf, with a median and two lateral lobes; and the phyllocyst acquires an elongated figure, with two lateral processes corresponding with these lobes. The inner surface of the hydrophyllium now, according to Leuckart, approaches the cœnosarc, and the two lateral lobes bend towards one another as if they were about to embrace it. From this time the lateral lobes grow rapidly, the emargination which separates them from the middle lobe is gradually effaced, and thus, when the organ has attained one fifth of a line in length, it lies like a saddle on the cœnosarc. The phyllocyst sends a long and slender canal downwards, parallel with the cœnosarc, a short process upwards, and two lateral processes at right angles to them.

"In the stage just described the hydrophyllium (Deckstück) has, as I have said, the form of a saddle: its lateral alæ are as yet isolated, so that the genital capsule—which now measures about one eighth of a line—projects outwards like a campanulate appendage between them. But these lateral alæ soon begin to coalesce, and the hydrophyllium enters into a new stage of development.

"The first traces of coalescence appear at the upper end of the alæ, which had previously approached one another in the middle line in front of the cœnosarc, and finally meet. The confluence proceeds rapidly downwards and inwards, so that the previously foliaceous hydrophyllium is very soon changed into a solid body, whose axis is traversed by the cœnosarc. In the lower half the coalescence is confined to the outer edges of the hydrophyllium. There remains here an internal dome-shaped cavity, whose bottom is pierced by the continuation of the hydrosoma, and, besides the polypite and tentacle, incloses the stem of the reproductive organ. At the point of insertion of the last, which now measures about a quarter of a line, and already has the form of a quadrangular pyramid with a contractile nectosac, the rudiment of a second reproductive capsule has appeared as a simple vesicular body, $\frac{1}{30}$th of a line long.

"At the commencement of the process just described, the outer surface of the hydrophyllium was tolerably evenly curved; but gradually four longitudinal ridges appear upon it, which run down at regular intervals, become bounded by plane surfaces, and gradually change the body into a cuboid, whose posterior surface is continued downwards into a hood-like (Schirmartig) appendage." [1]

Gegenbaur (' Zeitschrift für Wiss. Zool.,' v, p. 451) has objected that the hydrophyllium in *Abyla* does not grow round and embrace the cœnosarc, as Leuckart describes, but remains entirely on the side on which it was first formed ; and with this conclusion, notwithstanding the latter observer's reiteration of his own view (Z. N. K., p. 23), my own observations lead me to agree. The hydrophyllium figured in Pl. III, fig. 2 *d*, in fact, measured about $\frac{1}{60}$th of an inch in length, and yet, in opposition to Leuckart's statements quoted above, it had already assumed the cuboidal form ; and assuredly its lateral lobes had not coalesced round the cœnosarc. On the other hand, it seems very possible that the hydrophyllium may eventually infold the pedicle of the polypite.

The hydrophyllium attains, according to Leuckart, the length of half a line, while the cœnosarc is still entire. The polypite, tentacles, and gonophores associated with each hydrophyllium have also increased in size, and now the smallest shock, or even a sudden contraction of the cœnosarc, is sufficient to detach the group of organs as an independent Diphyozöoid, or " monogastric Diphyes."

Leuckart states (Z. U., p. 60) that he has repeatedly watched this process of separation under the microscope, which results from the cœnosarc breaking through midway between every two groups of organs, and that the young Diphyozöoid exhibits the projecting stump of the cœnosarc for a long time. Eventually the hydrophyllium enlarges to a length of $1\frac{1}{3}$ line, and has the form of a tall four-sided pyramid, with a square superior face and obliquely truncated inferior extremity, whose posterior wall is prolonged into a triangular blade, pointed below, and having a produced point on each margin. The inferior face presents the opening of a wide cavity, which extends upwards to the middle of the organ. The phyllocyst sends off a superior and an inferior narrow cæcum, and two very wide lateral branches, which embrace the dome-like roof of the cavity. The calyx of the reproductive organ attains a length of two lines and more, and is marked by four strong longitudinal crests, ending below in strong points. At the upper end is a conical process, whereby the organ adheres to the cœnosarc. Not infrequently, beside a gonophore of two lines long, another two thirds of a line in length, and already exhibiting contractions, may be seen. Leuckart terms the fully formed Diphyozöoid of *Abyla pentagona*, *Eudoxia cuboides*. But this organism differs widely from the *Eudoxia* of Eschscholz, and I believe it to be identical with one of the species of *Aglaismoides* (infrà), which in that case will form an additional synonym of *Abyla pentagona*.

Gegenbaur's account of the zöoids of *Abyla pentagona* agrees in all essential respects with that just cited from Leuckart, but he describes the phyllocyst as sometimes having four, instead of two, lateral lobes ; and states that the inferior extremity is emarginate and not pointed.

Vogt's figures and descriptions of the zöoids before their detachment are not very clear, but coincide, so far as they go, with those of Leuckart and Gegenbaur. In Kölliker's specimens the hydrophyllia appear to have been not yet developed, but he gives the first, and a remarkably clear, description of the nectocalyces and the mode of their adjustment to one another.

[1] Leuckart, Z. U., p. 59.

ABYLA BASSENSIS.  Pl. II, fig. 1.

*Diphyes Bassensis*, Quoy and Gaimard, 1833.
*Abyla quadrilatera*, De Blainville, 1830.
*Bassia quadrilatera*, Quoy and Gaimard, 1824.
*Calpe bassensis*, Lesson, 1843.
*Sphenoides* (?), Huxley (infrà).

The proximal nectocalyx has the same general form as in the foregoing species ; but, whereas in the latter, the base of the quadrate process, which contains the lower portion of the hydrœcium, does not occupy half the inferior face of the organ, it here takes up a much greater space, and is proportionally shorter and wider, its lower edges being somewhat everted.  The apex of the large and bell-shaped hydrœcium extends nearly to the middle of the organ, and is fully as long as the nectosac, which is wider and shorter, and has a proportionally narrower mouth.  The nectocalycine duct passes to its posterior face rather above its middle.  The somatocyst is ovoid, and has no narrow cæcal prolongation.

The distal nectocalyx is prismatic, and widest in the middle of its length.  The prism appears at first to have only four sides and as many longitudinal ridges, but in reality there are five ; that in the middle of the convex posterior face being almost obsolete, and marked only by a very small inferior pointed prolongation.

The postero-lateral crests are somewhat stronger, and their inferior points more prominent, and the antero-lateral ones are still more marked ; the right antero-lateral point is the strongest.  The anterior surface presents a deep longitudinal groove, bounded on each side by the antero-lateral ridges.  From the right-hand ridge a plate stretches transversely to the left-hand one, and is fixed to the latter for the greater part of its length, but it ends inferiorly in a free, convex, deeply serrated edge (fig. 1 a).  Beneath this plate may be seen indications of the existence of another, so that the anterior half of the hydrœcial canal is probably formed by the union of two plates, one from each antero-lateral ridge.

The inferior surface is truncated, and shelves downwards anteriorly into the septal ridge, which connects the terminations of the two antero-lateral crests.

The rounded aperture of the nectosac lies in the middle of the broad, flat inferior surface, of which it occupies only a small portion.  It is, as usual, surrounded by a membranous valve, and leads into a large nectosac, which gradually widens, attaining its greatest dimensions about the middle of the organ, and then narrowing again till it ends at about the junction of the upper with the next fifth of the long diameter of the organ.  The posterior and superior surface of the upper end shelves forwards and downwards, and where it joins the anterior surface, is the point of division of the nectoduct, which ascends thence obliquely to the floor of the hydrœcial canal.

The upper end of the distal nectocalyx is deeply notched, so as to present a sort of articular surface, into which the solid angle of the proximal nectocalyx, formed by the junction of the inferior and the posterior faces, is received.  The posterior facet of the notch looks forwards and upwards, and is formed by the upper face of that portion of the distal nectocalyx which contains the nectosac.  The lower half of the posterior face of the superior nectocalyx rests upon it.

small aperture of the nectosac, surrounded by a five-toothed raised margin. Posteriorly, the inferior face slopes very obliquely upwards and backwards, and presents a triangular space entirely occupied by the aperture of the hydrœcium.

The hydrœcium is bell-shaped and very large, occupying nearly the whole length of the organ. Its inferior aperture is narrow from side to side, but measured antero-posteriorly it equals about half the diameter of the nectocalyx in this direction.

The somatocyst—a large oval sac, occupying nearly all the space left between the posterior wall of the hydrœcium and the posterior contour of the organ—gives off no cæca. Its walls are highly vacuolated, and the duct by which it communicates with the cœnosarc opens into its apex.

The nectosac, finally, is subcylindrical, and tapers above to a point, against which the nectocalycine duct applies itself.

The distal nectocalyx (Pl. III, fig. 1 c) is pyramidal. Five more or less prominent longitudinal crests mark the outer surface of the organ, and are produced at its lower extremity into as many serrated points. The posterior of these is directed downwards and backwards; the lateral ones are curved sharply inwards; and the anterior pair pass downwards and forwards. Of these last that on the right-hand side is produced forwards into a crest which almost immediately becomes confounded with a large serrated perpendicular plate, which traverses the anterior face of the organ, and gives off from its inner surface a transverse plate, deeply toothed on its free edge.

The left-hand anterior point is prolonged upwards as a slight ridge for some distance, and then rises into a very strongly serrated vertical plate, which is overlapped by the transverse plate of the other side—the two enclosing the hydrœcial canal. Arrived at the conical, superior portion of the organ, the two crests diminish in height and become obsolete.

The nectosac is hardly more than two thirds as long as the whole organ, subcylindrical, and rounded above. The nectocalycine duct abuts against its apex.

The hydrophyllium is cuboidal, but narrower behind than in front, where it is somewhat excavated. The phyllocyst is oval, and two curved, narrow cæca proceed from it above.

<br>

| | | | |
|---|---|---|---|
| Length of the proximal nectocalyx | . | . | $\frac{5}{16}$ inch. |
| Length of the distal nectocalyx | . | . | $\frac{5}{8}$ ,, nearly. |

<br>

A single specimen of this species was taken in Torres Straits, off the south-east coast of New Guinea, on the 24th of July, 1849; but I observed it neither before nor afterwards.

The cœnosarc was imperfect and its appendages incompletely developed. The hydrophyllium described and figured was detached, but I have no doubt it belonged to this specimen. Its resemblance to the *Amphiroa alata* described below is so striking, that I imagine the latter must be the Diphyozöoid of *Abyla trigona*.

It is with some little hesitation that I identify this species with the *Abyla trigona* of Quoy and Gaimard, described and figured in the 'Annales des Sciences' for 1827, and subsequently in the 'Zoology of the Voyage of the Astrolabe,' t. iv, p. 87, pl. 3, iv, figs. 12—17; but there are so many points of similarity that I prefer to run the risk of making a species too few rather than one too many.

ABYLA LEUCKARTII. Pl. III, fig. 2.

The superior nectocalyx is long and broad, but thin and compressed from side to side, with six faces disposed around its longitudinal axis, and a single superior face which cuts the anterior and posterior ones nearly at right angles.

The anterior face (2 *b*) is flat and elongated, with four parallel sides. Its inferior angles are produced into two curved, serrated points.

The posterior face (2 *a*) is very narrow above, wider in the middle, and below ends in a point at the margin of the hydrœcium.

The antero-lateral faces are by far the largest; they are somewhat concave above, convex in the middle, and concave again below. They are separated by well-marked serrated ridges, concave forwards, from the narrow postero-lateral faces.

The superior face is hexagonal and somewhat concave; its posterior side is very small.

The inferior surface exhibits an anterior quadrate division facing downwards, and having in front the serrated points in which the lower angles of the anterior face end, while behind are two larger serrated points developed from the inferior edges of the lateral faces. Between these processes is the aperture of the nectosac itself, surrounded by four short, incurved points.

The posterior division is a triangular space which looks downwards and backwards and is wholly occupied by the aperture of the hydrœcium. The latter extends through nearly the whole length of the middle of the organ. Behind it is a large oval somatocyst with vacuolated walls, which occupies nearly all the space between it and the posterior face, and is connected by a duct from its apex with the cœnosarc.

The nectosac, cylindrical, narrow, and rounded above, extends as far upwards as the hydrœcium, and receives the short nectocalycine duct close behind its apex.

Length of the proximal nectocalyx . . $\frac{5}{16}$ inch.

A single specimen of this species, consisting of a detached superior nectocalyx, was taken in the South Pacific, not far from the east coast of Australia, in January, 1850.

Only one large polypite was attached to the remains of the cœnosarc, but several young ones were in the course of development.

I find no previous notice of this species, and I venture, therefore, to name it after the able Professor of Zoology at Giessen, to whom and to his colleague Frey, we are indebted for the most important improvement in the classification of the Animal Kingdom that has been made since the time of Cuvier—the establishment of the *Cœlenterata* as a sub-kingdom.

## *Fam.* SPHÆRONECTIDÆ.

### *Genus* SPHÆRONECTES (nov. gen.)

The proximal nectocalyx (which alone has been hitherto observed) is spheroidal, and of a gelatinous texture. The hydrœcium is completely closed behind. Hydrophyllia (?)

SPHÆRONECTES KÖLLIKERI. Pl. III, fig. 4.

*Rosacea*, Huxley, 1851.

Proximal nectocalyx a spheroid of gelatinous consistency, presenting anteriorly[1] a wide circular aperture, surrounded by a valvular membrane. This leads into a spacious, irregularly hemispherical sac, which reaches as far as the centre of the spheroid. Four canals run along the sides of the nectosac, and terminate above in a short, narrow duct, which passes to the closed extremity of a tubular hydrœcium, whose other end terminates in an aperture in front of the median plane of the spheroid. The hydrœcium traverses more than two thirds of the diameter of the spheroid, and contains the slender cœnosarc which is affixed to its closed end, and there receives the nectocalycine duct. It gives off a narrow cæcal somatocyst, which bends a little downwards, and ends near the proximal surface of the organ.

There was no second nectocalyx nor any indication of the attachment of one, nor were there any hydrophyllia developed.

Length of the superior nectocalyx . . $\frac{1}{4}$ inch.

I obtained altogether three specimens of a single species of this genus—in the Indian Ocean in 1847, on the east coast of Australia in 1848, and in Torres Straits, off the south coast of New Guinea, in 1849.

In all the cœnosarc was incomplete, though some of the polypites were fully developed and provided with tentacles of the ordinary characters. In one I observed rudimentary reproductive organs attached to the pedicle of a polypite.

The wall of the somatocyst was vacuolated in some specimens, in others not. There was a very distinct pyloric valve, and the tentacle arose immediately beneath it, from the wall of the polypite, into whose cavity its canal directly opened.

In one specimen the lip of the nectosac appeared to be obscurely four-lobed, and in all, the sacculi of the tentacles had a deep-red colour.

[1] Supposing the nectocalyx to have its hydrœcium vertical, which is the position in which *Diphyes* and *Abyla* have been described.

The absence of the hydrophyllia may have been accidental, but it does not seem easy to comprehend how any second nectocalyx could exist in this genus, at least, in its ordinary place attached to the proximal end of the cœnosarc.

From the description contained in Lesson's 'Acaléphes' I formerly imagined that this was the *Rosacea*[1] of Quoy and Gaimard, but it is clear that this species, though presenting many points of resemblance with *Praya* (= *Rosacea*, Q. and G.), cannot be included in that genus; the tubular form of the hydrœcium and the very large proportional size of the nectosac at once excluding it. I have, therefore, established a new genus for it, and I propose to call this species *S. Köllikeri*, after the distinguished author of 'Die Schwimmpolypen von Messina,' and of so many other valuable contributions of science.

---

[1] See 'Reports of the British Association,' 1851, p. 79.

*Fam.* PRAYIDÆ.

*Genus* PRAYA (*De Blainville*).

The proximal and distal nectocalyces are similar, and of a gelatinous texture. The hydrœcia of both the nectocalyces are open, groove-like, and applied together so as to form a tube in which the upper part of the cœnosarc lies. The hydrophyllia are thick, reniform, and gelatinous.

PRAYA DIPHYES?   Pl. III, fig. 3; and Pl. XII, fig. 5.

The body figured in Pl. III, fig. 3, 3 *a*, is thus described in my notes :

An ovate, reniform, gelatinous mass, presenting a small, hemispherical cavity at its lesser extremity, and widely excavated below. From the centre of this inferior excavation depended a twisted tubular cord (cœnosarc), surrounded in its upper part by a mass of nascent organs. The cord expanded into a broad muscular band at its point of attachment, and through the centre of this ran a narrow canal, which appeared to connect the cavity of the cord with a narrow, thick-walled cavity (somatocyst), extending along the roof of the inferior excavation from one extremity to the other. From this cavity a small canal was given off to the hemispherical natatorial cavity (nectosac), and on reaching it divided into four canals.

Length          .          .          .          .          $\frac{11}{16}$ inch.

This specimen was taken on the 23d June, 1847, in the Indian Ocean. I obtained another in Torres Straits in 1849, and one more in the South Atlantic in 1850; neither of these had any polypites.

In the last the hemispherical cavity was in active contraction, and the adjacent extremity of the organ was more distinctly bilobed.

I have little doubt that this fragmentary organism is the same as that described by Quoy and Gaimard under the name of *Rosacea plicata*. As Leuckart (Z. N. K., 39) has well pointed out, however, the two species of *Rosacea* described by the French naturalists are only isolated parts of what in its entire state is known as the genus *Praya*; and on comparing my figures with the excellent and well-illustrated accounts of this genus which have been recently published by Vogt, Kölliker, Leuckart, and Gegenbaur, I entertain no doubt that my specimens were merely the detached proximal nectocalyces of a *Praya*.

Leuckart states, indeed, that he has frequently found *Prayæ* which have lost one nectocalyx, with the other floating horizontally, and allowing the cœnosarc to depend perpendicularly from its under surface.

In order to enable those into whose hands this work may fall to comprehend the relations of this detached organism to *Praya*, I add the following short account of that genus, founded upon the statements of the authors just mentioned.

The nectocalyces are two, placed at the upper extremity of a cœnosarc, which sometimes (in *P. maxima* on Gegenbaur's authority), attains a length of three feet, and are nearly on the same level. One is usually smaller than, and more or less embraced by the edges of, the other. They are both of a gelatinous consistence, reniform, and more or less bilobed below. A shallow nectosac occupies the lower and outer end of each. Both nectocalyces are attached by a muscular expansion to the proximal end of the cœnosarc; and the somatocyst is a long, curved canal, which sends a blind process downwards between the nectosac and the hydrœcium. The latter is a widely open groove, or shallow pit, in both nectocalyces, and the chamber into which the cœnosarc is retracted is formed by the application of the edges of these grooves to one another.

In the natural position, therefore, the long axis of this composite hydrœcium is vertical, and, consequently, the long axes of the nectocalyces are also vertical; and the mouths of their nectosacs are directed outwards and downwards.

Each hydrophyllium is a thick, gelatinous, and reniform body, bent upon itself, rounded and solid at one extremity, and divided at the other into a median thick and two lateral lamellar lobes. The phyllocyst is prolonged into four cæcal processes.

The calyx of the reproductive organ is provided with two strong, longitudinal crests, and the same hydrosoma presents gonophores of both sexes.

Two species of doubtful distinctness[1] (*P. diphyes* and *P. maxima*) are described. They have been taken in the Mediterranean and in the tropical parts of the Atlantic and Pacific Oceans.

---

[1] See Leuckart, Z. N. K., p. 40.

*Fam.* HIPPOPODIIDÆ.

*Genus* HIPPOPODIUS (*Quoy* and *Gaimard*).

The nectocalyces are numerous, horse-shoe shaped, smoothly convex on their inner faces, and form a double series along the (deflexed) proximal end of the cœnosarc.

H. GLEBA.    Pl. XII, fig. 6.

> *Gleba hippopus*, Forskäl, 1775.
> — *excisa*,[1]   Otto, 1823.
> *Hippopodius luteus*, Quoy and Gaimard, 1827.
> *Hippopus excisus*, Delle Chiaje.
> *Protomedea lutea*, De Blainville, 1830.
> *Stephanomia hippopoda*, Quoy and Gaimard, 1833.
> *Elephantopes Neapolitanus*, Lesson, 1843.
> *Hippopodius Neapolitanus*, Kölliker, 1853.
> — *luteus*, Vogt, 1854.
> — *gleba*, Leuckart, 1854.

I have not observed this or any other member of the genus *Hippopodius*, but, in order to give completeness to my account of the *Calycophoridæ*, I subjoin an abstract of Leuckart's description of it, referring to his and the other works just cited for further details.

Each nectocalyx is shaped like a horse's hoof, with its lower face turned upwards. It is a wedge-shaped bevelled segment of a cone, in which may be distinguished an upper surface which forms an angle with the longitudinal axis of the cone formed by the union of all the nectocalyces, a less inclined lower surface, and a horseshoe-shaped lateral surface. The upper face is turned towards the axis, and is provided with a deep longitudinal groove with strongly produced edges, which end below and internally in two obtuse processes, between which is a rounded projection. The lower, smaller, face of the nectocalyx exhibits a large circular aperture which leads into a flat nectosac. At the anterior edge (or that turned away from the axis) of the nectosac the ridge between the lower and lateral or anterior face of the nectocalyx is raised up into four well-marked prominences, which are separated by concavities, and die away superiorly upon the anterior surface of the organ. The upper edge of this surface also shows one median and two lateral prominences, which correspond with the intervals between the prominences of the lower edge.

---

[1] Though Forskäl only figures the animal he discovered, Otto, who adopts his genus, gives not only a figure but a description of the nectocalyces. Ought not the genus therefore to be termed *Gleba* ?

The substance of the nectocalyces has a semicartilaginous consistence. Their number amounts to as many as twelve. The lowest are the largest, and new ones are constantly budding forth at the upper end of the series.

The nectocalyces of opposite sides are wedged together by their inner faces—each one receiving the end of its opposite neighbour and the lower surface of that which lies above it, between the ridges of that face. The apertures of the nectosacs of the two lowermost nectocalyces alone are uncovered, the rest being hidden by the upper surface of the nectocalyx below them. As usual, there is a muscular valve, which is narrower below than above.

The axis of the cone formed by the nectocalyces appears to be, as it were, a branch from the upper end of the cœnosarc; but, from Leuckart's observations, it results that this apparent branch is, in reality, merely the upper end of the cœnosarc bent down upon itself: for, in the youngest individuals, which may not have more than two nectocalyces, the arrangement of the parts is just as in *Diphyes* or *Abyla*. The cœnosarc gives off a series of nectocalycine ducts, one below the other, along the same lateral line; though, in consequence of the position of the nectocalyces, they appear to be right and left.

The extended cœnosarc sometimes measures full six inches, and bears twenty or thirty well-developed groups of organs, besides the numerous buds which remain inclosed within the cone formed by the nectocalyces.

The tentacles are like those of the other *Calycophoridæ*. *Hippopodius* is monœcious, and the gonophores are remarkable for the brevity of their gonocalyces and the length of their manubria. The genus has not hitherto been taken beyond the limits of the Mediterranean.

### Genus VOGTIA (*Kölliker*).

The nectocalyces are numerous, similar, and convex on their inner sides ; externally they are concave, and produced into five points, of which the three upper are much longer and stronger than the two lower.   The nectosac is small and rounded.

VOGTIA PENTACANTHA.   Pl. XII, fig. 7.

*Vogtia pentacantha*, Kölliker, 1853.

Only a single species of the genus *Vogtia* has been discovered, and we are indebted to Professor Kölliker for all we know of its structure.   Unfortunately, only two specimens passed into that observer's hands, and hence his account is necessarily brief and incomplete.

The nectocalyces, whose form has been described in defining the genus, are four or five ines wide.   Their arrangement upon the cœnosarc has not been accurately determined, out they formed a double opposed series with their convex faces turned towards one another.

The cœnosarc of *Vogtia* is like that of *Hippopodius*, but it is shorter and somewhat thickened at the lower end, where it bears the polypites and the other organs.   The polypites were only two and large ; each had a tentacle similar to those of *Hippopodius*.   Gonophores of both sexes were borne by both specimens, and were attached by short peduncles to the cœnosarc close to each polypite—a single long gynophore being accompanied by two still larger androphores.   The gonocalyces are like those of *Hippopodius*, but shorter in proportion to the long manubria.

*Vogtia* has hitherto been observed only in the Mediterranean.

## THE DIPHYOZÖOIDS.

Eschscholz, in defining his genera of Diphydan *Siphonophoræ*, lays great stress upon the character of the digestive apparatus. Certain genera have a "tubulus suctorius unicus," others have the "ductus nutritorius (cœnosarc) tubulis pluribus obsitus."

As I have already had occasion to mention, Lesson seizing upon the distinction thus indicated, divided his "*Diphydæ*" into two very natural groups—the *Polygastricæ* (tubulis pluribus) and the *Monogastricæ* (tubulo unico).

In the first division he arranged the genera *Diphyes, Calpe,* and *Abyla;* in the second, *Cymba, Enneagonum, Cuboides, Cucubalus, Cucullus, Eudoxia, Amphiroa, Ersæa,* and *Aglaisma.*

Neither by Will, Busch, nor myself was the true nature of the "monogastric Diphydæ" suspected, but Leuckart's investigations cited above, appear to me to leave no doubt that these apparently independent forms are nothing more than detached zöoid forms, or independent portions of the "polygastric Diphydæ." I have grouped them together, therefore, under the head of "Diphyozöoids;" and though it is necessary, so long as the genesis of each Diphyozöoid has not been worked out, to retain their distinct generic and specific titles, and even to invent new ones for undescribed forms, yet these names can only be regarded as provisional.

*Genus* EUDOXIA (*Eschscholz*).

*Diphyozöoids derived from* DIPHYES (?).

The hydrophyllium is lamellar and evenly convex externally. The walls of the cavity which contains the polypite are incomplete on one side. The phyllocyst is simple and conical.

EUDOXIA LESSONII (*Eschscholz*). Pl. III, fig. 6.

> *Ersæa Quoyi,* Eschscholz, 1829.
> —— *Gaimardi,* Idem.
> *Diphyes cucullus,* Quoy and Gaimard, 1833.
> *Ersæa pyramidalis,* ? Will, 1844.
> *Eudoxia Eschscholzii,* ? Busch, 1851.
> —— *campanula,* Leuckart, 1853.
> *Galeolariæ pullus,* Vogt, 1854.

This Diphyozöoid attains the length of four tenths of an inch. The hydrophyllium occupies from less than a half, to two thirds of the whole dimensions. It is thick and irregularly conical, terminating in a rounded apex.   One face—the anterior—is excavated in its superior half by a wide and shallow groove, which is continued into the wide cavity which occupies the inferior half, and which has somewhat the form of a pyramid with a truncated apex. The posterior wall of the cavity is tolerably thick, and terminates below in a short, transversely truncated margin.   The lateral walls of the cavity become very thin at their anterior margins, which are cut away from above downwards and backwards.   The right-hand margin slopes gradually into the inferior edge of the posterior face.   The left-hand margin, on the other hand, cuts the edge at an obtuse angle, which is produced into a point.

The phyllocyst is about two thirds as long as the interval between the apex of the hydrophyllium and that of its inferior cavity.   It is usually broad at the base, tapers to an obtuse point above, and has no lateral processes.   Its walls are largely vacuolated.

The calyx varies a good deal in size and proportion.   It is a little convex anteriorly and posteriorly, and its edges are sharply serrated; superiorly and posteriorly it is prolonged into a short process traversed by a canal which divides into the ordinary four radiating canals a little below the apex of the nectosac.

Length of the hydrophyllium, one fifth of an inch.   Length of the calyx, one fifth of an inch.

*Eudoxia Lessonii* is one of the commonest of Diphyozöoids.   I took it in all the seas which the " Rattlesnake " traversed in her circumnavigatory voyage, and it appears to be common in the Mediterranean and Adriatic.

Eschscholz characterised the genus *Eudoxia* ('Isis,' 1825, and 'System') thus: " Tubulus suctorius unicus.   Pars corporis organa nutritoria fovens simplex (cavitate natatoria haud instructa);" a definition which will apply equally well to any Diphyozöoid whatever.

In the 'System' another genus, *Ersœa*, immediately follows.   It is defined, " Tubulus suctorius unicus.   Pars corporis nutritoria cavitate parva natatoria, tubuli instar prominenti, instructa."   And Eschscholz states that the only distinction between *Ersœa* and *Eudoxia* is the presence in the former, of a very small swimming cavity, which projects like a short tube from the nutritive piece, or hydrophyllium.   Of this genus he makes two species, *E. Quoyi* and *E. Gaimardi*.

On comparing Eschscholz's figures and descriptions with the various states in which I have observed *Eudoxia Lessonii*, I entertain no doubt that his two *Ersœæ* are merely *Eudoxia Lessonii* with differently developed calyces.

I have found it to be the rule in this species that there should be a single large calyx, devoid of any manubrium, and, consequently, presenting the appearance of an ordinary nectocalyx, while one or two much smaller gonocalyces containing manubria, with ova or spermatozoa, are attached to the pedicle of the polypite.   Sometimes there were two such large empty calyces.

It was the constancy with which these empty calyces occurred which, more than anything else, led me to believe the monogastric *Diphydæ* to be independent existences; and it may still be a question whether these empty calyces are all gonocalyces whose manubria have discharged their contents and disappeared, or whether they are sometimes or always true nectocalyces.[1]

[1] Consult on this point Leuckart's excellent history of *Eudoxia campanula* (=*Lessonii*), in Z. U.,

Leuckart (Z. U., p. 69), has conclusively shown that his *Eudoxia campanula* is the Diphyozöoid of his *Diphyes acuminata*. But I can find no distinction between *E. campanula* and *E. Lessonii*, and I have already endeavoured to prove that *Diphyes acuminata* is identical with *D. appendiculata*. Consequently, *Eudoxia Lessonii* must be regarded as one of the synonyms of the latter species, and the other *Eudoxiæ* are probably nothing but Diphyozöoids of other species of *Diphyes*.

**EUDOXIA BOJANI** (*Eschscholz*). Pl. III, fig. 7.

This species, of which I only obtained one specimen, is distinguished by the more flattened form and symmetrically oval outline of the hydrophyllium, whose margin is produced into a point on each side, at about the junction of the lower with the two upper thirds. The inferior edge is convex and rounded, not truncated.

In the sole specimen obtained the phyllocyst, broad at the base, was very short and irregular. I suspect that it had undergone some abnormal alteration.

The calyx is greatly elongated, and its edges smooth.

The gonocalyces, which in the present instance were male, were subcylindrical, smooth, and rounded, without those strong crests so characteristic of the preceding species.

Length of the hydrophyllium, three sixteenths of an inch.

This species agrees so well with the figure and description of *E. Bojani* given by Eschscholz, that, notwithstanding one or two minor differences, such as the lateral points of the hydrophyllium, which Eschscholz does not notice, I feel justified in supposing it to be the same. It was taken on the southern coast of New Guinea.

*Genus* **EUDOXOIDES** (nov. gen.)

*Diphyozöoids derived from —————?*

The hydrophyllium is elongated and pointed, flattened on one face, evenly convex on the other, and is provided with a deep conical cavity for the polypite. Phyllocyst simply conical.

**EUDOXOIDES SAGITTATA.** Pl. IV, fig. 1.

I have seen only four specimens of the hydrophyllium of this species, and each of these was devoid of a calyx, and had only imperfectly developed tentacles and reproductive organs. Nevertheless, the form of the hydrophyllium is so peculiar that I am compelled to distinguish it generically from other Diphyozöoids. It is narrow and pointed superiorly, and its anterior face is flat, the inferior angles of this face being pointed and well defined. The conical cavity in which the polypite is lodged occupies rather less than half the length of the piece, and is closed in for the greater part of its extent anteriorly. The phyllocyst, slightly pyramidal, has no processes, and ends near the apex of the organ.

Length of the hydrophyllium, one fifth of an inch.

This species was also obtained on the southern coast of New Guinea.

## Genus AGLAISMOIDES (nov. gen.)

*Diphyozöoids derived from* ABYLA (?).

The hydrophyllium is a frustrum of a pentagonal prism, with one face partially bevelled off. The phyllocyst has four cæcal processes. The cavity for the polypite is deep and conical, or hemispherical.

AGLAISMOIDES ESCHSCHOLZII. Pl. IV, fig. 2.

The hydrophyllium is a pentahedral prism with truncated, more or less concave, terminal planes, whose edges are usually strongly serrated. In the position in which all these *Calycophoridæ* are described the posterior face of the hydrophyllium is formed by one of the terminal planes, and is consequently pentagonal. One of the five angles is directed downwards, and, therefore, one of the five faces of the prism is directed upwards. The lower half of the anterior face is, as it were, bevelled off below, and the bevelled area corresponds with the extent of the lower opening of the cavity which shelters the polypite, which is almost hemispherical, and has its axis directed upwards and backwards.

It extends through not quite half the diameter of the organ, and the edge of its inferior boundary is produced on each side into a tooth.

The phyllocyst is short and wide, and gives off four cæcal processes. Of these two are slender and vertical, the longer passing towards the inferior angle of the hydrophyllium, the other approaching the middle of its superior face, and being inclined backwards towards the posterior face. The two lateral processes are shorter and wider than the vertical ones, and pass forwards and outwards towards the antero-lateral angles, exhibiting a slight curvature or bend about the middle of their length.

The calyx is four-sided, with serrated edges, and a broad, truncated, and slightly excavated inferior surface, in the middle of which is the small aperture of the nectosac. This cavity has an elongated bell shape, and the duct connecting the radiating canals with the cœnosarc terminates close to its apex. The calyx exhibited no manubrium.

Length of the hydrophyllium, one eighth of an inch.

This Diphyozöoid occurred in all the seas which I traversed. Its curious resemblance to the *Aglaisma* form of *Abyla*, with which it used constantly to be taken, is indicated by its name; and its general characters, more particularly the form of its phyllocyst, leave no doubt on my mind that it is the Diphyozöoid of an *Abyla*.

## AGLAISMOIDES ELONGATA.   Pl. IV, fig. 3.

The hydrophyllium is a vertically elongated prism ; its superior face is square and flat, and a little narrower than the inferior ; the lateral and anterior faces are more or less convex, and cut off square below ;  the posterior face is pentagonal, being prolonged inferiorly into a short, triangular process, which bends a little forwards.

The inferior face is excavated by a large conical cavity whose apex reaches the centre of the organ in a vertical direction.   In width the cavity occupies about the posterior half of the hydrophyllium.   The posterior wall of this cavity is prolonged by the triangular process above mentioned, and on the face of this are seen two short longitudinal crests, which run down from the side walls of the cavity and terminate abruptly below.   These inferior angles are pointed and curved.   The phyllocyst gives off, or rather is divided into, four processes : Two of these, wide, lateral, pass at first horizontally outwards, and then are deflected at right angles forwards to terminate in cæca which are bent downwards.   Another process is very slender, and passes vertically upwards, nearly reaching the superior face of the hydrophyllium. The last, equally slender, runs downwards and backwards parallel with and close to, the posterior wall of the chamber, and ends nearly opposite the commencement of the triangular process.

The gonocalyces are four-sided prisms tapering to a conical end above, and having their edges produced into crests which end below in four inflected points.

Length of the hydrophyllium, one tenth of an inch.

*Aglaismoides elongata* occurred on the east coast of Australia, in Torres Straits, and about the Louisiade Archipelago.

It is impossible to compare these species of *Aglaismoides* with the figures and descriptions which Leuckart and Gegenbaur give of the detached zöoids of *Abyla pentagona*, without being struck by the many points of resemblance which they offer.

Indeed, if I had only Leuckart's figures before me, I should be inclined to identify my *A. Eschscholzii* with those zöoids, but I cannot reconcile Gegenbaur's account of the same objects with my own figures and notes.   I prefer therefore to leave the question open.

In the first specimens which I obtained the gonocalyx was very small, not extending beyond the cavity of the hydrophyllium.   Subsequently, I found not only large single gynophores, but on one occasion two large androphores and a small gynophore attached to one polypozöoid (Pl. IV, fig. 3 *b*).

### Genus SPHENOIDES (nov. gen.)

#### Diphyozöoids derived from ABYLA (?).

The hydrophyllium is wedge-shaped below, but is bevelled into four quadrate faces on its upper surface.   The cavity for the polypite is open in front.   The phyllocyst is like that of *Eudoxia,* but has a long, slender, cæcal diverticulum from its posterior and inferior part.

SPHENOIDES AUSTRALIS.    Pl. IV, fig. 4.

*Sphenia* (mihi), 1851.

Hydrophyllium wedge-shaped, presenting a sharp inferior edge and a wide superior surface, produced into a point in the middle, round which four quadrate facets are symmetrically arranged; the two posterior are slightly excavated and look backwards and outwards.    The two anterior look forwards and outwards, and are separated anteriorly by a deep triangular notch.    The posterior wall is broad and convex above, but ends below in a point.    It has four sides, the two upper of which are much shorter than the two lower. The lateral faces are broad and irregularly pentagonal, their anterior edges being somewhat concave.    Close to the lower termination they give off a sharp downwardly directed point.

The anterior face is occupied by the wide triangular aperture of the cavity of the organ, which extends much further back in its lower than in its upper moiety, so that its posterior contour is very convex forwards above, and equally concave below.

Where this contour cuts the centre of the hydrophyllium the phyllocyst arises, and is continued for more than half the distance to the apex of the organ, where it ends in a point.    Just above its origin it sends down in the middle line posteriorly a slender cæcum, which runs parallel with and close to, the posterior contour of the cavity, and ends near its lower boundary.

The gonocalyx has the form of a four-sided prism whose edges are produced into four more or less marked crests, ending below in as many points, which surround a flat space in which the circular aperture of the nectosac lies.    The summit of the organ is roof-shaped; two of the faces of the prism being, as it were, bevelled off, and the calycine duct leads to one gable end of this roof, by which, therefore, the gonocalyx is attached to the cœnosarc.

The elongated nectosac extends through the length of the prismatic portion of the organ, and four longitudinal canals, ending in a circular canal around its mouth, run down its walls from the calycine duct.    It contains a large manubrium with well-developed ova or spermatozoa.    When the gonocalyx has attained its full size it becomes detached, and swims about as an independent organism.

Length of the hydrophyllium, half an inch.    Length of the detached gonocalyx, one fourth of an inch.

I first found this species on the 8th of February, 1848, in Bass's Straits, where it abounded.    Subsequently, I took it off Timor, and in different parts of the Pacific and Indian Oceans.

The individuals figured in Pl. IV, fig. 4*, are probably only the young of the others. I am strongly inclined to suspect that this is the Diphyozöoid of *Abyla Bassensis*.    In fact, the hydrophyllium of the latter requires very little modification to convert it into that of *Sphenoides*.    The abundance of the species in Bass's Straits is in accordance with this view.[1]

[1] I have briefly referred to the characters of this Diphyozöoid, and more particularly to those of its reproductive organs, in my note, ' Ueber die Sexual organe der Diphyden und Physophoriden,' published in Müller's 'Archiv,' for 1851.

## Genus CUBOIDES (*Quoy* and *Gaimard*).

### *Diphyozöoids derived from* ABYLA (?)

Hydrophyllium with six flattened and four-sided faces. The chamber for the polypite is deep and conical, and its inferior aperture occupies one face of the cube. The phyllocyst is pyriform or narrow above, and very broad and slightly bilobed below.

CUBOIDES VITREUS, *Quoy and Gaimard*. Pl. IV, fig. 5.

Hydrophyllium with six equal, slightly concave faces, and prominent angles. The inferior face is occupied by a wide infundibuliform cavity, whose apex reaches to the centre of the cube. The phyllocyst is pyriform, with a broad base, which is much dilated and bilobed anteriorly, while above it narrows into a short cæcum which approaches the upper face of the organ within about a fifth of the whole diameter.

Gonocalyx a quadrilateral prism with its edges produced into four strong, serrated crests, ending below in sharp points. The upper portion of the organ is prolonged into a large pyramidal process, which is traversed by the calycine duct, and forms a strong, longitudinal crest posteriorly.

Length of the hydrophyllium, one fourth of an inch. Length of the gonocalyx, one eighth of an inch.

This species was taken twice, once on the east coast of Australia, and once on the south coast of New Guinea.

The genus *Cuboides* was established by Quoy and Gaimard ('Annales des Sc. Nat.,' x, 1827, p. 19), on apparently the very same species as that which I have described and figured. Leuckart (Z. N. K., p. 20) imagines that *Cuboides vitreus* may be the Diphyozöoid of *Abyla pentagona*, but this idea seems to me to be negatived by the form of the hydrophyllium—more especially of its phyllocyst. On the other hand it might very well be derived from the species which I have named *A. Vogtii*, as a comparison of Pl. II, fig. 3 *b*, with *Cuboides* will readily show.

## Genus AMPHIROA (*Lesueur*).

### *Diphyozöoids derived from* ABYLA (?).

Hydrophyllium with a trapezoidal section, the longer side being convex; inferior face obliquely truncated in front (where the wide and deep chamber for the polypite opens); four-sided behind. The phyllocyst is large and oval, with two slender, curved, lateral and superior cæca.

**AMPHIROA ALATA** (*Lesueur*).   Pl. V, fig. 1.

The hydrophyllium is depressed and broad, with six unequal faces; the superior face is a little convex and four-sided; its anterior side is convex and very much longer than the posterior, which is straight; the lateral edges of this face are nearly straight. The anterior face is a parallelogram, elongated, and convex from side to side. The lateral faces are slightly concave and four-sided; their inferior edges are concave and prolonged downwards posteriorly. The posterior face is a vertically elongated parallelogram. The inferior face is flat and four-sided posteriorly, but anteriorly it is obliquely truncated and occupied by a wide aperture leading into a conical cavity, which extends beyond the centre of the organ vertically. A very short, narrow duct runs from the apex of this cavity to just below the summit of a great oval phyllocyst with vacuolated walls, which occupies almost all the space between the posterior wall of the cavity and the posterior face of the hydrophyllium. From the upper end of this there is given off on each side a long, slender cæcum, slightly concave upwards, which ends close to the junction of the anterior and lateral faces.

The gonocalyx is a prism of apparently four sides, but its lower face is surrounded by five points like those in the nectocalyces of *Abyla* and *Diphyes*, with which the organ presented a further resemblance in the junction of two of the points by a strong, transverse plate, and their continuity upwards with strong crests, between which a deep groove is included. The upper end of the organ is pyramidal.

Length of the hydrophyllium, one fourth of an inch. Length of the gonocalyx, one fourth of an inch.

*Amphiroa alata* occurred only in Torres Straits.

In one specimen of this Diphyozöoid (Pl. V, fig. 1 *b*) obtained July 26th, 1849, I found three reproductive calyces; one was very small, the other two large and fully developed. Of these, the larger contained an ovisac, in which were four or five large ova. The smaller contained a sperm-sac, with incompletely developed spermatozoa.

This is one of the species drawn and named by Lesueur, but first published by De Blainville, in his 'Actinologie.' The description given in the latter work is very imperfect, but the figure leaves no doubt in my mind as to the identity of Lesueur's species with mine.

I suspect this *Amphiroa* to be the Diphyozöoid of *Abyla trigona;* at least, the hydrophyllium of the latter (Pl. III, fig. 1 *e*) has the same general form and large oval phyllocyst, with slender lateral processes.

**AMPHIROA ANGULATA.**   Pl. V, fig. 2.

The hydrophyllium has the same general form as in the foregoing species, but its anterior face is concave instead of convex, and its upper edge is angulated in the centre, while its lower edge is notched opposite the same point. Furthermore, the posterior wall of the cavity is prolonged beyond the general level of the truncated flat part of the lower face, and the lateral walls send down thin processes, deeply notched on their free edges, to meet this prolongation.

| | | | | |
|---|---|---|---|---|
| Length of the hydrophyllium | . | . | . | ⅛th inch |
| Breadth   ,,   ,, | . | . | . | ,, |
| Length of the gonocalyx | . | . | . | ,, |

*Amphiroa angulata* was only taken once, in Torres Straits, and I am strongly inclined to believe that it may be nothing but a younger form of the last species.

## Genus ENNEAGONOIDES (nov. gen.)

*Diphyozöoids derived from ----------- (?).*

Hydrophyllium having the general form of a cube with produced angles, but a pointed process is developed from one solid edge, so that this and the adjacent face are pentagonal, and the body exhibits altogether nine points. The chamber for the polypite is conical. The phyllocyst is simple and oval.

### ENNEAGONOIDES QUOYI. Pl. IV, fig. 6.

Hydrophyllium six-sided, with four quadrangular and two pentagonal faces, and much produced solid angles. One of the faces is inferior, and presents towards one angle the rounded aperture of the cavity for the polypite, which is conical, and is connected above with a small elongated phyllocyst. Supposing the side on which this opening lies to be anterior, then the axis of the cavity and that of the phyllocyst are directed obliquely backwards, upwards, and to the right side.

The superior, anterior, left lateral, and posterior, faces are square, but the right lateral face is pentagonal.

The organ would be a simple cuboid, were it not for the development of the triangular process (β, fig. 6 *a*, *b*, *c*), which converts the two adjacent sides into pentagons.

I regret to find that I have omitted to note the size of this Diphyozöoid, which was taken on the east coast of Australia in 1849.

I obtained but one specimen of *Enneagonoides Quoyi* and it had neither polypite nor reproductive organs.

I was at first inclined to regard this species as the *Enneagonum hyalinum* of **Quoy** and **Gaimard** ('Annales de Sc. Nat.,' 1827), but they state that the hydrophyllium of their genus contains two oblong, lateral cavities, besides that which lodges the swimming organ, and one would be led by their figure to imagine that one of these cavities is a natatorial cavity, and that their *Enneagonum* is nothing but an ill understood "Aglaisma-form" of *Abyla*. I can testify that it is no easy matter to obtain a clear conception of the complex figure of the singularly shaped hydrophyllium of this and other *Calycophoridæ*.

―――――――

The genera *Cymba* and *Cucubalus* of Quoy and Gaimard appear to be Diphyozöoids; but the figures and descriptions given by these naturalists are not such as to enable me to arrive at any very confident opinion on this point.

Gegenbaur (Beiträge, p. 9) carefully describes and figures a species, *Diplophysa inermis*, which appears to be very distinct from any of those enumerated above. However, it has some resemblance to the *Cucubalus* of the French voyagers.

## SECT. V.  THE GENERA AND SPECIES OF THE PHYSOPHORIDÆ.

The systematic arrangement of the *Physophoridæ* is beset with difficulties which are partly due to the nature of the animals themselves, but still more to the confusion introduced by the mistakes of systematists.

The term "Physsophora" was first used by Forskål, and under it may be found, in his 'Descriptiones Animalium,' good and clear descriptions of three very distinct though allied animals—*Physsophora hydrostatica, Physsophora rosacea,* and *Physsophora filiformis,* all of which were discovered in the Mediterranean.

Peron and Lesueur ('Voyage aux Terres Australes') represent a *Physophora muzonema,* obviously closely allied to the *P. hydrostatica* of Forskål, and they give the name of *Rhizophysa planestoma* to another Physophorid, which is as nearly related to *P. filiformis.* At the same time they figure two new forms, *Stephanomia amphitridis,* and *S. uvaria,* without expressing any opinion as to their zoological relations.[1]  Subsequently, on the return of these naturalists from a visit to the French coasts of the Mediterranean, Lesueur communicated to the Société Philomatique (from whose bulletin it was copied into the 'Journal de Physique' for 1813, t. lxxvi, p. 119, under the title of 'Mémoire sur quelque nouvelles espèces d'Animaux Mollusques et Radiaires recueillies dans la Méditerranée près de Nice') a notice of some of the animals which they had observed, and which are stated to "belong to the genera *Salpa, Stephania* (sic), *Physsophora, Pyrosoma* and *Hyalæa.*"

The word "*Stephania*" appears to be a misprint for *Stephanomia,* but I can find no evidence respecting the relation of this *Stephanomia* to that already figured.

Eschscholz ('System' &c.) separated the *Stephanomia uvaria* (the original drawing of which, in the Banksian Museum, he had carefully examined) with great justice from the *Stephanomia amphitridis,* and erected the first into a new genus, *Apolemia,* while he restricted *Stephanomia* to the latter.

Forskål's *Physsophora hydrostatica,* Peron's *Physophora,* and a species described by Quoy and Gaimard (*P. Forskálii*), are combined by Eschscholz into the restricted genus *Physophora,* while the *Ph. rosacea* of Forskål is very properly united with the *Rhizophysa heliantha* of Quoy and Gaimard into a new genus, *Athorybia.*

Eschscholz is less happy in his treatment of the third Forskålian "Physsophora," *P. filiformis.*  Imagining that this was simply a mutilated individual of some Physophorid

---

[1] Peron does indeed give a highly coloured and poetical popular sketch of *Steph. amphitridis* (t. i, p. 45), but it has no scientific value.

normally provided with nectocalyces, he makes a new genus (*Epibulia*) of it, with the definition, "Tentacula sacculis simplicibus obsita. Partes cartilagineæ adhuc incognitæ;" and separates it from Peron's *Rhizophysa*, whose swimming organs he also imagines he has seen. Lamarck had taken a more just view in uniting both Peron's and Forskål's species under the common head of *Rhizophysa*, but, on the other hand, he had erred, as Eschscholz points out, in including Forskål's *P. rosacea* in the same category.

The genus *Agalma* is a new and most important addition to the list of *Physophoridæ*. Eschscholz includes under it, and I suspect rightly, the *Stephanomia Amphitrite* of Chamisso (*Cuneolaria incisa* of Eysenhardt), which is certainly not the species of that name figured by Peron, and the *Pontocardia cruciata* of Lesson.

To these genera of *Physophoridæ*, Eschscholz adds the *Hippopodius* and *Discolabe* of Quoy and Gaimard, and the long known *Physalia* of Lamarck, while *Velella*, *Rataria*, and *Porpita* are united into a family by themselves, the *Velellidæ*.

Leaving out *Epibulia*, Eschscholz's family of *Physophoridæ* contains nine genera: three, *Physophora*, *Athorybia*, and *Rhizophysa*, founded on Forskål's three *Physsophoræ*; one, *Stephanomia*, on Peron and Lesueur's *St. Amphitridis*; another, *Apolemia*, on their *St. uvaria*; two being Quoy and Gaimard's *Hippopodius* and *Discolabe*; one Lamarck's *Physalia*; and one altogether new, *Agalma*. Excluded from this group, and forming the distinct family of the *Velellidæ* are the *Velella* and *Porpita* of Lamarck, and a new genus, *Rataria*. *Hippopodius* has since been shown to be one of the *Calycophoridæ*, and *Rataria* is only the young of *Velella*. *Discolabe* is doubtful. The rest are all, I believe, good, sound genera.

Although Eschscholz separated the *Velellidæ* as a distinct family from the *Physophoridæ*, he very clearly apprehended the close relations of the two; he refers particularly (p. 166) to the resemblance of the "shell" of *Rataria* and *Velella* to the air-vesicle of *Physalia*, and it seems to have been only the fancied resemblance between *Porpita* and *Fungia*, which led him to separate the two families.

I find the two groups first united, though in an indirect sort of way, by Deshayes, in the second edition of Lamarck (1840), tome iii, p. 94, and Index, p. 764.

Neither Quoy and Gaimard, nor Lesson, nor De Blainville, in their various publications, have, so far as I have been able to discern, added a single real genus to those established by Eschscholz, while in many respects their works are far behind his; and those of Quoy and Gaimard, and of Lesson, have introduced the most lamentable confusion, especially in regard to the limits of the genus *Stephanomia*.

The masterly investigations of Milne Edwards published in the 'Annales des Sciences Naturelles' for 1841, inaugurated a new epoch in the study of these singular animals, and they were well seconded by the author of the 'Fauna Litteralis Norvegiæ' (1846), which contains a remarkable memoir on some *Physophoridæ* and *Calycophoridæ* taken on the shores of the Island of Floröe, in the high northern latitude of $61\frac{1}{2}°$. Sars considers (though at p. 55 he seems to have some misgivings on the subject) that they all belonged to the same species of a new genus, *Agalmopsis*, which he thus defines:

"Partes cartilagineæ superiores seu natatoriæ ut in agalmate; inferiores numerosæ solidæ, triangulares, sparsæ, non tubum componentes, sed modo una earum extremitate canali reproductorio affixæ ceterumque liberæ, pro emissione tubulorum suctoriorum ac tentaculorum ubicunque fissuras præbentes. Canalis reproductorius longissimus, tubulos suctorios, vesiculos variæ formæ et tentacula offerens. Tentacula sacculis clavalis (*clava variæ formæ*) obsita."

Sars remarks (p. 40) upon the features which this genus has in common with both the *Agalma* of Eschscholz and the *Stephanomia* (*Amphitridis*) of Peron, and, indeed, it would be difficult to separate it by any character, save that assigned to the tentacula, from *Agalma*. If the tentacula really have a "clava variæ formæ,' *Agalmopsis* differs not only from *Agalma*, but from all *Physophoridæ* at present known, except *Rhizophysa*, whose tentacles, however, are so differently and so much more simply constructed, that they can hardly serve as terms of comparison.

After a careful study of Sars' memoir, I must confess that I am strongly inclined to believe that his *Agalmopsis elegans* embraces in reality species of two distinct genera, one a true *Agalma*, with the tentacles characteristic of that genus, the other a form closely allied to what I have described below as *Stephanomia*, believing it to be the *S. Amphitridis* of Peron.

Sars' "first kind of tentacles" (l. c., tab. v, figs. 5 and 6, p. 35) are, in fact, exactly like those which I have figured in *Stephanomia*, and unlike those of any other genus of *Physophoridæ* with which I am acquainted. The "*Agalmopses*," enumerated by Sars at p. 36, under (*c*), which were the largest, and were taken from the end of November until March, possessed only this one kind of tentacle; and the most of those taken in autumn, and enumerated under (*a*) p. 35, had only these, and those peculiar organs whose structure is not very clearly represented in Tab. VI, fig. 10. I suspect these were all *Stephanomiæ*.

The individuals enumerated under (*b*), taken contemporaneously with the last named, had tentacles exactly like those of *Agalma*, and tentacles of the first kind, in addition, according to Sars. But with every respect for the accuracy of observation of the justly-esteemed Norwegian naturalist, I think it very possible that he may have overlooked the real mode of termination of the younger tentacles of this form, and have been led to imagine their ends single when they were really trifid. In this case they would all belong to *Agalma*.

Whatever be the real nature of the species described by Sars under the head of *Agalmopsis*, however, there is, as Vogt has justly pointed out, an insuperable objection to the genus, as defined by its author; the sole distinctive character given by him being accidental, and depending on the extended state of his specimens, whose solid appendages would, had they been contracted, have formed a tube, as in *Agalma*.

Leuckart (Z. N. K., p. 73), admitting the justice of Vogt's elimination of the genus *Agalmopsis*, as defined by Sars, appears, nevertheless, to wish to retain the term, as the designation of that section of *Agalma* which has naked tentacular sacs, and a long, straight cœnosarc. Unfortunately, in this case, the sub-genus *Agalmopsis* would not contain either of Sars' species, so that there would be considerable risk of confusion. Under these circumstances, I propose to retain the name *Agalma* for those species whose tentacular sacs are provided with two filaments and a median lobe, and to give to the *Agalma rubrum* of Vogt, and its allies, the generic appellation of *Halistemma*.

The following systematic arrangement of the *Physophoridæ* appears to me to be in accordance with our present knowledge. Under each genus I have given the names of those species which have been carefully examined and may be considered to be established.

### I. *Fam.* APOLEMIADÆ.

Physophoridæ provided with nectocalyces and hydrophyllia; the latter united with the other organs into groups, which are arranged at considerable intervals along the cœnosarc. Tentacula without lateral branches. Pneumatocyst small. Cœnosarc filiform.

Genus I. APOLEMIA (*Eschscholz*).

*A. uvaria.*

### II. *Fam.* STEPHANOMIADÆ.

Physophoridæ provided with nectocalyces and hydrophyllia; the latter arranged with the other organs in a continuous series. Tentacula with lateral branches terminated by sacculi. Pneumatocyst small. Cœnosarc filiform.

*A.* Sacculi without involucra, and ending in a single filament.

*a.* With biserial nectocalyces.

Genus II. HALISTEMMA (*mihi*).

*H. rubrum* (*elegans* ?)

*b.* With multiserial nectocalyces.

Genus III. FORSKALIA (*Kölliker*).

*F. contorta.*
*F. Edwardsii.*
*F. Ophiura.*
*F. prolifera.*

*B.* Sacculi provided with involucra. Filament single.

Genus IV. STEPHANOMIA (*Peron* and *Lesueur*).

*S. Amphitridis.*

*C.* Sacculi with involucra. Filaments two, with a median lobe.

Genus V. AGALMA (*Eschscholz*).

*A. Sarsii.*
*A. clavatum.*
*A. Okenii.*

### III. *Fam.* PHYSOPHORIADÆ.

Physophoridæ with nectocalyces, but without hydrophyllia. The distal end of the filiform cœnosarc dilated. Tentacular branches with involucrate sacculi. Pneumatocyst small.

Genus VI. PHYSOPHORA (*Forskål*).

*P. hydrostatica.*
*P. musonema* ?

IV. *Fam.* ATHORYBIADÆ.

Physophoridæ without nectocalyces, and with hydrophyllia. Tentacular branches with involucrate sacculi, with two filaments and a median lobe. Pneumatocyst occupying almost the whole of the globular cœnosarc.

*Genus* VII. ATHORYBIA (*Eschscholz*).

*A. rosacea.*

*A. melo.*

V. *Fam.* RHIZOPHYSIADÆ.

Physophoridæ with a small pneumatocyst and a filiform cœnosarc; without either nectocalyces or hydrophyllia, and having lateral branches without sacculi, to their tentacula.

*Genus* VIII. RHIZOPHYSA (*Peron and Lesueur*).

*R. filiformis.*

VI. *Fam.* PHYSALIADÆ.

Physophoridæ with a pneumatocyst which occupies almost the whole of the thick and irregularly fusiform cœnosarc; without either nectocalyces or hydrophyllia; and without lateral branches to the tentacula, which are provided with basal sacs.

*Genus* IX. PHYSALIA (*Lamarck*).

*P. caravella.*

VII. *Fam.* VELELLIDÆ.

Physophoridæ without nectocalyces or hydrophyllia; with short, clavate, simple, or branched, submarginal tentacles. A single central, principal polypite. Pneumatocyst flattened, divided into chambers by numerous concentric partitions, and occupying almost the whole of the discoidal cœnosarc.

*a.* Pneumatocyst cristate. Tentacula simple.

*Genus* X. VELELLA (*Lamarck*).

*b.* Pneumatocyst without a crest. Tentacula branched.

*Genus* XI. PORPITA (*Lamarck*).

## Fam. STEPHANOMIADÆ.[1]

### Genus STEPHANOMIA (*Peron* and *Lesueur*).

Nectocalyces and pneumatophore unknown. Tentacula with lateral branches terminated by an involucrate sacculus with a single filament.

### STEPHANOMIA AMPHITRIDIS. Pl. VII.

On the 4th of May, 1848, during a calm which had already lasted some days, I saw from the deck, floating at the surface of the sea near the ship, the beautiful organism a part of which is figured of the natural size in Plate II, fig. 1. I threw the towing net over it, and succeeded in capturing it and transferring it, apparently uninjured, to a basin of sea-water, where it remained entire all that day ; by the next morning, however, all the hydrophyllia had become detached though the polypites remained perfectly lively. I did not perceive any motion in the individual hydrophyllia, but when the living mass was irritated, either by the least touch or even by pinching one of the depending tentacles, the cœnosarc shortened, and thus brought them into close contact. The ordinary position was horizontal, with the tentacles hanging down in the water, and when I first saw the animal it was curved to one side.

The hydrophyllia were perfectly colourless, and so transparent as to be almost imperceptible when in the water ; the cœnosarc had a whitish hue ; the enlarged portion of the polypites was pink or scarlet. The reproductive organs were colourless, as were the stems and lateral branches and filaments of the tentacles, while the tentacular sacs were scarlet.

The body bore handling very well, and a piece could be cut off from one end without causing any detachment of other parts.

The cœnosarc had a diameter of about one twentieth of an inch, with thick, muscular walls. It was obviously broken at each end.

The hydrophyllia surrounded the cœnosarc in whorls of four (figs. 2, 3) ; they were attached by triangular, striated processes of the ectoderm, whose base was inserted upon a triangular ridge, which traversed the middle of the internal face of each hydrophyllium (fig. 4). From this a clear linear canal is continued almost to the extremity of the organ. The hydrophyllia were in general leaf-shaped, and it appeared to me that a distinction might be drawn between those which were situated at the sides and those which were superior and inferior ; the latter (fig. 5, 5 *a*) being distinguished by a sort of shoulder on one side of their upper extremity, which is absent in the lateral hydrophyllia (figs. 6, 6 *a*, 6 *b*).

---

[1] I commence with this genus because I have had no opportunity of examining any *Apolemia, Halistemma*, or *Forskália*.

The polypites are of two kinds, large and small; the former are attached at regular intervals along one side of the cœnosarc by a short peduncle, measure six tenths of an inch to one inch in length, and resemble those of other *Physophoridæ*.

Their ventricose enlarged portion is marked by numerous red striæ, which are simply elevations of the endoderm, containing thread-cells and colouring granules, and are homologous with the villi of the *Calycophoridæ* (Pl. VI, fig. 11).

The small polypites (hydrocysts?) are attached to the cœnosarc between the large ones. They possess no coloured villi, and I am not sure that their extremities are open; they are frequently as long as the large stomachs, but never nearly so wide; and their apices are commonly provided with large thread-cells. A rudimentary tentacle is developed from one side of their base (fig. 12).

The tentacles are attached to the pedicle of the large polypites, or to their base close to the pedicle, but which I could not determine. They consist of a stem, which gives rise on one side to a series of branches, which carry at their extremity deep-red sacculi. In structure most of these parts resemble those of the *Calycophoridæ*, but the sac requires especial notice. It is very long, and is usually coiled up and partly inclosed within a cup-shaped, hood-like process of the ectoderm of the peduncle. On each side of the ordinary imbricated series of thread-cells there is a single row of larger thread-cells; the latter are oval, and $\frac{1}{150}$th of an inch in length, while the others are elongated, somewhat curved, and not more than $\frac{1}{300}$th of an inch in length. The thin wall of the sac contains a quadruple series of peculiar bodies, represented in Pl. V, fig. 9. They are elongated, slightly curved, and pointed at one end, while the other end is obtuse, and presents three or four elevations. They are disposed transversely to the axis of the sacculus.

The filament, which terminates the sacculus, is long and cylindrical, and contains a vast number of thread-cells of $\frac{1}{800}$th of an inch in length.

The mode of development of these organs exactly resembles that of their homologues in the *Calycophoridæ*. They commence as cæcal processes, which elongate and become constricted into three portions—pedicle, sac, and filament. The thread-cells are at this time all alike, and not more than $\frac{1}{3500}$th of an inch in diameter. The involucrum commences as a circular projection of the ectoderm of the peduncle.

The gonophores (fig. 12) are attached by branched footstalks to the cœnosarc, between the larger polypites. There was no very great regularity in their occurrence, but I think that, as a general rule, there were both ovarian and seminal organs between every two polypites. The same stem that supported them frequently gave rise to a small polypite, or hydrocyst.

The androphores are distinguishable from the gynophores by their greater absolute length, their more elongated form, and by their greater clearness and transparency. The largest androphore I measured was one tenth of an inch long; the largest gynophore three fortieths of an inch.

The calyx of the androphore is terminated by four obtuse elevations, containing large thread-cells. In essential structure it exactly resembles the corresponding part in *Diphyes*. The thickened outer wall of the spermsac contains round vesicles, about $\frac{1}{2500}$th of an inch in diameter, none of which were developed into perfect spermatozoa in the specimen I observed. The androphores were developed from simple papillæ, in the same way as those of *Diphyes*.

The gynophores, or female organs, in their essential structure and mode of development, resembled those of *Diphyes ;* but they offered two points of difference : 1. They never contained more than a single ovum ; 2. The surface of this ovum appeared as if wrinkled or covered with anastomosing canals ; but this appearance arises, as in *Athorybia,* merely from the irregular separation of the ovisac from the walls of the calyx.

*Genus* AGALMA (*Eschscholz*).

Nectocalyces biserial. Branches of the tentacula terminated by involucrate sacculi, with two filaments and a median lobe.

AGALMA BREVE. Pl. VII.

> *A. Okenii* (?) Eschscholz, 1829.
> *A. intermedia* (?) Quoy and Gaimard, 1833.

To the naked eye this animal appeared like a prismatic mass of crystal, traversed by a delicate filament, terminated at one extremity by a pink spot, and at the other by an irregular pink mass. The pink spot is the pneumatophore, or float; the filament, the cœnosarc; the pink mass, the polypites and their appendages; while the crystalline prism is formed above by the nectocalyces, below by the solid hydrophyllia, which are appended to and embrace the cœnosarc.

The pneumatophore is oval, and measures about $\frac{1}{40}$th of an inch in length. In the first specimen I examined the walls of the organ were of so deep a colour that all the details of its structure could not be made out; but in the second, which was somewhat smaller, the pneumatophore was colourless, and the arrangement of its internal parts was easily determined.

The pneumatocyst appears to be open below; but however this may be, its cavity does not communicate with that of the cœnosarc, for the endoderm, which is reflected upon and closely adheres to its outer surface, does not stop short of the lips of the aperture, but extends completely over it. It is not tightly stretched over the aperture, but forms a sort of loose, bag-like end, extending far below it. The contents of the pneumatocyst could be readily forced into this sac, and they returned again when the pressure was removed.

The sac thus formed by the reflected endoderm does not hang loosely and freely in the cavity of the pneumatophore, but is connected with the walls of the latter by a number of vertical, mesentery-like, partitions. These terminate in free arcuated edges opposite the lower end of the reflected endodermal sac. Immediately below the pneumatophore a number of budding nectocalyces, in all stages of development, make their appearance, the youngest being the highest. Of the fully-formed and functionally active nectocalyces, however, there were only five, three on one side, and two on the other. Viewed laterally, these organs appear fusiform, while from above they have a horseshoe shape, in consequence of the deep concavity of their internal edges. Above and below they present a deep and wide groove, whose edges are bounded by well-defined ridges, or rather crests.

The nectosac has a comparatively narrow, oval, or rounded aperture, fringed by the usual valvular membrane. Its cavity near the aperture is subcylindrical, gradually widening internally. It then suddenly dilates, and forms a very wide, blind, sac, more or less divided into two lobes by a median constriction. The cavity is much wider than it is deep.

Below the nectocalyces four thick and solid hydrophyllia are attached, so as to lie nearly in the same plane. They have the form of pyramidal wedges, with square bases.[1] The latter are turned outwards, while the apices are connected with the cœnosarc by a duct which extends, as a cæcal phyllocyst, through the axis of the hydrophyllium, terminating at some distance from its base. In some specimens there was a second set of such appendages, but in others, these hydrophyllia were succeeded by four different ones, much larger and more foliaceous, though still very thick. Internally, they are concave; superiorly, convex. Externally, they present two or more somewhat excavated facets, separated by thick ridges. Their lateral edges are sharp, and coarsely serrate, and they taper more or less to a point below. Like the preceding, these organs contain long and narrow cæcal phyllocysts, which traverse their axes, and nearly reach their apices.

The polypites lie amongst and between the hydrophyllia. Bunches of what appear to be young polypites (hydrocysts), accompanied by rudimentary hydrophyllia and tentacles, are attached to the cœnosarc, between the fully formed ones, and are either on the same pedicle with, or close to, the reproductive organs.

The sacculi of the tentacula are nearly a sixth of an inch long, and possess a long median prolongation or lobe, flanked on each side by a filament of about double its length. The involucrum is very large, and apparently capable of containing the whole sacculus.

The reproductive organs are developed more particularly towards the lower end of the cœnosarc, the male and female organs being placed close to one another. The gynophores are very numerous, and about half as large as the androphores, which are fewer in number. The gynophores are borne upon special stems, or gonoblastidia, each of which is simply a process of the cœnosarc, and contains, of course, a diverticulum of the somatic cavity. On all sides the gonoblastidium gives off short bud-like processes, whose development is always the more advanced the nearer they are to the free end. It would appear, therefore, that new ones are continually developed at the base of the gonoblastidium. The smallest of these processes is a mere cæcal process of the endoderm and ectoderm, and is rather less than $\frac{1}{500}$th of an inch in length. It next becomes pyriform, and the endoderm acquires so great a thickness at the apex and at the neck of the organ, that the included cavity assumes a more spherical form, with a narrower neck. The thickened apical endoderm now presents a clear space of about $\frac{1}{1450}$th of an inch in diameter, containing a spheroidal, pale, solid body. These are the rudiments of the germinal vesicle and spot.

The largest gynophores are oval bodies, attached by a short pedicle, and about $\frac{1}{100}$th of

[1] In describing his *Agalma Okenii* Eschscholz states that, of the solid, cartilaginous pieces, " some are similar to a very depressed pyramid, whose base presents two longer and two shorter sides. The broader lateral faces meet at the apex of the pyramid earlier than those which ascend from the narrower sides. Other pieces are very irregular; they present a broad base, then a large, convex surface, and many small excavated ones, which cause one side of the piece to be notched (*zackig*)." Figs. 1 *e*, 1 *f* of pl. xiii, which represent these solid pieces, have a close resemblance to mine.

an inch long.   The contained ovum is nearly as large as the gynophore, and has a pale, granular yelk, a clear, spherical germinal vesicle of $\frac{1}{300}$th of an inch, and a thick-walled, vesicular, germinal spot of $\frac{1}{1250}$th of an inch.

The gonocalyx remains in a very rudimentary state, closely embracing the ovum.   It exhibited no terminal aperture in any specimen I examined, and its canals were narrow, straight, and unconnected by any circular canal at their extremities.   The inner wall of the calyx was only separated from the wall of the ovisac or manubrium over irregular spaces, thus giving rise to a system of canals like those in the same position in the gynophore of *Athorybia*, only less complete.

The androphores are oval bodies, seated on very short peduncles, and $\frac{1}{100}$th of an inch or more in length.   They commence their development as processes of the endoderm and ectoderm, in which the four canals are developed in the ordinary way ; but some of these would appear to become obliterated with age, as those which were fully formed rarely possessed more than from two to three canals, and exhibited only indications of the circular canal.

The manubrial spermsac was not distinctly separated from the calyx in the largest specimen I examined, nor did any exhibit fully-developed spermatozoa.

I obtained on one occasion the young *Agalma* (possibly of this species), about two lines long, which is represented in Pl. VII, fig. 12.   The unilateral attachment of all the appendages was very obvious in this young individual.   There were—1stly, immediately below the pneumatophore, a series of young nectocalyces, the largest of which measured about $\frac{1}{180}$th of inch in length, and had an apical opening to its rudimentary nectosac, with four canals not yet united by a circular canal ; 2dly, a series of cæca, the rudiments of the hydrophyllia ; 3dly, polypites in various stages of development.   The only perfect one was terminal, and half as large as the rest of the animal.   It was suspended by a pedicle, and presented a pyloric valve at its junction therewith.   The upper third of the polypite had a globular form, and was of a dark reddish colour.   Its endoderm was raised up into longitudinal ridges, in which a great number of round fatty-looking particles were imbedded.   Besides these, other smaller villous processes, similar to those in the polypites of *Diphyes*, were scattered about.   A coiled filament, probably the rudiment of a tentacle, arose from the neck of the polypite, and gave off lateral buds, the most fully developed of which were cylindrical processes, terminated by rounded heads containing many thread-cells.

I am unable to identify the *Agalma* which has just been described with any published species.   It presents some points of resemblance with the *A. Okenii* of Eschscholz, others with the *Stephanomia intermedia* of Quoy and Gaimard ; but there are well-marked differences in each case.   I therefore give it the specific name of *A. breve*.

### *Fam.* PHYSOPHORIADÆ.

### *Genus* PHYSOPHORA (*Eschscholz*).

Cœnosarc dilated at its distal end; provided below the pneumatophore with necto-calyces. No hydrophyllia. Hydrocysts forming a series on the proximal side of the polypites. A spheroidal involucrum completely inclosing the sacculus.

PHYSOPHORA (sp. ?) Pl. VIII, figs. 1—12.

The anatomy of certain species of *Physophora* has been studied of late years by Philippi,[1] Vogt, and Kölliker. Only three specimens presented themselves during my voyage, and neither of these was an adult, while two were exceedingly small. Nevertheless, as I paid particular attention to points which happen to have been comparatively neglected by Vogt and Kölliker, I trust that the additions which I am able to make to their account of this interesting genus will not be without value.

The hydrosoma in the largest of Vogt's specimens measured rather more than two inches in length, and Kölliker's appear to have had about the same dimensions ($2\frac{1}{2}$ inches). In my largest specimen the hydrosoma was only three quarters of an inch long.[2]

The cœnosarc enlarges above into the pyriform pneumatophore; below this it is slender and cord-like, and gives attachment to a variable number of nectocalyces. Its inferior extremity is enlarged, and supports the remaining appendages.

With regard to the structure of the pneumatophore, Kölliker states only that it has an apical pigment-spot; and Vogt appears to me not to have comprehended its organization at all, inasmuch as, in his description of the adult *Physophora*, he mistakes the walls of the pneumatophore for those of the pneumatocyst, having apparently overlooked the latter.[3] This is the more singular as, in his account of the young *Physophora*, at p. 58, he states that

[1] Ueber den Bau der Physophoren und eine neue art derselben, *Physophora tetrasticha*. 'Müller's Archiv.,' 1843, pp. 59—67, tab. v.

[2] Peron and Lesueur's *P. muzonema* is stated to have been four inches long; the *P. Forskálii* of Quoy and Gaimard two inches; while Forskål's original *P. hydrostatica* had a length of only an inch and a half. The axis of Philippi's *P. tetrasticha* had apparently a length of about two inches.

[3] La bulle d'air est entourée immédiatement comme je viens de le dire, d'une expansion muscu-laire faisant suite aux couches musculaires du tronc" (p. 43). Philippi denies the existence of any air in the pneumatophore (p. 63).

the air-vesicle " has the form of a pear, and is enclosed in a fibro-flocculent tissue, which lines the interior of the pneumatophore (*partie pyriforme*), surrounds the pigment-spot, and descends, forming four organs, in the midst of which passes down a rounded mass of the same substance, and closely invests the air-bubble, which thus perfectly resembles the clapper suspended in the middle of a bell."

I found the structure of the pneumatophore to be quite similar to that which obtains in *Agalma;* that is to say, the air is contained in a distinct pneumatocyst, enclosed within a reflection of the endoderm of the pneumatophore. No cellular processes, like those of *Rhizophysa*, were observed to proceed from the under part of the reflected endoderm, and I could discover no pore communicating with the exterior, even in the youngest specimens.

The cœnosarc, immediately below the pneumatophore, gives attachment to a number of budding nectocalyces, which are succeeded by a double series of perfect ones. Of these there may be as many as five on each side.[1]

Kölliker says that these are so like those of his *Agalmopsis*, that it is unnecessary to describe their form particularly; they alternate and embrace the cœnosarc by their excavated sides. This was also the case in Vogt's specimens and in mine. According to the last-named investigator, the nectocalyces are horseshoe shaped, with an orbicular aperture on the truncated summit of their external curve, surrounded by a membranous valve, and leading into a nectosac, which is "very small, and does not extend through more than half the thickness of the organ."

M. Vogt's figures, however, represent the nectosac with much larger relative proportions, and Kölliker represents the nectosac with much the same proportions as in my specimen, in which the nectocalyces were about a quarter of an inch long, and had an irregularly cordate form. Each was attached by a broad, thick pedicle to the cœnosarc, and its axis was inclined (as Vogt notices) at an angle of 45° to the latter. The inferior and external face of the organ was broad and convex above, but suddenly narrowed towards its free end. The superior and internal face was deeply excavated in the middle line, so as to present a convex lobe on each side, between which arose the pedicle of attachment. The excavation was continued into the internal and inferior face, while the inferior and external face was truncated and almost wholly occupied by the rounded, or somewhat four-sided, aperture of the nectosac, provided with its narrow membranous valve.

The edge of junction of the inferior internal, and inferior external, faces is prolonged into a thin, broad, subquadrate plate, whose lower free edge is emarginate in the middle line, and pointed at the angles.

The sides of this plate are continued into two ridges, which run along the margins of the inferior internal face to about its middle, and then become constricted, but are continued upwards, on each side, on to the superior internal face, and thence downwards on the superior external face, as far as its truncated inferior edge, where they end in obtuse points. Superiorly and internally these ridges form broad plates, which overlap

---

[1] In *P. tetrasticha* Philippi found four series of nectocalyces, each series containing four of these organs (p. 59). It would appear, nevertheless, that they were all really attached to one side of the cœnosarc.

those of the opposite nectocalyces, and thus enclose the cœnosarc in a sort of hydrœcial canal.    The nectosac occupies nearly the whole cavity of the organ.    Near its mouth it is subcylindrical, but almost immediately it becomes exceedingly wide and is divided into two lobes, by an inflexion corresponding with the groove in the internal face of the nectocalyx.

On very careful examination, the ends of four delicate canals could be traced opening into a circular canal which surrounded the aperture of the nectosac, and the origins of these canals could be seen radiating from the end of the canal of the pedicle, but in the fully formed organs I could not satisfactorily trace their intermediate portions.

M. Vogt says of these canals, which he calls "bâtonnets" (though he recognises them to be canals): "Une entoure l'iris orbiculaire de l'ouverture en servant de support à ce rideau musculaire,[1] tandis qu'un autre se porte d'arrière en avant.    Deux courbes latérales embrassent le bouton median[2] par laquelle la cloche est fixée en arrière, se réunissent au bâtonnet qui court dans le ligne médiane, tandis que deux autres se dessinent sur les ailes postérieures proéminentes de la cloche" (p. 42).

I do not quite understand this description, and I will, therefore, without further comment, state the results of a careful study of the development of these organs in my *Physophora*.    The smallest buds measured $\frac{1}{150}$th of an inch in length, and were simple cæcal processes of the ectoderm and endoderm of the cœnosarc, immediately beneath the pneumatophore, with an internal cavity, whose walls were ciliated, and which was in free communication with the somatic cavity (Pl. VIII, fig. 10 *a*).

In a bud of $\frac{1}{150}$th of an inch in diameter, the apical region of the wall had developed a large, internal, spheroidal prominence, and its cavity had thus become cup-shaped (fig. 10 *b*). In buds of one eightieth of an inch in length, the cavity had become divided into four canals, and a central hollow began to appear in the spheroidal prominence (fig. 10 *c*).

In a bud of one sixtieth of an inch long, the central hollow, or rudimentary nectosac, had acquired a very large size, but was not open at its apex ; and the four canals were united by a circular canal.    The whole organ had become broader in proportion to its length, principally by the widening of its base.    This was still more marked in young nectocalyces of one fiftieth of an inch in length, in which the nectosac had a larger cavity, and proportionally thinner walls.    In these the lateral canals had acquired a slight double curvature, so as to have the outline of an italic *s* (fig. 10 *d*).

A nectocalyx, one twenty-fourth of an inch long, consisted of an extremely broad and expanded base attached to a short pedicle, and not yet excavated internally, surmounted by a short, truncated, and subcylindrical apical portion.    There was no aperture in this, nor were any of the characteristic crests of the adult organ developed.    While the median longitudinal canals remained unchanged, the lateral ones had become singularly contorted (fig. 10 *e*). Supposing the pedicle of the organ to be posterior, and its natural superior and external face superior, the lateral canals pass at first outwards, and then turn sharply inwards on the under face, where each forms a loop by bending as suddenly outwards again.    On reaching the lateral face, it curves upwards and backwards to attain the superior face, on which it passes inwards, and afterwards bends at right angles forwards ; it then passes inwards again and finally forwards to the circular canal.    I traced the development of the organ no further

---

[1] The membranous valve.                                    [2] The pedicle.

than this, but it is probable that in the adult organ the convolutions of the lateral canals are even more complicated.

Kölliker considers the lower enlarged end of the stem of *Physophora* to be a simple dilatation of the cœnosarc; but Vogt affirms that it is not only enlarged, but bent upon itself, so that its discoid form is more apparent than real; and he adds, that the more developed appendages are always situated at the distal end of this coiled enlargement of the cœnosarc; the young buds of the hydrocysts and polypites being situated at its proximal end, or where it joins the narrow stem-like portion of the cœnosarc.

Philippi states that, in *P. tetrasticha,* a membranous fold runs down one side of the axis, to which, without doubt, the nectocalyces were attached. Below, the axis becomes somewhat wider, makes a turn, and ends in a tolerably large vesicle, which, in the living animal, is hidden by the appendages. It is placed not in the middle, but on one side; upon the other side it exhibits a wide aperture surrounded by a plaited membranous fold like a collar. Philippi supposes that this aperture is the mouth, and the cavity into which it leads the stomach, wherein he is undoubtedly mistaken. Externally, he found no trace of the attachment of the hydrocysts, but, from the middle line below, the racemose reproductive organs depended.

In my notes upon the small *Physophoræ,* I find it stated that the bulbous expansion of the stem ends below in a sort of solid papilla, in which there were no indications of any inferior aperture; and on this last point Vogt and Kölliker are also agreed against Philippi.

According to Philippi and Kölliker, the hydrocysts are arranged, most externally, in a complete circle around the inferior enlargement, and internal to these are the polypites, with a tentacle attached to each. The male and female reproductive organs are attached in pairs beside (neben) the polypites. According to Vogt, the hydrocysts are external, the polypites internal, and the groups of reproductive organs lie between them.

In my specimens the hydrocysts were external, the polypites internal; but I can say nothing about the reproductive organs, as they were not developed.

The hydrocysts are closed sacs with pointed apices and broad bases, by which they are fixed into the cœnosarc. Vogt says, "L'extrémité par laquelle le tentacule est fixé au disque, est taillée comme un bec de plume de manière à s'adapter à la surface arrondie du disque. Cette extrémité n'est point fermée; elle s'adapte facilement sur une ouverture conduisant du disque dans la cavité du tentacule. En arrachant ce dernier on remarque qu'un fil de matière élastique entre dans le disque même et sert ainsi d'attache" (p. 45).

In my specimens this was by no means the way in which the hydrocysts were connected with the cœnosarc, but the broad bases of the former coalesced completely with the wall of the latter (fig. 3), which extended inwards so as to leave only a narrow, oblique, valvular aperture of communication between the cavity of the hydrocyst and that of the cœnosarc.[1]

[1] Philippi (p. 61) describes the hydrocysts as having "flattened articular surfaces." "In the middle of the articular surface is a small knob (Höcker), probably the point of attachment, and down from its upper part depends a fine thread, which, when extended, is longer than the hydrocyst, but is often spirally coiled up, and then is hardly a line long" (p. 61). According to this observer, the hydrocysts are true "prehensile arms" (Fangarme), for, on placing the end of a forceps in their neighbourhood, "they all seized it, held it fast, and loosened their hold only in a couple of seconds."

The endoderm and ectoderm were exceedingly distinct in the walls of the young hydrocysts. There were no villi; but the apices of the organs contained several large thread-cells.

Vogt does not mention or figure any small tentacular appendages to the hydrocysts, and Kölliker distinctly states (p. 22) that he "could find no trace of the fine tentacles observed by Philippi attached to these organs in *P. tetrasticha*." In the young forms of my specimens, on the other hand, they were very obvious as delicate, filiform processes of the ectoderm and endoderm of the hydrocyst, which arose from the upper wall, close to its attachment to the cœnosarc. The internal cavity of each tentacle communicated freely with that of the hydrocyst, and towards its apex delicate thread-cells were imbedded in its outer wall. I did not particularly examine the polypites, but Vogt and Kölliker agree in stating that they are affixed by slender pedicles, and that the tentacles are attached at the junction of these pedicles with the enlarged digestive division of the organ. Villi are developed from the endoderm of the latter.

The stem of the tentacle[1] is as usual single, and carries a number of lateral branches, to whose extremities very singular saccular bodies are attached, of whose structure I can speak with some confidence, as I worked out the principal steps of their development.

In their early stages these lateral branches exactly resemble those of the tentacles of the *Calycophoridæ*, that is to say, they commence as simple, cæcal, double-walled processes of the stem, which gradually elongate, and become divided into three portions. The one wall of the middle division becomes greatly thickened, and rows of elongated thread-cells disposed vertically to its plane are developed in it. The distal division remains short, and acquires only small thread-cells.

The proximal division elongates and becomes a slender pedicle, devoid of thread-cells in the greater part of its length. When it joins the middle division, however, it becomes dilated, and not only small thread-cells, but several very large oval ones, appear in it. Similar thread-cells make their appearance in the proximal end of the middle division. Thus far the development of the organ (which has now a length of about one fortieth of an inch) exactly resembles that of the corresponding part in *Diphyes*, and it is obvious that the basal division answers to the pedicle and involucrum, the middle division to the sacculus, and the distal to the filament (fig. 5).

The next change that takes place is, that the sacculus lengthens and becomes coiled upon itself, while the involucrum at the same time dilates and acquires a quadrate outline (fig. 6).

In the most perfect organ (which measured about one sixtieth of an inch in diameter, but was still colourless, and, consequently, incomplete) the involucrum has become immensely dilated, so as to form a sort of hemispherical cup closed on all sides, except at one point, where a small aperture is left, through which the extremity of the filament, divided into three lobes, protrudes[2] (figs. 7, 8).

---

[1] Attaining as much as a foot in length in *P. tetrasticha*, Philippi, l. c., p. 61.

[2] Compare Philippi's fig. 9. The lobes are described as "a few short cirri." But this observer has not comprehended the structure of those singular organs, and while he definitely asserts they are not prehensile organs, supposes they may be branchiæ.

The structure of this involucrum differs from that of the corresponding part in *Stephanomia* and *Agalma*, inasmuch as it is only partially formed by a lamellar expansion of the ectocyst; the greater part of its wall being constituted by a cup-shaped dilatation of the pedicle itself, from whose edges the proper involucrum rises. As a consequence of this enlargement of the pedicle, the attached end of the sacculus, distinguishable at once by its large oval thread-cells, has been carried to the distal extremity of the involucrum, instead of remaining at its proximal end. And at the same time, as the sacculus has increased in length far beyond the diameter of the sac, it has become coiled into a helix with several close turns. By pressure it can be extruded from the involucrum.

As I have stated, none of those organs which I examined were fully formed. Indeed, they must have been far removed from their adult condition, for they were not more than one sixtieth of an inch in diameter; while, according to Philippi and Kölliker, the fully formed sacs measure a line or a line and a half. Both Kölliker and Vogt, however, figure and describe intermediate states, which completely bridge over the interval between the adult forms which they more particularly investigated, and the very young ones of which I have just given an account, but of which they say nothing.

Vogt's pl. v, fig. 10, and Kolliker's pl. v, fig. 3, represent successive intermediate stages; Vogt's being but little more advanced than my oldest. The sacculus here makes seven or eight turns, and its proximal end is represented as lying free, while the distal end, containing many large oval thread-cells, is attached to the wall of the involucrum.

Kölliker's figure represents a rather more advanced stage, the distal extremity of the involucrum being produced into a point; otherwise, so far as the figure is concerned, I should have said there was no essential change. His description, however, presents difficulties.

"These (organs) consist of an oval vesicle produced into a point at its free end, and whose thick granular walls, composed apparently of small cells, inclose an oval cavity (provided with a small aperture near the pedicle), which contains a clear fluid and a large spirally coiled filament. This commences at the upper (distal) end of the investing capsule, with a rounded free end, runs down, making six or seven turns, towards the pedicle, and ends near the aperture in a narrow cord, which ascends through the cavity of the spiral, and is inserted into the upper (distal) end of the capsule. On examination the spiral thread turns out to be a cylinder full of thread-cells, and the cord to be a muscle, which, divided into two bands, is continued on to the spiral thread, and runs along its concave side to its free end" (p. 22).

From this description it will be observed that the general structure of the organ appears to be the same as that which I have described, except that the spiral is turned round, its free end being distal instead of proximal, and the proximal end remaining connected with the original place of attachment by a muscular band.

Such a *bouleversement* is almost inconceivable, and Kölliker's fig. 2, and Vogt's figs. 9 and 11, convince me that it really has not taken place, for in all these I find the end of the spiral cord, which contains the large oval thread-cells, distal, *i. e.*, in the same position as in my figures.

I conceive, in fact, that the real state of the case is this. As the sacculus enlarges, a strong band of muscular fibres is developed within its thin wall, and it is the edge of this band which, in the retracted state, appears like a distinct muscular cord traversing the axis of the spire.   I am strengthened in this view by Vogt's statement (p. 51) that when the sacculus (his "banderola") is protruded, "it is accompanied through its whole length by a very delicate muscular filament, which is attached to its inner edge, so that it is hidden completely by the folds of the 'banderola' when the latter is retracted into the capsule."   It is true that Vogt figures (fig. 9) the end of the sacculus, which contains the large thread-cells, free; but as the lining membrane of the involucrum is forced out of the aperture, this may well be the result of pressure.

In other respects the structure of the adult organ, as described by Kölliker and Vogt, is readily reducible to the type of the young form.   The cavity of the base of the involucrum appears to become filled up by vacuolated tissue, so that Kölliker describes the wall of the capsule as consisting of three layers.   "Close round the inner cavity (whose outline is never twice alike, and which always presents a sinus towards its apex), in fact, is a granular substance, having the same appearance as the wall of younger capsules, only that a reddish colouring matter is deposited on one side of it.   This is succeeded (but on one side only, toward the apex) by a conical appendage formed of coarsely vesicular tissue; and, lastly, the whole is invested by a partly striated, partly vesicular-looking substance, whose extreme point is also coloured reddish" (p. 23).   This innermost layer is, I doubt not, the inner wall of the dilated base of the involucrum.   If the latter (as it appears to do) gradually grew out into a cone beyond the sacculus, and the endoderm of its cavity became vacuolated, as is so constantly the case in the appendages of these animals, we should have the "conical appendage with coarsely vesicular tissue."   And if the ectoderm thickened and altered, it would give rise to the striated or vesicular outer substance.

The reproductive organs are stated by Kölliker to resemble exactly those of his *Agalmopsis* (*Agalma*).   Vogt's account of their structure and development is not very clear, and, if I may judge by the analogy of other *Physophoridæ*, is in many respects not quite correct; but it tends towards the same conclusion.

The largest of my *Physophoræ* was taken in the southern part of the Indian Ocean on the 17th of June, 1847.   With it I obtained a very small one, not more than one third of an inch long, and one of the same size had been obtained on a previous day (June 7th, 1847).

In these small specimens (fig. 2) the ectoderm of the stem-like portion of the cœnosarc appeared to consist of longitudinal fibres $\frac{1}{6000}$th of an inch in diameter.   The lower end of the cœnosarc expanded into a somewhat obliquely set, spheroidal, or elliptical, bulbous enlargement, round which were arranged three hydrocysts, two large and one small, which I took at the time for young polypites.   These, which have been described above, were arranged nearly in one plane.   Below them were numerous small buds, which appeared to be nascent polypites.   Arising from one side of the cœnosarc, just below the pneumatophore, were several rudimentary nectocalyces; the largest and lowest, one sixtieth of an inch in length, had four straight longitudinal canals united by a circular canal, but its nectosac was not yet open.   This is, I believe, the youngest state in which *Physophora* has yet been observed, as the young form described by Vogt has four large hydrocysts and a polypite with open mouth and long tentacle; however, I confess I can understand neither the figures nor the description of the young tentacular sacs of this specimen.

I will not attempt to refer my *Physophoræ* to any of the species yet described, for I doubt whether it is possible, with our present information, to separate one species of *Physophora* satisfactorily from another. I will only remark that if the hydrocysts of *P. Philippi* (Köll.) and *P. hydrostatica* (Vogt), which I am strongly inclined to think with Leuckart are one and the same, are really devoid of tentacles, mine is a totally distinct species.

In conclusion, I will remind the reader that fig. 1, Pl. VIII, is no better than a diagram, the original sketch having been very hasty and imperfect. I imagined I should meet with plenty more *Physophoræ*, and could finish my drawing at any time; but in three years and a half I never took another. The other drawings were made very carefully, and are, I believe, accurate.

## *Fam.* ATHORYBIADÆ.

### *Genus* ATHORYBIA (*Eschscholz*).

The hydrosoma, which is not distinctly separated into pneumatophore and cœnosarc, is spheroidal, the pneumatocyst nearly filling its cavity. There are no nectocalyces. The hydrophyllia are arranged around the cœnosarc, on the proximal side of the other appendages.

ATHORYBIA ROSACEA (?). Pl. IX.

> *Athorybia rosacea*, Eschscholz. 1829.
> — — Kölliker. 1853.

That portion of the hydrosoma which represents the pneumatophore is spheroidal, but somewhat pointed above, and has its apex surrounded by a series of radiating dark-brown striæ, each made up of dots. Its general colour is pink. The polypites have a lightish-red hue, shading off into pink at their apices. The tentacles are yellowish or colourless, with dark-brown sacculi.

The hydrophyllia are lanceolate, tolerably straight in their upper halves, but greatly incurved below. The upper and outer surface of each is convex, the lower and inner concave. Six longitudinal rows of small thread-cells mark the outer surface. The basal or upper portion of the hydrophyllium is broad, and presents, on each side, a notch or shoulder, where it joins with the narrower neck, by which it is connected with the broad lanceolate blade. These shoulders overlap, or are overlapped by, those of neighbouring hydrophyllia. The axis of each hydrophyllium is traversed by a narrow, tubular, cæcal phyllocyst, which runs nearer the inferior surface, and is wider and ciliated internally in the younger organs. The larger and more conspicuous hydrophyllia are arranged in a circle around the globular hydrosoma above its equator, but a few smaller ones are to be observed among the appendages of the under surface. These were polypites, tentacles, and reproductive organs.

Of the polypites, the distal ones,[1] or those attached more towards the centre of the under surface, especially one or two, were the larger and more active. Their inner wall was provided with villi for about its basal two thirds; some of these villi were short and thick, others thinner and elongated. The latter were often jagged or produced into small points at their extremity. The villi contained large clear spaces (vacuolæ) in their interior.

Young undeveloped polypites were scattered among the perfect forms.

The tentacles sometimes appeared to come off from the wall of the cœnosarc itself,

---

[1] The upper and outer series were so similar to the others that they are not specially distinguished in my notes, so that I cannot say whether they have the structure described by Kölliker in the " Fühler," or hydrocysts of his *Athorybia*, or not.

but in other cases I could distinctly observe that they arose from the pedicle of the polypites. In their perfect state they were similar to those of the *Calycophoridæ*, except in the structure of the sacculus, which nearly resembles that of *Agalma*.

This organ is very long, and is coiled up within a large involucrum. The distal end of the sacculus is prolonged into a conical median lobe, devoid of thread-cells, and two lateral, comparatively short, filaments (fig. 9 *f*).

The involucrum and the filaments contain many small thread-cells ($\frac{1}{4000}$th inch); those which lie in the thickened wall of the sac are, as usual, elongated, about $\frac{1}{1000}$th of an inch long, and of a deep-brown colour. Thread-cells of a different kind are disposed obliquely to these and imbedded in the proximal half of the walls of the sacculus; they are from two to eight in number on each side, measure $\frac{1}{350}$th of an inch in length, and have an elongated oval form.

The lateral branches of the tentacula are first visible as papillæ about $\frac{1}{100}$th of an inch in length, composed of the endoderm and ectoderm, and containing a diverticulum of the somatic cavity. These papillæ elongate and become tricuspid at their extremities, small thread-cells at the same time making their appearance in their walls towards the proximal end; next a constriction appears in the middle of the papilla, and one wall becomes much thicker than the other. The lateral processes of the tricuspid distal end now elongate rapidly, the central one remaining comparatively stationary, and the thread-cells acquire their characteristic forms (figs. 9 *a*—9 *e*).

The involucrum finally makes its appearance as a process of the ectoderm of the basal division of the organ. Up to this time the sacculus has remained straight; its coiling up only takes place subsequently.

The reproductive organs are scattered irregularly upon independent branched stalks or gonoblastidia (fig. 12), one pedicle (always ?) carrying both androphores and gynophores. Small hydrocysts are also developed on the same pedicle. The androphores are longer and rather thicker than the gynophores. The calyx of the former presents a terminal circular aperture, and the characteristic longitudinal canals, though I am not sure there were four of them.

In the most advanced androphores the manubrium had a reddish colour, and its apex projected beyond the mouth of the calyx; it contained nearly fully developed spermatozoa. Each gynophore contained but a single ovum. The calyx exhibited its four regular canals, united, in the fully developed organ, by a circular canal surrounding a terminal aperture.

The gynophore appeared to contain many large superficial anastomosing canals, an appearance produced, as in the case of *Agalma*, by the irregular and incomplete separation of the outer surface of the manubrium from the inner surface of the calyx.

I took this *Athorybia* in the Indian Ocean in April, 1847; on the East Coast of Australia in May, 1848.

The only complete anatomical description of any *Athorybia* extant is that given by Kölliker of *A. rosacea*, which occurred abundantly at Messina, and presented many varieties. The hydrophyllia were attached below the air-vesicle to the short, depressed, conical cœnosarcal portion of the hydrosoma, in two or three circles, of which the uppermost was sometimes the shortest, so as to suggest that here, as in other *Physophoridæ*, the youngest organs are nearest the proximal end of the body. Some of these organs were lanceolate and compressed at the base, others obliquely truncated at the base, and rounded at the apex. Five or six lines of thread-cells ornamented their outer surface, and each contained a narrow canal which nearly reached its apex, and was not ciliated. The hydrophyllia could be raised and depressed, and the animal could propel itself by alternating these movements.

There were twenty to forty hydrophyllia, but never more than eight polypites.

Irregular cavities occur in the walls of the latter organs, which Kölliker considers to be glandular.

A series of hydrocysts (Fühler), some fourteen or twenty in number, and always more numerous than the polypites, are attached by short peduncles around the margins of the hydrosoma. Their walls are muscular and ciliated internally and externally, and their apices are surrounded by thread-cells.

There is a tentacle for each polype, whose general structure appears to be very similar to what I have described above, but there is a good deal of apparent difference in the sacculi and their appendages.

Kölliker says—"The saccculi (nesselknöpfe) consist of many parts. Their pedicle divides into two organs; a stalked, elongated capsule, and a crescentic, proper urticating cord (nesselstrang); to whose extremity two prehensile filaments (fang-fäden) and a pyriform vesicle are attached. All of these parts are hollow, and contain the same clear liquid as the stem. The urticating cord shows the ordinary structure. First, large thread-cells, one of which is shown with its thread projected in fig. 10; then smaller thread-cells, inserted in rows in the thickened wall, between which a reddish-brown pigment is deposited. Finally, there are two muscular cords in the concave part of the organ. The prehensile filaments are thread-like, short, and very contractile, so that they can shrink into a very small space, and are beset throughout with small thread-cells; while on the other hand, the pyriform sac appears clear, and although quite similar in form and position to the analogous organ in *Agalmopsis Sarsii*, exhibits no movements and is not ciliated. The stalked elongated capsule, lastly, exhibits in its walls, and, as it would seem, also, in its interior, a beautiful reticulation, in whose spaces, besides a clear fluid, yellowish or reddish fatty-looking globules are often contained. Besides, the yellow middle part is (though not always) surrounded by transverse fibres, and, at one point, covered with dark organs like urticating organs, and drops of fat. The signification of this vesicle, which, like the other parts, was observed colourless, especially among the uppermost of these organs, is altogether doubtful. In the younger and youngest sacculi, such as were frequently to be observed at the root of the tentacles, it was not unusually closely applied to the concave side of the urticating cord, but I could find no close relation between the two parts, nor did it seem that the capsule took any share in the movements of the urticating cord, for, indeed, it exhibited none itself."

On comparing this description and its accompanying figures with my own notes and drawings, I entertain no doubt that the structure of the tentacles in the two *Anthorybiæ* is essentially the same; that, in fact, the "stalked elongated capsule" is the involucrum; the "urticating cord" the sacculus; the pyriform sac the dilated median lobe; and the "small tentacles" the filaments.

The reproductive organs of both sexes are found combined in *A. rosacea*, as in my species, but, apparently, they are somewhat differently arranged. A solitary androphore and a bunch of female organs are attached to the under surface of the hydrosoma, beside each polypite. The male organs have essentially the same structure as that I have described. As to the female organs, Kölliker confirms the account which I had given in 'Müller's Archiv' of the peculiar canals which lie between the ovisac and the calyx, and shows that their structure is in all essential respects the same as in my species. The entire calyx is, he says, covered with cilia, and when detached swims about by their agency.

Forskål gives the length of the hydrophyllia in *A. rosacea* as half an inch, whence the diameter of the whole animal must be about an inch. Lesson says, "Largeur 1 pouce," but Kölliker's specimens would not seem to have attained half that size, which is about the dimensions of those I observed. Notwithstanding the apparent discrepancies, I am inclined to regard the forms I have described as of the same species as that described by Kölliker. It will be better at any rate to do so provisionally, for M. Kölliker's observations show that the *Athorybiæ* are liable to great variation, and it is anything but clear that the *A. heliantha* of Eschscholz and the *A. melo* of Quoy and Gaimard are distinct from *A. rosacea*.

### *Fam.* RHIZOPHYSIDÆ.

### *Genus* RHIZOPHYSA (*Peron* and *Lesueur*).

Hydrosoma filiform; neither nectocalyces nor hydrophyllia. Tentacula branched, the branches peculiarly modified at their extremities, but without true sacculi.

RHIZOPHYSA FILIFORMIS ?   Pl. VIII, fig. 13.

> *Physsophora filiformis,* Forskål, 1775.
> *Epibulia filiformis,* Eschscholz, 1829.
> *Rhizophysa filiformis,* Gegenbaur, 1853.

The pneumatophore is pyriform, and, like the rest of the body, of a pale, pinkish hue, but with a very deep red patch surrounding the aperture of the pneumatocyst.[1]

The cœnosarc, long and cylindrical, is hardly at all twisted upon itself, and gives attachment at intervals to slender polypites, about half an inch long.

The endoderm of these organs exhibits short villi, containing clear spaces. A tentacle arises at the junction of the polypite with its pedicle, and the stem of this organ when contracted is not more than an inch long, thick at its base, thin at its extremity, and usually coiled upon itself. It is capable of great extension (to as much as two or three inches in length), and then appears like a slender thread. Floating at the top of the water in a glass vessel two or three inches deep, the animal could fix itself by means of the lowermost branches of its tentacles to the bottom, and holding on by them, raise and lower itself at will.

The stem of the tentacle gives off a series of lateral branches in which no distinction into pedicle, sacculus, and filament is discernible. These branches arise from only one side of the stem, and those which are nearest the attached end are mere small, oval buds, while the distal ones are delicate threads as much as half an inch in length. Each thread is a double-walled, cæcal tube, with one wall thicker than the other in the proximal portion, and alone containing the thread-cells, which are scattered over the whole surface in the lower part of the organ. The thread-cells are spheroidal, and measure about $\frac{1}{800}$th of an inch in diameter.

The polypites appear to be attached indifferently to either side of the cœnosarc (?), and at the base of the pneumatophore several small and partially developed ones could be observed. There was no indication of any nectocalyces.

---

[1] Whose structure is particularly described above.

I sought carefully for reproductive organs, but the only trace of them to be discovered was two bunches of small, oval bodies, situated at the base of and between, two of the polypites. These were oval, double-walled diverticula of the cœnosarc, with a ciliated internal cavity, and about $\frac{1}{130}$th of an inch in length. Their ectoderm contained a few thread-cells.

I took a single specimen of this species in the Indian Ocean on the 2d of January, 1849.

It was in this animal, as I have stated above, that I saw the air spontaneously expelled from the orifice of the pneumatocyst.

The only account of any species of *Rhizophysa* which suffices the wants of the modern naturalist is the excellent description of *R. filiformis* by Gegenbaur, in the 'Beiträge,' to which I have so often had occasion to refer. This animal attains a foot and a quarter in length, but has about the same sized pneumatophore and general thickness as that which I have just described.

In Gegenbaur's description of the structure of the pneumatophore, the facts agree pretty closely with those which I have observed, but his interpretation of them is different. He seems, in fact, to regard the layer of endoderm, reflected over the outer wall of the pneumatocyst, as the whole wall of the pneumatophore, and hence he imagines that the apex of the pneumatocyst is, at the superior pore, naked. The ciliated, cellular processes are described just as I saw them. I did not observe the layers of small, round, yellowish cells which he describes between the endoderm and the air-sac, whose presence, however, is extremely interesting when we consider the position of the liver in *Velella*.

Gegenbaur having supposed the reflected endoderm to be the ectoderm, naturally denies that the apical pore can have any communication with the interior of the air-sac; but its real connexions are in favour of such a communication, and, as I have stated, I distinctly saw air-bubbles escape from it.

The young polypite is at first, according to Gegenbaur, a simple process of the wall of the cœnosarc, whose cavity at first freely communicates with that of the latter. The rudiment of the tentacle buds forth from the base of the polypite as this budded from the cœnosarc; and at the same time a process arises just in front of this rudiment, and gradually reduces the communicating passage to a narrow canal, which can be completely shut by muscular contraction. Eventually, the polypite opens at its apex, becomes functionally active, and villi appear on its inner surface.

Thus far Gegenbaur's observations agree so closely with my own that I can see no ground for supposing that we examined different species, but, in his account of the tentacles, he describes structures which, I think, I could hardly have overlooked, though, as I examined but one specimen, I may have done so; or, perhaps, they were not developed in the tentacles I examined. They consist, he states, of a stem with secondary branches, whose buds are closely aggregated at the root of the stem. At the end of each branch are small, mostly greenish capitula, which, when microscopically examined, appear as prehensile organs (fang-organe) of a structure quite different from what obtains in other "polypi nechalei." Their forms are various, but they may be reduced to the different states of three typical forms.

In the first, the end of the branch is somewhat dilated and divided into three lobes, each of which is beset with large thread-cells.

In the second, the expanded end of the branch divides dichotomously (so as to resemble one of the oral tentacles of a *Bougainvillia*), and a single large thread-cell is contained in the end of each of the terminal branches.

Of the third kind there is not one for ten of the others. The end of the branch enlarges into a globular knot, containing many thread-cells, and sending out, at a right angle to the axis of the branch, a firm, conical process. "It is composed of a few cells, and carries on one side a coat of clear, muscular fibres, by means of which it is frequently set in motion, being usually bent towards that side on which the muscular fibres lie, and then starting back into its first position.

"At the root of this beak-like process a great number of fusiform bodies are attached, one end being buried in the organ, the other free. No motion was observed in them. Their contents are finely granular and condensed towards the middle, where the outlines of a nucleus are sometimes discoverable. The points are almost always clear and glassy."

Fully developed sexual organs were found by Gegenbaur in none of the numerous specimens which he examined. But he describes vesicular bodies seated on the cœnosarc between the polypites, which he believes were their rudiments. He found, however, no trace of either generative products or medusiform buds, so that the real nature of these organs is still open to doubt.

Lesson ('Acalèphes,' p. 490) gives a figure of *Rhizophysa filiformis*, to whose cœnosarc, spheroidal, granular masses are attached between the polypites. These he calls in the text "paquets d'ovaries," and in his definition of the species these "paquets d'ovaries" are said to be "jaunes." Nevertheless, in the figure they are of a lively pink hue! By way of making the confusion perfect, Lesson praises Delle Chiaje's "description de cet Acalèphe," which he subjoins, and which obviously relates to a totally different animal.

## Fam. PHYSALIADÆ.

### Genus PHYSALIA (*Lamarck*).

Hydrosoma irregularly pyriform. Pneumatocyst occupying almost the whole of the somatic cavity, and produced into cæca, arranged in a longitudinal series. Tentacula without branches, but provided with reniform enlargements along one edge, and with basal sacs.

The term *Physalia* was employed by Lamarck to denote certain remarkable animals which, before his time, had passed under the various scientific names of *Urtica marina*, *Arethusa*, *Holothuria*, *Salacia*, &c., and were popularly known by the titles of "Portuguese man-of-war," "Kriegschiff," "Galère," "Caravella," "By-the-wind Zeyler," &c. appellations, which the *Physaliæ* enjoy in common with the *Velella*, and all expressive of the fact, that the great bladder which constitutes the most conspicuous part of the animal is impelled hither and thither by the winds, as it floats on the surface of the sea.

Cuvier discerned the true position of *Physalia* in the animal kingdom, and Eysenhardt's essay, 'Zur Anatomie und Naturgeschichte der Quallen,'[1] contains some valuable notes upon its structure. He points out the analogy of the polypites of *Physalia* with the mouths of the *Rhizostomidæ*, and of the central cavities and canals of each, but he considers the long tentacles to be external genital organs, and seems not to understand the true nature of the pneumatocyst.

Eichwald again ('Observationis nonnullæ circa fabricam Physaliæ, auctore Dr. E. Eichwald[2]) describes the manner in which the tentacles are, as it were, gathered up, along the line of their attachment to their basal sacs, but he considers them to be reproductive organs ("funiculos proliferos, cognominare liceat," l. c., p. 456). The attachment of the pneumatocyst to one point only of the hydrosoma, and the free communication of the cavity interposed between the pneumatocyst and the wall of the hydrosoma, with the cavities of all the appendages, are noted. The crest, which Eichwald calls a branchia, and certain vessels distributed upon it, are fully described, but the reproductive organs are supposed to be polypites in various stages of development (p. 461), while the author's conception of the reproductive process is expressed in the following paragraph (p. 468):

"Hisce forsitan concludendum, physalias veluti infusoria seu polypos hydriformes prolem gemmæ instar, in funiculis proliferis progignere, qui tunc per fimbrias ei nutrimentum adducerent donec tubuli suctorii ab initio filis tenuibus comparandi ei evolverentur."

A somewhat more satisfactory account of the anatomy of *Physalia* is due to Eschscholz ('System,' p. 147, et seq.)

[1] Nova Acta, t. xvii, pt. 2, 1821.

[2] 'Mém. de l'Acad. Imp. des Sc. de St. Petersbourg,' t. ix, p. 453, 1824. (The essay was read in 1822.)

" The very large swimming bladder is distended with air," says this excellent observer, ' in such a manner that its longest diameter is horizontal.   In all the species there may be remarked at one end of the bladder a prolongation, also full of air, which is not provided with suckers or prehensile filaments, and at whose surface, near the end, a distinct pit is perceptible, which, as soon as the bladder is compressed, opens and allows of the exit of the contained air. In some species this part equals half the entire length of the bladder, while in others it is very short.   The opposite end of the bladder, on the other hand, is, in all species, covered on one side with suckers, which, in young individuals, are much more imperfect than the others which lie in the middle of the vesicle.   This end also possesses a pit on its upper surface, which appears to be an opening of the bladder,[1] and is in some species provided with a particular solid process.   Along the upper surface of the bladder there runs a plaited ridge, which, in its common condition, is also filled with air ; but the animal can, at will, press the air out of it, when the ridge collapses into a membranous fold, but the bladder becomes thicker and more distended.

" The bladder consists of a double membrane, an outer solid, and an inner much more delicate one ; when the animal has lain in spirit, the inner membrane can be separated from the outer as a separate bladder.

" On the lower side of the bladder are the organs of nutrition, which consist of suckers and prehensile filaments.    The former arise either singly[2] from the bladder, or many spring together from a common stem.    The prehensile filaments are so far to be called simple that they neither branch nor give off lateral offsets.    They consist of a rounded filament, which is covered throughout its whole length on one side with a series of reniform acetabula (saug-warzen), and on the other side is supported by a narrow membrane, which accompanies it from the root to the point.

" At the root of each prehensile filament, of which there are many of different sizes on a single animal, is a long, pointed receptacle of fluid (flüssigkeits-behälter), attached throughout almost its whole length to the filament, and only free at its apex.    The acetabula of the prehensile filaments appear to be the organs which secrete the mucus which produces the well-known urtication of the human skin, and by which animals which are seized are at once paralysed."

Eschscholz compares the receptacles at the bases of the tentacles to the ambulacral vesicles of the *Echinodermata*.

After denying the justice of the statement of a Dr. Blume respecting the existence of a nervous system in *Physalia*, Eschscholz goes on to say :

" That the *Physaliæ* have the power of emptying the air out of their bladder, and so diving down, as the older writers relate (though their statements are only suppositions), rests upon no direct observation.   *Physaliæ* which are touched, pricked, cut, irritated with acrid substances, or placed in brandy, would certainly not fail to dive if they could, in order to escape such treatment.   But it is only by actual compression of the bladder that I have

---

[1] This observation has not been verified by subsequent observers.

[2] I entertain great doubts whether this is ever the case in adult *Physaliæ*.   Leuckart denies it in *Ph. utriculus* (' Ueber den Bau der Physalien,' p. 195), which is in perfect accordance with my own observations.

succeeded in pressing the air out of the aperture.    However, a young *Physalia* of five lines in length possessed this power : after I had touched the animal a few times, it suddenly expelled all the air from its bladder, and sank to the bottom of the glass.

" Besides the prehensile filaments and suckers, we find between these organs, on the under surface of the bladder, one or many bundles of short threads, which may be regarded as young.    Different parts are distinguishable in these bundles, namely, a long thread closed at its apex ; then a tubular or funnel-shaped body ; and a small globe at the root of the two preceding.    These parts of the bundle were easily detached when the animal was touched, which clearly showed them to be young, as this phenomenon is observed in all the lower animals.    Of the three organs here mentioned I hold the first, the long thread, to be the receptacle of fluid of an undeveloped prehensile thread, the funnel-shaped body for a sucker, and the small globe for the vesicular body, which is not yet filled with air.    So that these three parts form together the most essential parts of the body of the *Physalia*."

De Blainville ('Manuel,' p. 113) has fallen into the most marvellous errors respecting *Physalia*.    Not content with discovering its mouth and an anus, he attributes to the *Physaliæ* a stomach (the air-bladder), a foot (the crest), branchiæ (the tentacles), and generative apertures, besides a hepatic plate, vessels, and a central circulatory organ !    No wonder, then, that he places *Physalia* among the Molluscs.

Von Olfers, the author of the next essay of importance on the structure of the *Physaliæ*,[1] has not added very much to what was made known by Eschscholz.

He describes the chambered structure of the crest, and mentions the sphincter of the aperture, but he affirms that a probe introduced into the latter leads into the space between the outer bladder and the inner, in which last he was unable to detect any opening. Like Eichwald he ascribes to the inner, air-containing, bladder cæcal processes, which lie in the compartments of the crest.

Von Olfers further mentions the villi of the polypites (or large and small suckers), and the communication of the cavity of the latter with the cavity which lies between the external vesicle, or body-wall, and the internal proper air-bladder.    Less accurate in some respects than his predecessor, he affirms the tentacular receptacles to have an aperture at their apex, though he admits he has never seen the supposed mouths in a state of dilatation.

The thread-cells, while *in situ* in the villi and tentacles, are described as small, round glands ; while, when partially detached and adherent by their thread only, to the latter, Von Olfers has mistaken them for *Vorticellæ*.

The supposed budding young, or " brut," of Eschscholz, are called " keimbündel"— germ-bundles, and are carefully analysed by Von Olfers into bodies of three kinds : 1. Small suckers, similar to the large ones, but smaller ; 2. Club-shaped bodies ; 3. Ovate or pyriform bodies.

Von Olfers states particularly that he does not consider these to be reproductive organs (l. c., p. 163), nor does he agree in Eschscholz's view of their nature ; but he imagines that the ovate or pyriform bodies are " the germs of young *Physaliæ*, which, probably, become

---

[1] 'Ueber die grosse Seeblase (*Physalia arethusa*) und die Gattung der Seeblasen im Allgemeinen.' Abhandlungen der Kön. Akademie d. Wissenschaften zu Berlin, 1831.

developed into the clavate bodies and then fall off, either alone or in connexion with one of the small suckers as young buds."

In 1847, during the voyage of H.M.S. 'Rattlesnake,' I[1] sent from Australia to the Linnean Society, a memoir on the structure of *Physalia*, which was read before that learned body on the 21st of November and the 5th of December, 1848, but the following abstract from the 'Proceedings of the Linnean Society,' vol. ii, p. 3, 1855, is all that has appeared of its contents.

"The specimens of *Physalia* on which Mr. Huxley's observations were made, were collected on board the 'Rattlesnake,' between the 25th of February and the 3d of March, between lat. 25° and 37° south, and long. 5° and 7° west. They varied in size from one sixth of an inch to two inches, in the long diameter of the float. The author first describes the general appearance of the specimens, of which he doubts whether the largest were adult, and then proceeds to a minute examination of their details, dividing them for this purpose into the float, air-bladder, and the appendages, of greater or less length, which depend from it, when the animal is in its natural position at the surface of the water. The smaller specimens he states to be the best adapted for examination.

"The float is described as consisting of an outer coat, an inner coat, and an air-sac, contained within them, attached only to one spot of their parietes, and there communicating with the exterior by a small constricted aperture, which was always found on the upper surface. The disposition of the appendages is very irregular, but the larger tentacles are generally placed more externally, the smaller and nascent organs more towards the centre. These appendages are of three kinds, and consist of stomachal sacs, tentacles, and cyathiform bodies.

"Of each of these the author gives a detailed description, in their more perfect form, as well as in their undeveloped state, as nascent organs; and then proceeds to inquire, first, what is the physiological importance of the organs described, and, secondly, what zoological place should be occupied by an animal provided with such organs, so disposed.

"Each of these questions the author treats at considerable length. Of the function of the stomachal sacs in receiving the prey there can be little question; but it may be doubted whether the digested nutritive matter circulates in the ciliated water-carrying canals, or is absorbed into totally different channels.

"In the latter case, the purpose of the stomachal villi would plainly seem to be to absorb nutritive matter, and convey it, through their central canal, to the wide interspace existing between the outer and the inner membrane; but the author states that he has never seen in this interspace any corpuscles analogous to those described by Will[2] as blood-corpuscles. He suggests that the villosities noticed by Dr. Milne Edwards in the stomachal sacs of *Apolemia* are the same organs, and not ovaries, as Dr. Milne Edwards considers them; and observes that similar organs exist in a *Diphya* (*Eudoxia*), hereafter to be more fully described.

"The functions of the tentacles, both as prehensile and defensive organs, admit of little doubt, and on this subject the author notices an erroneous view of M. Lesson, who describes

[1] By accident, the author of the communication is called '*William*' Huxley in the 'Proceedings.'

[2] I should state that Will's 'Horæ Tergestinæ' was one of my few books, and that for a long time I made great efforts to see the vascular system which he has imagined to exist in many *Hydrozoa*.

them merely as ducts for conveying a (hypothetical) acrid fluid from a (hypothetical) poison-gland. He also controverts M. Lesson's opinion that certain of the colourless tentacles are to be regarded as branchiæ; being quite sure that there is no difference between these and the ordinary tentacles, except in the absence of colour. As regards the function of the cyathiform bodies, he has no other than analogical evidence to offer. The only organs in the *Acalephæ* with which he conceives them to have any resemblance are the natatorial organs of the *Physophoræ*. But their little adaptation to a similar purpose, and the entire absence even of their rudiments in young *Physaliæ*, discourage this comparison; while, on the other hand, they bear a singular resemblance to the female generative organs of a *Diphya*, and this resemblance extends even to the younger stages of both.

"Mr. Huxley concludes by referring Physalia to the position assigned to it by Eschscholz among *Physophoræ*, and near *Discolabe* or *Angela*. In fact, he regards *Physalia* as, in all its essential elements, nothing but a *Physophora*, whose terminal dilatation has increased at the expense of the rest of the stem, and hence carries all its organs at the base of this dilatation.

"The paper was illustrated by pencil drawings of the structures described."

In 1851, Professor Leuckart published a very valuable essay, 'On the Structure of the *Physaliæ* and of the *Siphonophoræ* in general,' which contains some important additions to our knowledge of the structure of these animals. On one or two points, respecting which Leuckart's observations are more complete than Von Olfers' and my own, I will quote him at length.

"The crest is an integral part of the outer wall of the body, and may be regarded as a duplication of it. Between its two lamellæ there remains a cavity, which is not continuous through its whole length, being divided by a number of transverse septa, which are visible even from without, into a corresponding number of cæcal chambers or compartments.

"These septa are especially formed by the inferior muscular layer of the wall of the body, whose elements here consist of large, trabecular, transverse fibres, composed of fine fibrillæ.

"The length of the septa is very different, and they are alternately larger and smaller.

"According to these differences, four groups of septa may be distinguished. The first group contains the longest, which traverse the whole height of the crest, from its ridge to its base. Of such septa I count six in the present species, a number which, notwithstanding the difference in size (I examined individuals of two to three and a half inches in length) of the body, appeared to be constant.[1] These six septa divide the cavity of the crest into seven successive chambers. Each such chamber is divided in the middle by a septum of the second order, which extends from the ridge half-way down. In this way fourteen chambers are formed in the upper part of the crest, and this number is increased by further repetition of the dichotomous division to twenty-eight and fifty-six. The last septa are the shortest, being little more than constrictions of the outermost ridge of the crest.

"The position of the crest is commonly stated to be on the upper surface of the bladder.

---

[1] Leuckart adds in a note: "This character would, therefore, seem to be not without importance in distinguishing species. In *Ph. arethusa* I counted twelve such septa, with which the statements and figures of Von Olfers agree."

This, however, is not exactly the case. At least, if the place of attachment of the appendages is decisive, and the opposite surface is to be regarded as the upper, the crest lies horizontally and on one side, hardly more remote from the under than from the upper surface."

With respect to the "keim-bündeln," Leuckart's account of their structure contains no addition to that of Von Olfers, which is not to be wondered at, as only spirit specimens were at his disposal. He states (p. 209):

"So much is certain, that these vesicles (the ovate and club-shaped bodies of *Physalia*— medusoid bodies of other *Siphonophoridæ*) are not sexual organs, but are more or less developed individuals of a second generation, which arise asexually by budding and are capable of sexual propagation, whilst the *Siphonophoridæ* themselves remain constantly without sexes."

As we shall see, Leuckart nearly, though not quite, divines the true nature of these bodies in this passage.

In the same year 1851, the lamented Johannes Müller, the great anatomist of Berlin, published in his 'Archiv' a translation of a brief communication which I had addressed to him,[1] and which comprised among other matters a description and figures of the reproductive organs of *Physalia*, based upon the observations and drawings which will be given in the present work.

The last memoir upon *Physalia* to which it is necessary I should advert, is that published in the 'Annales des Sciences Naturelles,' for 1853, by M. De Quatrefages.

The author justly corrects the statement of Leuckart which I have quoted above, so far as to point out that, in the natural position of the animal, the crest is vertical, while the appendages are lateral; and he describes extremely well and faithfully the singular somersaults which the *Physalia* describes during life by raising up the pointed end of its body, changing its centre of gravity and tumbling over; but I must confess that I cannot regard the fact of the performance of these manœuvres as any proof that the *Physaliæ* are in the habit of tacking (virent de bord), or that it " décèle une volonté bien déterminée et comme réflechie" (p. 114). On the contrary, as I have over and over again watched the operation going on with great vigour in a dead calm, I cannot but think that if the *Physaliæ* really imagine they are tacking or wearing ship, they exhibit a remarkable absence of reflective capacity.

In discussing the functions of the pore, M. De Quatrefages contributes the following remarkable observation:

"One of my *Physaliæ*, which had already served for many investigations, suddenly began to collapse. The loss of the gaseous matter evidently took place through the pore in question. The bladder collapsed completely and floated on the surface of the vessel, without giving any other signs of life than obvious contractions when I irritated it.

"I believed the animal was dead, and setting it down for such in my notes, resumed the occupation with which I was then engaged. A quarter of an hour afterwards, at the most, having chanced to cast a glance at my *Physalia*, I was greatly surprised to see it distended anew, although a little smaller than it was at first, and erecting its crest in the air at the surface of the water, just as when it was first brought to me."

---

[1] 'Ueber die Sexual-organe der Diphydæ und Physophoridæ.' Müller's 'Archiv,' 1851, p. 380, **taf.** xvii.

M. De Quatrefages goes on to say, that, to account for this reappearance of the air, we must suppose either that it is secreted, or that it enters by the pore, and he adopts the latter hypothesis, conceiving that the walls of the air-vesicle are so strong and elastic as to act like a perforated, hollow, caoutchouc ball, which yields its air when compressed by the hand, and, expanding when the compression is removed, sucks it in again. The muscular fibres of the body-wall act, in M. De Quatrefages' opinion, as the compressing force, and when they are relaxed the vesicle resumes its primitive form. I must say that this hypothesis appears to me to be quite inadmissible. The wall of the pneumatocyst is, so far as my recollection serves, kept tense by the air which it contains, so that when it is pricked or cut, the organ at once collapses, by its own elasticity, quite independently of the muscular body-wall. And the extreme thinness of the membrane of the pneumatocyst is, to my mind, incompatible with the notion that its elasticity is sufficient to overcome the weight of the wall of the hydrosoma.

As little can I agree in M. De Quatrefages' view of the functions of the air-vesicle, which he supposes to be respiratory. A chemist, I think, would not lay much weight on the two eudiometrical experiments whose results are given ; and the dense and tough, though thin, elastic membrane of the pneumatocyst, covered as it is by the endoderm (the mucous layer of M. De Quatrefages), is hardly the structure in which a physiologist can recognise a special respiratory apparatus.

On injecting a *Physalia* by one of the polypites, M. De Quatrefages made an observation which seems to point to the existence of a system of canals in this Physophorid similar to those which cover the upper surface of the pneumatophore in *Velella* and *Porpita*.

"I saw that the coloured liquid had passed into a perfectly free cavity on almost the whole of the lower face and a part of the sides of the body, but, beyond a certain limit, this cavity seemed to me to become changed into an extremely close network[1] of canaliculi, ascending even on to the upper face. Muscular (?) bands passing from the parietes of the body to the air-vesicle, properly so called, kept the two concentric bladders in connexion and traversed the cavity. I regret not having ascertained if this last, or the network, which is a prolongation of it, passed into the crest, but I am led to believe it did so."

I do not propose to discuss the histological details into which the author enters, but I must remark that he has unfortunately confounded the tentacular sacs with polypites, while he supposes the latter to be hepatic organs. The account of the development of the polypites and of the reproductive organs is also, in many respects, imperfect.

The perusal of the works of the various writers who have occupied themselves with the establishment of specific distinctions among the *Physaliæ*, simply makes one long for the advent of a Caliph Omar in this department of zoological literature. A sort of unpleasant vertigo is the only result I can report of my study of the systematic labours of Von Olfers, Lesson, and Lamarck, but those who are inclined to take up the inquiry will find a very elaborate discussion of the synonymy and characters of the various so-called species in the already-cited memoir of the first named of these naturalists.

Eschscholz, on the other hand, is, as usual, clear and intelligible, and, as his species are

---

[1] This network seems to have been first noticed by Tilesius. See Eysenhardt, l. c., p. 414.

founded upon personal observation of the animals in their living state, they might very advisably (if their distinctive characters are really well founded) be taken as the starting point by future observers.   I therefore subjoin his definitions.


### 1. PHYSALIA CARAVELLA.

The first species is *Physalia caravella*, especially distinguished, according to Eschscholz, by the fact that the polypites arise from a common stem.   There is a considerable number of tentacles of equal size, and the polypites and tentacles are all crowded together at one end of the hydrosoma, which is obtuse, in such a manner that the rest of the organ, which is naked, and produced into a proboscidiform process, is almost twice as long as the part provided with polypites.

When the hydrosoma is so placed that its naked end is anterior, the left side is nearly straight; the right side, on the other hand, widens towards the middle, and behind this is strongly concave.   The series of polypites begins here, and continues to the posterior very blunt end; at a corresponding point the crest is emarginate, and it terminates at both ends of the hydrosoma, in specimens where this measures eight inches, at one inch from the end.   The colour is bright purplish red, with dark extremities, and blue lines in the folds of the crest.   The polypites are violet, with whitish points; the larger tentacles are red, with dark purple acetabula; the smaller tentacles blue; the bundles of buds are reddish.

This species attains a length of eight inches, and a width of two and a half inches, and inhabits the Atlantic from the Azores to the Brazilian coast.


### 2. PHYSALIA PELAGICA.

The polypites arise singly, and one of the tentacula is often much larger than the others. That end of the body which bears the polypites, &c., has no fleshy process, but is filled to its point with air.  The hinder end of the body is bent towards the right side, while the appendages are attached to the left side on a median prominence.   The naked end of the hydrosoma is not separated by any marked excavation from the rest; and is a third or a fourth part as long as the whole.   The crest begins as a slight elevation in the neighbourhood of the anterior naked end, gradually increases in height posteriorly, and ceases suddenly, opposite the root of that posterior process which bears the appendages.

In young individuals, the hydrosoma is only pale blue.   In the adult, both ends are green, and the crest appears to be purple in its highest part.   The tentacles are blue, with dark acetabula.   In the older individuals, besides the large tentacle, there is a second, smaller one, distinguishable from the rest.   The polypites are dark blue, with yellow points. Between the posterior process and the middle part of the hydrosoma, there is a naked spot, where the series of appendages is interrupted.   This species attains a length of two and a half inches, and inhabits the Atlantic, especially about the Cape of Good Hope.

## 3. PHYSALIA UTRICULUS.

A long, fleshy, proboscidiform process at that end of the hydrosoma, which is provided with appendages, distinguishes this species at first sight from the two preceding; the polypites arising singly from the hydrosoma, and the inequality of the tentacles, among which one is very much larger than the other, are characters which it has in common with *P. pelagica*.

In the largest specimens, the naked anterior end of the hydrosoma elongates into a narrow, conical process, which is almost longer than the other part, provided with appendages. At its extreme end, a small, fleshy, conical process of half a line in length is observable, and is to be regarded as a part of the hydrosoma containing no air. In like manner, the posterior end, beset on one side with short polypites, is not filled with air, but appears as a narrow, fleshy, and thence moveable process, six lines long, which is continued by two crura into the sides of the hydrosoma. Behind the middle there is observable on the lower surface, a great, round, bluish spot, which arises from a flat, fleshy part connected with the other thicker, fleshy streak. The long and not high crest commences six lines behind the anterior end, and does not extend to the root of the posterior process. *Physalia utriculus* attains a length of three and a half inches. As to its colour, the crest and the middle part of the pneumatophore are greenish, the two extremities blue. It inhabits the tropical regions of the Pacific.

I must confess I feel anything but satisfied that these are really distinct species, but this is a point which can only be settled by those who study these singular animals with modern appliances and a knowledge of what has already been done.

To such observers I would suggest that the number of primary and secondary septa in the crest, and the exact mode of grouping of the appendages are more likely to yield good distinctions than any other characters.

PHYSALIA UTRICULUS ? (*Esch.*)  Pl. X; Pl. XII, fig. 1.

The *Physaliæ* which I examined appeared to me to belong to one species, whose description I subjoin as I find it in my notes.

The hydrosoma tapers to a point at one end, whence it gradually enlarges, and becomes subcylindrical about the middle; the other end is somewhat suddenly widened, so that, viewed from above, the organ has, roughly speaking, a **T** shape. Along the middle of the upper surface of the subcylindrical and pointed part of the hydrosoma, its wall is raised up into a transversely plaited crest, which dies away on the enlarged end. The rest of the upper surface and the greater part of the under surface of the pointed and subcylindrical portions are quite smooth, and distended by the air contained in the pneumatocyst. The under surface of the transversely enlarged end, on the other hand, is very irregular, and gives attachment to the numerous appendages.

The general colour of the hydrosoma is a pale, delicate green, passing gradually into a dark, indigo blue on the under surface.

The ridge of the crest is tipped with lake, and the pointed end is stained deep bluish green about the aperture of the pneumatocyst.

The bases of the large tentacles are deep blue; the polypites deep blue at their bases, and frequently bright yellow at their apices; the velvetty masses of reproductive organs and buds on the under surface are light green.

This description applies to individuals whose hydrosoma is four inches long and upwards. In young specimens, the form and colour are apt to vary much.

The structure of the hydrosoma is best made out in very young individuals, small enough to be placed bodily under the microscope, as, in consequence of the extreme contractility of the walls of this organ in the larger ones, it commonly collapses and contracts into a formless mass the moment an incision is made into it.

In such young *Physaliæ*, of one fifth to three eighths of an inch in length (Pl. X, figs. 1, 2), the wall of the hydrosoma, which presents a minute, closely shut aperture or pore at one extremity, is very obviously composed of two distinct membranes,[1] the outer, or ectoderm, being denser and more transparent, while the inner, or endoderm, is softer, more opaque, and ciliated on its inner free surface.

In the region of the pore (fig. 3), the endoderm is reflected on to the outer surface of an ovate sac, which occupies only a comparatively small portion of the cavity of the hydrosoma. The walls of this pneumatocyst are dense, thick, and elastic, and its inner surface is covered with a thin layer of granular matter. The end of the pneumatocyst on to which the endoderm is reflected, is in close contact with the ectoderm, and when viewed from within presents a depression, surrounded by circular fibres, and towards which short, radiating folds of the membrane converge, which corresponds with the pore visible upon the outer surface, and is the inner end of the pneumatic aperture. By pressure, the air contained in the pneumatocyst could be made to pass out through this aperture.

In adult specimens, the outer crescentic aperture of the pneumatocyst is visible on the upper surface of the pointed apex of the hydrosoma, about half an inch from the end.

The ectoderm is composed of parallel, elongated, cœllœform masses, arranged perpendicularly to the plane of its surface; the endoderm of an outer layer of delicate (muscular?) fibres about $\frac{1}{5000}$th of an inch in diameter, invested by a granular, internal substance, which is richly ciliated.

The appendages are large tentacles, small tentacles, polypites, gonoblastidia, and reproductive organs.

The tentacular appendages arise from the outermost of the numerous protuberances developed from the under surface of the hydrosoma, or what is in reality the representative of the stem-like cœnosarc of other *Physophoridæ*.

The larger tentacles of large specimens sometimes attain a length of many feet, and are

---

[1] I do not find this structure distinctly alluded to by my predecessors. They often speak of an inner membrane, indeed, but always mean thereby the wall of the pneumatocyst. M. De Quatrefages refers to it in other parts of the organism, as the mucous layer.

remarkable for their deep blue colour, which is not merely confined to the reniform elevations, containing thread-cells, with which they are beset, but extends in a less degree on to the stem of the organ.

Each tentacle consists of two very distinct parts—the short, broad, basal sac ($c^6$), and the filiform tentacle proper ($c^1$) (fig. 11).

The former is a sort of conical bag, attached by a broad base, and terminating in a free, pointed apex, which is nothing more than a cæcal process of the hydrosoma, containing a diverticulum of the somatic cavity. Its inner surface is ciliated. The outer presents many thread-cells, whose number increases towards its base.

On one side, the edge of the sac is rounded and thick; on the other, it thins and expands into a broad, muscular membrane, which is continued down into the muscular band of the tentacle.

The tentacle proper has a common base with the sac, but is otherwise separate from it. It is essentially a cæcal tube, whose canal communicates with the cavity of the sac and with that of the hydrosoma, by means of the common base. On the side turned away from the basal sac, the ectoderm of the tube is much thicker than on the opposite side, where it expands into a thin muscular band, continuous above with the muscular expansion of the basal sac. The endoderm of the tentacle is ciliated.

The proximal end of the tentacle is gathered up into folds, which are attached to the edge of the tentacular sac by the muscular membranous expansion, just as the folds of an intestine are held by a mesentery. The rest of the tentacle hangs down straight.

At the attached end of the convoluted part of the tentacle, the thickened wall was quite even and smooth, but a little lower down, the wall had become sacculated (fig. 11 $a$), each sacculation involving both the ectoderm and the endoderm, and containing a short, broad cæcum of the tentacular cavity. At first, the sacculations involve only a small segment of the tentacular wall, but by degrees they extend transversely until, at length, they leave between their extremities only sufficient space for the longitudinal band of muscular fibres, into which the ectoderm of the opposite wall of the tentacle is metamorphosed, and for the tentacular canal, which, within the cavity of each fold, expands into a cæcum, corresponding with the fold in shape. Throughout the convoluted part of the tentacle the folds are very close together; but, in the beginning of the straight portion, they separate from one another, and throughout the rest of its length they are, in the uncontracted state of the organ, a long way apart.

When fully formed and extended, consequently, the tentacle looks like a delicate, narrow ribbon, having transverse, reniform thickenings at regular intervals (fig. 12). The substance of each thickening has a dark blue colour, and imbedded within it are myriads of close-set, colourless, spherical thread-cells, varying from $\frac{1}{300}$th of an inch in diameter, to a sixth of that size. Under a low power a number of fine filaments, the extruded threads of many of these cells, might be seen radiating from the surface of each reniform thickening.

The small tentacles arise indiscriminately among the appendages of the rest of the hydrosoma; they precisely resemble the larger ones in structure, but they are, in addition to their small size, distinguished by their pale colour, the blue coloration being either absent or entirely confined to the reniform bodies.

The *polypites* (fig. 4) attain a length of three quarters of an inch or more. Like the tentacles they exhibit great irritability and contractility, and are in constant motion, at the same time assuming every variety of form from that of a cylinder to that of a pear, or that of a wide-mouthed and narrow-necked flask. The latter is the shape most commonly assumed.

The lip is covered with many thread-cells, and is usually colourless or yellowish white; the dilated body of the organ is blue, and appears, even to the naked eye, to be dotted over with numerous dark spots ($b^1$). The ectoderm of the polypite is thin and dense. The endoderm, thicker, occasionally exhibits an appearance as if it were longitudinally fibrillated, and its inner surface is covered with long and beautiful cilia, which are especially obvious about the oral aperture. The ectoderm and endoderm are in close contact about the mouth of the polypite, but elsewhere a narrow, clear space exists between them; and in the enlarged, globular portion of the polypite this space was increased at intervals by the endoderm becoming folded (fig. 6). The folds were not at regular intervals, nor, so far as I could observe, did they ever extend completely round the circumference of the sac. They were certainly not produced by any mere contraction of the endoderm, inasmuch as the state of extension of the polypite had no influence whatever upon their existence. The space left between the endoderm and ectoderm appeared (as might be expected) greenish, and as if filled by a liquid, but no trace of globules or granules could be detected in it.

The dark spots which have been referred to above, arose from the presence of delicate villous processes of the endoderm (figs. 5—7). These villi were found wherever the folds existed; and, whenever I succeeded in tracing a villus completely to its attachment, I found its base to pass into one of these folds. The villi were especially numerous towards the proximal end of the polypite. They were cylindrical, or slightly conical, but became almost dendritic when compressed, in consequence of the thrusting asunder of the large globular masses, of which their free ends appeared to be composed. These masses were but indistinctly visible towards the base of the villus, but, towards its apex, they projected, so as to give the extremity of the organ a slightly lobed appearance, and were filled with densely packed, coloured granules.

The surface of the villi was richly ciliated, and thread-cells were imbedded here and there in their substance. The axis of the villus was traversed by a clear canal, continuous at its basal end with the interspace between the endoderm and ectoderm. The apical termination of this canal was obscured by the pigment of the villi. It would seem as if the endoderm had a distinct basement membrane, for, in two instances, where the soft investment of the villi had been torn asunder and compressed, they remained connected with the endoderm of the polypite by a delicate membranous tube of the same diameter as the central canal.

The greater part of the surface of the cœnosarc is covered by a bluish-green, granular mass, mixed with small polypites and numerous tentacles of the smaller sort (figs. 13, 13a, 13b). On microscopic examination, it is seen that the granular mass is formed by an infinity of small appendages, attached to the extremity of ramified processes of the hydrosoma, whose internal cavities are, of course, continuous with that of the hydrosoma.

Most of these appendages are imperfect, and are to be found in every stage of development. They are—1, polypites; 2, tentacles; 3, hydrocysts; 4, androphores; 5, medusiform bodies, probably gynophores.[1]

1. In their youngest condition (fig. 9) the polypites are pyriform processes of the ectoderm and endoderm (the latter ciliated internally) about $\frac{1}{100}$th of an inch in diameter. From these rudiments a regular series of gradations could be traced up to elongated sacs about one fortieth of an inch long, and $\frac{1}{200}$th of an inch wide, with rather pointed apices, about which more especially, thread-cells were accumulated (fig. 10). The endoderm, ciliated on its inner surface, sometimes presented an appearance of longitudinal fibrillation, and a distinct interval, or, at any rate, a clear space, was visible between the endoderm and ectoderm. Towards the proximal end, the transverse folds and villi of the latter had begun to make their appearance. The villi are at first papillary, obtuse eminences, without any trace of an internal cavity. As they become larger, clear vacuolar spaces appear in their interior, so that they resemble the villi of the *Calycophoridæ*, and dark pigment granules are deposited in their apices. In polypites of larger dimensions, the folds and villi were fully developed, but their distal extremities were still closed. Eventually, these open and the polypites are complete.

2. The rudiments of the tentacles (fig. 11 *b*) are, in the youngest state, hardly distinguishable from those of the polypites. The first formed part is the sac, and from the side of the base of this, the tentacle buds out as a cylindrical process, one of whose walls eventually thickens and becomes sacculated in the way described above.

Many of the protuberances of the hydrosoma are covered with nothing but these polypites and tentacles, but others, distinguishable even by the naked eye by their rounded, velvetty appearance, exhibit only one or two small polypites arising from the midst of a mass of branched, tubular processes of the hydrosoma (gonoblastidia), to which the three remaining kinds of appendages are attached.

3. The hydrocysts (fig. 13) I find described in my notes as "young stomachs," or polypites, which, indeed, they resembled in every respect, save being open at the extremity. They were usually placed at the extremities of the branches of the gonoblastidia.

4. The gynophores (fig. 15) seemed also to be very generally situated towards the end of a branch, though this appearance may possibly be due to their long pedicles. They first appeared as rounded papillæ, about $\frac{1}{180}$th of an inch in length, and having the endoderm at their apex much thickened, so that it projects into the cavity of the papilla (fig. 15 *a*).

The series of changes from this condition to that of the fully formed medusiform bud (fig. 15 *e*), is quite similar to that passed through by the nectocalyces of other *Physophoridæ*, and, therefore, need not be detailed. In the largest of these (fig. 15 *e*) the ectoderm of the calyx was thick and yellowish. Four wide, straight nectocalycine canals opened into a circular canal, which surrounded the prominent mouth of the organ. Broad transverse fibres were distinguishable in the thick inner wall. The peduncle of attachment, thick and subcylindrical, contained a canal which widened at the base of the medusiform body into a cavity whence the four longitudinal canals arose.

[1] Called "cyathiform bodies" in my memoir, communicated to the Linnean Society (*suprà*) in 1847. At that time I had not discovered the androphores, which, however, were briefly described and figured in my paper in 'Müller's Archiv' for 1851, above referred to.

These bodies attain a diameter of one sixteenth of an inch or more.

5. The androphores (fig. 14) commence as papillary elevations of the lateral walls of the branches of the gonoblastidia, whose endoderm rapidly thickens, and consists of pale, circular granules $\frac{1}{2500}$th of an inch in diameter. A small, cæcal prolongation of the central cavity next extends up one (or probably both) sides of the organ (fig. 14 $b$).

When these rudimentary androphores have attained a length of about $\frac{1}{125}$th of an inch (fig. 14 $c$), they are more completely pedunculated. The canal of the peduncle sends a short, broad process, in the middle line, into the thickened apical mass, which now consists of two portions—an inner membranous wall, resembling in all respects, and, apparently, continuous with, the endoderm of the peduncle, and an outer thick mass lying between this and the ectoderm, which consists of an aggregation of pale, spherical granules $\frac{1}{2500}$th of an inch in diameter. Two narrow, opposite canals pass from the upper end of the cavity of the peduncle, and run close to its outer wall to terminate in blind ends.

Finally, the organ increases in size, and its contents assume more and more the form of spermatozoa (fig. 14 $d$).

I can produce no direct evidence of the fact, but I entertain little doubt that the gynophores are detached as free swimming medusiform zöoids, as in *Velella*, and only develope their ova subsequently. The androphores, on the other hand, must dehisce while still attached. It might seem at first as if this arrangement were not very well calculated to ensure the impregnation of the ova, but when we consider in what enormous troops the *Physaliæ* are ordinarily found, the difficulty disappears.

All my *Physaliæ* were taken either in the South Atlantic or in the Indian Ocean.

## *Fam.* VELELLIDÆ.

### *Genus* VELELLA (*Lamarck*).

The flattened pneumatocyst, which has more or less the form of a parallelogram, is provided with a diagonal vertical crest. The tentacles are simple.

Under the head of *Holothuria spirans*, Forskål ('Descriptiones,' p. 104, and 'Icones,' tab. xxvi, fig. *k*, and $k^1$ to $k^5$) gave the first, and, at the same time, the best, concise scientific account of a *Velella* extant. He was acquainted with the concentric chambers of the pneumatophore, and with the fact that air is contained in them ("Nucleus annulis ovatis concentricis." . . . "In ejusdem nuclei annulis bullæ aeris residui se manifestant vario motu." . . . "Haud raro fundum vasculi petiverunt emisso prius aere"); being, in these respects, far in advance of some of his successors. The descriptions of Bosc ('Histoire Naturelle des Vers,' 1802); of Leach ('Tuckey's Voyage,' 1818, p. 419); of Chamisso and Eysenhardt ('De Animalibus quibusdum,' Nova Acta, 1821); of Quoy and Gaimard ('Voy. de l'Uranie, Zoologie,' 1824, p. 586); of Eschscholz ('System,' 1829); and of Lesson ('Voyage de la Coquille, Zoologie,' 1830, t. ii, part 2, p. 48); contain no additions of importance to the facts which Forskål had made known.

De Blainville ('Actinologie,' 1834, p. 306) threw out the suggestion that the "*Rataria*" of Eschscholz would turn out to be the young of *Velella*, a surmise which has proved correct. Delle Chiaje ('Descrizione e Notomia,' tomo 4to, 1841, pp. 105-8) figures and describes at some length the vascular system. He points out the communication of the chambers of the pneumatocyst with one another, and notices the gonocalyces, which he suspects to be the genital organs.

M. Hollard ("Sur l'Organisation des Velelles," 'Annales des Sciences Naturelles,' 1845) endeavoured to prove that the small polypites or gonoblastidia of *Velella* are "aquiferous tubes," and not digestive organs. On the other hand, he is the first to have pointed out very distinctly the nature of the liver (though Delle Chiaje called it "fegato"), and, apparently unacquainted with Delle Chiaje's work, he draws particular attention to the gonocalyces, which he considers to be ovaria. The thread-cells which they contain he takes for embryonic *Velellæ*, while the yellow corpuscles are ova less advanced.

Krohn ("Notiz über die anwesenheit eigenthümlicher Luftkanäle bei *Velella* und *Porpita*," Wiegmann's 'Archiv.,' 1848) confirmed Delle Chiaje's statements as to the communication between the chambers of the pneumatocyst, and at the same time communicated the important discovery of the existence of tubular prolongations of the under wall of the pneumatocyst containing air. Krohn adds a fuller account of the liver than had been given by either Delle Chiaje or Hollard.

Forskâl pointed out the peculiarity in the direction of the crest, in his species of *Velella*: "Ab uno ejus margine ad alterum oblique transiens ita ut quamcunque extremitatem advertas, pone ad dextram ante ad sinistram spectet;" and Chamisso and Eysenhardt, supposing that direction to be constant, made it the basis of their subsections of the genus, distinguishing right-handed and left-handed *Velellæ*.

" Falli autem videtur, si unicam Velellarum speciem existere, contendit, tres enim formæ facile distinguuntur, si ad directionem velæ respexeris et longitudinem corporis cum ejus latitudine comparaveris. Vela semper obliqua est, quod auctores omnes annotavere; sed duplici modo. Cum enim laterum corporis longiorum alterum dextrum, alterum sinistrum et breviorum alterum anticum, alterum posticum nominaveris, tunc vela vel ab antica parte ad posticam simulque a sinistra ad dextrum tendit (Vela sinistra, *Velella sinistra*), vel ab antica parte ad posticum simulque a dextra ad sinistram cursum dirigit (Vela dextra, *Velella oblonga* et *lata*). Directio hæc cum ratione diametri sequentes constituit formas."[1]

Chamisso then goes on to describe his three species, but a statement of Eschscholz, who was his companion in Kotzebue's voyage, renders it difficult to understand what value is to be attached to them.

" During the voyage of the Rurick with Captain Kotzebue, we observed that *the direction of the shell in the membrane which surrounds it* is not always the same. In some, the nearer end of the shell was to the right hand, in others, to the left. Chamisso described these *Velellæ*, in 1823 [*sic*], in the tenth volume of the ' Nova Acta Akad. Leop.-Carol.,' t. xxxii, and *drew attention to the variation in the position of the shell;* but unfortunately both descriptions and figures reverse everything (geben alles verkehrt an). But, inasmuch as I drew and described the animals at the same time, I can rearrange them. No great weight, however, can be placed upon the position of the shell, for having taken three specimens out of a fleet of *Velellæ* in the Atlantic, I observed that in two the shell lay from right to left, while, in the other, it lay from left to right."[2]

I cannot understand this statement of Eschscholz, for it will be observed that Chamisso does not speak of the position of the shell, but of that of the crest; and to complete the confusion, on comparing Eschscholz's figures with this description I find that they also are all reversed. Thus it is said to be the character of the first division that " If one of the longer sides of the animal is turned towards the observer the shell lies from the anterior angle of the left side to the posterior angle of the right side." On turning to the figure of *V. septentrionalis* (fig. 1, t. xv), I find that in placing it in the position indicated the shell lies from the anterior angle of the right side to the posterior angle of the left side.

In addition, Eschscholz establishes the genus *Rataria*, but I have no doubt whatsoever that, as De Blainville supposed, these are nothing but young *Velellæ*, such as I have figured in Pl. XI, fig. 9. Eschscholz describes, altogether, ten species, but I doubt the sufficiency of his definitions.

My own observations on this genus are but fragmentary, relating chiefly to the development of the gonocalyces, which eventually become free medusiform zöoids; the distribution of the vascular canals in the soft parts; and the structure of the young forms. In the following

[1] ' System der Akalephen,' p. 169.

[2] ' De Animalibus quibusdam,' Nova Acta, tom. x, pars secunda, 1821.

pages I shall therefore borrow freely from the excellent memoirs of Kölliker and Vogt, contained in the works which I have so often had occasion to quote.

The body of *Velella* (fig. 1) presents a firm, horizontal, rhomboidal disc, convex upwards or proximally, in the middle and fringed by a delicate membranous limb. The crest passes diagonally from one angle of the rhomboid to the other, and, like the horizontal disc, presents a firm central portion, and a soft marginal limb. It is triangular in shape (at any rate in most species), the apex of the triangle being immediately over the centre of the horizontal disc.

In its natural position the *Velella* floats on the surface of the sea, with its crest vertical and exposed to the air,[1] so as to act as a veritable sail; and, consequently, very little is to be seen of its appendages, which are all situated on the under surface of the horizontal disc; and indeed of its firm part, as none are attached to the membranous limb.

The large central polypite presents a projecting, conical, often plaited, oral extremity, which is susceptible of considerable dilatation. Its base is more particularly prominent in the line of the crest, so that the polypite is not altogether symmetrical. On its base, and on the under surface of all firm portions of the horizontal disc, are scattered innumerable minute polypites, which perform the office of gonoblastidia, and slender simple tentacles, with slightly enlarged extremities, spring in a single series from the line of junction between the firm part and the membranous limb.

The difference between the "firm part" and the membranous "limb" in the horizontal and vertical portions of the body of the *Velella*, is caused by the presence in the former of a hard resisting body, which is commonly known as the shell of the *Velella*, and consists of a horizontal and a vertical plate, which are perfectly continuous with one another. The notion entertained by Lesson that this shell, the pneumatocyst, is composed of several pieces, has arisen, as Kölliker has well pointed out, from a mistaken view of the nature of certain markings on its surface. Thus there is a linear groove-like depression (fig. 1 $w, w$), which traverses the upper face of the horizontal portion of the pneumatocyst, nearly at right angles to the crest, and rises upon this in the middle line until it reaches its apex. A slight ridge on the under surface of the pneumatocyst answers to this groove, while a longitudinal depression, increasing in depth from the margins to the centre, corresponds with the attachment of the crest.

The horizontal division of the pneumatocyst (accidently inverted in fig. 2) consists of two thin laminæ, passing into one another at their free edges, and united by a number of concentric[2] vertical septa, between which are corresponding chambers filled with air. All these chambers communicate together by means of apertures in the septa. Of these each septum presents two, placed at opposite points of its circumference, and all nearly in the middle line of the pneumatocyst. Kölliker made the interesting discovery that many of the chambers have an additional opening, by which they communicate directly with the exterior. These apertures are situated in the proximal or upper wall of the chambers, along a line about midway between that of the openings just described and that of the vertical plate of the pneumatocyst. Of the thirteen apertures observed by Kölliker, six lay on one side of the

[1] At least, I always observed it in this position. Delle Chiaje and Kölliker, on the other hand, seem to have seen it with the crest turned downwards.

[2] Vogt and others have affirmed the horizontal portion of the pneumatocyst to be formed of a spirally coiled tube; but this is an error.

vertical plate and seven on the other ; one aperture lies in the wall of the central chamber, the other six at tolerably even intervals between this and the margin. Consequently, as there are more than six concentric chambers, some of them must communicate with these stigmata, only indirectly.

The vertical plate of the pneumatocyst is a thin solid plate, wholly without chambers. Its concentric markings are due to mere ridges on its surface.

A character which distinguishes the pneumatocysts of *Velella* and *Porpita* from those of other *Physophoridæ* is the attachment to their distal or under surfaces of the long filamentous processes containing air, discovered by Krohn, whose cavity is subdivided at intervals by imperfect partitions, whence they appear jointed. In *Velella* there are, according to Kölliker, ten or fifteen of these " pneumatic filaments" attached to the five or six innermost chambers ; and this observer agrees with their discoverer in asserting that they traverse the liver without branching, and end cæcally in the walls of the central polypite.

Vogt, on the other hand, states that these filaments are inserted into the centre of the disc (" par quatre canaux disposés en croix"), and ramify in the liver. Leuckart ('Z. N. K.,' p. 115) is uncertain as to the mode of origin of the canals, but confirms their ramification.

The substance of the pneumatocyst is structureless, and consists of a nitrogenous substance, similar to, if not identical with, chitin. (See Leuckart, 'Z. N. K.,' p. 114.)

This singularly modified pneumatocyst is inclosed on all sides by the soft parts of the body or hydrosoma which extend beyond its free edges, and constitute the limb to which I have already referred.

If the crest is cut off and examined under the microscope (fig. 3), the soft parts over the vertical plate of the pneumatocyst will be found to be traversed on each side by a series of canals, about $\frac{1}{270}$th of an inch in diameter, which radiate from the central third of the base of the crest towards its free margin. The innermost of these canals are nearly straight ; the outermost are more or less curved, in correspondence with the free margin of the crest. From these canals branches are given off, some of which terminate in cæca, while others anastomose together, so that an irregular network of vessels spreads over the whole surface of the crest. Near the termination of the vertical plate of the pneumatocyst, the canals, becoming wider and less marked, take on a decided blue colour, and pass into a canal, which runs along the line of junction of the vertical plate of the pneumatocyst with the limb ($p^1$). From the outer side of this canal, again, branches are given off into the limb, which run obliquely towards its margin, and in their course give off wide cæcal processes on each side, which but rarely anastomose.[1] Arrived near the edge of the limb, the ends of all the branches are connected by a blue marginal canal ($p^2$), which gives off numerous short cæca on its outer side. The walls of all these canals are ciliated.[2]

---

[1] Vogt (p. 19) says, in describing these canals, " Ils s'anastomosent nulle part entre eux ;" but so far as the species I observed is concerned, this is certainly not the case.

[2] They were certainly so in my specimens. M. Vogt, however, states, " Le dois remarquer que je n'ai jamais pu observer aucun mouvement dans toutes ces ramificationes vasculaires, même en observant des individus pleins de vie qui tout en étant placés librement sous le microscope, nagaient dans l'eau." p . 21.) Kölliker, on the other hand, finds a ciliated epithelium in all the larger canals. (p. 51.)

The proximal wall of the hydrosoma, or that which covers the upper surface of the disc, presents a system of similarly ciliated, wide, anastomosing canals, which communicate with a longitudinal canal, situated over the diagonal groove which marks the upper surface of the horizontal portion of the pneumatocyst.[1] On the limb of the disc these canals divide dichotomously into straight sacculated branches, which end in a marginal canal.

All these ciliated sinuses are continuous with a series of similar sinuses in the distal layer of the hydrosoma investing the under surface of the animal, which eventually communicate with the cavities of the great central polypite and of the small or gonoblastidial polypites.

The roof of the wide digestive cavity of the central polypite is, in fact, formed by a dark-brown mass, which fills the inferior hollow of the pneumatocyst, and may probably be regarded as a liver, while, according to Kölliker, it is traversed in all directions by thin-walled canals or sinuses, $\frac{1}{200}$th — $\frac{1}{330}$th of an inch in diameter, containing cells with brownish granular contents. The canals commence in a series of cleft-like apertures, discovered by Krohn, which are readily visible with the naked eye, in the roof of the cavity of the polypite, and from these, forming many anastomoses, the sinuses pass towards the convex surface of the organ. Here they communicate with a whitish network of superficial canals, containing cells, like those of the liver, but colourless.

At the margins of the liver these whitish vessels become continuous with the system of dorsal canals above described, and, according to Kölliker, in the following way. Very numerous and close-set offshoots of the whitish vessels pass from the margin of the liver on all sides, into that portion of the soft substance of the body which covers the under surface of the horizontal division of the pneumatocyst, and, frequently dividing and anastomosing, pass beyond the points of attachment of the gonoblastidial polypites and tentacles to the margin of the pneumatocyst. Here they divide into two sets. Some pass into the limb, and, keeping near its under surface, subdivide and anastomose, becoming continually smaller, until they nearly reach the free edge; the others, on the other hand, bend upwards, round the edge of the pneumatocyst, and enter those which ramify on its upper surface.

The sinus which I have described as running along the edge of the vertical plate of the pneumatocyst appears to be what Kölliker describes as the " marginal vessels of the crest" (Randgefässe der senkrechten platte), which he states arise from the ends of the liver, and passing along the line of insertion of the membranous limb, meet and open into one another.

Besides these ramifications the sinuses of the distal layer of the hydrosoma all communicate with the cavities of the small polypites, the canals of whose peduncles open into them.

The tentacles (fig. 3) of those *Velellæ* which I examined, appeared to be nearly solid, the endoderm being, as in many *Sertulariadæ*, so extensively vacuolated, that the sides meet and nearly obliterate the central cavity. Thread-cells[2] abound more particularly towards their slightly enlarged ends. Kölliker's account of the structure of the tentacles, however, differs widely from this, since he states that, in *V. spirans*, they possess an external longitudinally

---

[1] According to Kölliker this canal is continued on to the crest in the prolongation of the groove upon the vertical plate noticed above.

[2] These are, according to Kölliker, arranged in two rows in *Velella spirans*. In a species from the Pacific Leuckart observed four rows.

fibrous and an internal circularly fibrous muscular coat; and he says that a "cavity occupies their whole length," and opens at its base into a vessel.

Vogt (p. 22), in describing the same species, says, " these tentacles are hollow cylinders, completely closed at their extremities . . . . . One might regard them as very strong, thick, and muscular tubes, whose interior is filled by a transparent liquid, which doubtless plays a certain part in the process of elongation of these organs. The principal muscular fibres which form this tube seem to be disposed in ogives, so as to present the summit of the ogive towards the interior of the tube. Other bundles are distinguishable which run circularly, while still others are disposed longitudinally. Some of these bundles traverse the interior tube in such a way as to simulate a cellular structure, which does not appear to me really to exist." From this description I am inclined to believe that the structure of the tentacles in the Mediterranean species is in reality similar to what I have observed.

Vogt (p. 22) describes a peculiar glandular structure in the margin of the limb of the horizontal disc of *Velella spirans* in the following terms: " I have already frequently mentioned the clear blue line which runs along the edge of the limb. On microscopic examination it is seen that this is composed of a simple series of great glandular sacs arranged side by side, whose circular apertures are all situated on the dorsal face of the limb, and which secrete a transparent and viscous mucus. The structure of these glandular sacs is very curious, for they are wholly made up of great cylindrical cells, disposed in a radiating manner, so that the free and rounded extremities of the cells are turned towards the centre of the sac, whilst the other extremity is fitted into its wall. On the edge of the latter the rounded contour of the cells intended to replace the cylindrical cells (of which there are apparently many series) is visible. . . . . The inferior face of the limb is covered only by the ordinary integument, and exhibits the bottom of those glandular sacs, which here have no aperture." Kölliker (p. 60) would seem to have observed these glands, and similar ones in *Porpita*, and Leuckart ('Z. N. K.,' p. 115) confirms Vogt's discovery in *Velella*.

The smaller polypites, or gonoblastidia (fig. 4), as they might, perhaps, be more correctly termed, are supported upon longish, slender, peduncles. Their apical ends are very variable in shape, sometimes wide and trumpet-shaped, with everted lips, sometimes contracted and plaited. The wall of the polypite[1] is, as usual, composed of a distinct ectoderm and endoderm; the former being provided with villous elevations on its inner surface.[2] The outer surface of the ectoderm also presents many rounded elevations, each of which contains a great number of spherical thread-cells.[3]

The wall of the peduncle has the same composition as that of the polypite itself.

[1] Kölliker (p. 53), however, states that he has seen no hepatic striæ or glandular cavities in the walls of the small polypes.

[2] Vogt has observed the two membranes of which the wall of these buds is composed, but imagines that the endoderm is a structure peculiar to them (p. 27), whereas it is continuous with the endoderm of the polypite. As I have stated above, these buds were discovered by Delle Chiaje, and have since been observed by Hollard (who entirely mistook their nature), Leuckart, Kölliker, and all the later investigators.

[3] Half digested *Crustacea*, &c., have been observed in these organs by Lesson, Vogt, and Kölliker, so that there is no doubt as to their function.

Attached to its outer surface are numerous groups of little oval bodies (figs. 5, 6, 7), the smallest of which are simple cæcal diverticula of the ectoderm and endoderm of the peduncle. These, as they increase in size, undergo all those changes which have been described as characterising the development of a medusiform zöoid, so that in such bodies of less than $\frac{1}{100}$th of an inch in length, one is able to distinguish a circular aperture in the free truncated end of the calyx, and four wide, longitudinal canals in its walls. Along the sides of these canals many peculiar, reddish-yellow vesicles, of about $\frac{1}{1000}$th of an inch in diameter, containing two or three small granules, are discernible, and round thread-cells appear in the outer wall of the calyx.[1]

On the 23d of August, 1850, while traversing the South Atlantic Ocean, I found in the vessel in which a full-grown *Velella* that I was examining was contained, a number of free bodies more or less like these medusiform buds (fig. 8). The smallest were not more than $\frac{1}{150}$th of an inch in length, and were motionless. They very closely resembled the still attached zöoids, but there was an indication of four lobes around the mouth of the calyx, and a small ovate sac containing much dark pigment, depended from the summit of the roof of the calyx into its cavity. From these every intermediate stage could be found to little "*Medusæ*," one sixtieth of an inch in length, or thereabouts, which propelled themselves by the vigorous contractions of their bell-shaped calyces (fig. 8 *a*).

The circular mouth of the deep nectosac is surrounded by a narrow membranous valve, and externally to this by four rounded lobes, whose surface, like that of the calyx, is here and there beset with thread-cells. Four longitudinal canals traverse the calyx close to its inner surface, and end below in cæcal extremities, lines of the brownish-yellow vesicles marking their course. An oval sac of $\frac{1}{300}$th of an inch in length depends from the summit of the cavity. It is closed at its extremity, and near its base is coloured by much dark pigment. No trace of their original attachment is visible in these free gonophores.

The substance of the above observations, accompanied by illustrative figures, was published in Müller's 'Archiv.'[2] for 1851. They were, in the main, confirmed by M. Vogt, in his 'Recherches,' published in 1854, but in the meanwhile Professor Gegenbaur had indicated the ultimate fate of the *Velella*-zöoids. This naturalist observed free-swimming medusiform bodies perfectly similar to those just described; and in the larger ones he found two tentacles, with greatly enlarged ends, developed from opposite sides of the rim, at points corresponding with the ends of two of the longitudinal canals. In these the yellow vesicles formed eight series, and indications of the development of four more longitudinal canals, in the intervals of the old ones, from the common cavity were discoverable.

In fact, Gegenbaur adduces reasons for believing that, eventually, sixteen such canals are developed, and that the zooid becomes the "*Medusa*," which he has termed *Chrysomitra striata* (Pl. XII, fig. 13).

The calyx of *Chrysomitra* is about three lines high, and has the same diameter at the mouth. In the centre it is about a line thick, becoming gradually thinner towards the edge.

---

[1] Vogt gives a view of one of the medusiform buds, like my figure, but he has missed the four canals. He states, further, that "the yellow cells lie in the interior of the canals;" but this, as Gegenbaur has pointed out, is certainly incorrect.

[2] 'Ueber die sexual-organe der Diphyiden und Physophoriden.'

The inner surface has a deep-yellow colour, and the conical manubrium or polypite presents four reddish-brown lateral enlargements, which are the sexual organs.

From the common cavity at the base of the manubrium sixteen radial canals arise, and pass to a circular vessel surrounding the edge of the calyx.

On the surface of the calyx there are sixteen radiating rows of thread-cells, one corresponding with each longitudinal canal. Where the latter opens into the circular canal there is a semicircular dilatation, containing externally a whitish body, formed of vesicles like drops of oil, the larger of which are coloured brown, red, or violet. The valvular membrane lies within these enlargements, and is seen with difficulty. There are neither lithocysts nor ocelli.

Only one of Gegenbaur's specimens possessed a tentacle, and that was single. It arose by a broad base from one of the enlargements just described, and attained a length of half a line, ending below in a knob with a depressed centre.

The yellow colour of the inner surface of the calyx is produced by yellow cells, which form close networks between the longitudinal canals. Two of the specimens observed were male, and one female, but the sexual products were in none fully developed.

Of the earliest stages of the development of *Velella* nothing is known, but a very young form (younger than almost any hitherto observed[1]) is depicted in Pl. XI, fig. 9. The animal was not one tenth of an inch long, and the horizontal disc of the adult was represented by a bell-shaped, membranous expansion, continued above into a broad crest, half as high as the whole depth of the animal. It was symmetrically disposed, and, its superior edge, far from being pointed, was rather concave, and in the centre presented a curious thickening.

The central polypite was already open at its distal extremity, and around its base were a few short, cæcal processes, the rudiments of the gonoblastidia or of the tentacles. The margin of the disc was occupied by a single series of large, oval vesicles.

The somatic cavity was divided by a series of vertical septa, which passed continuously over the pneumatocyst into the crest, near whose free edge they terminated abruptly. At their other ends, or near the margin of the disc, they also ended abruptly, and between them other very short septa were interposed. The somatic cavity and its continuation into the crest were thus broken up into a series of parallel canals, united at their ends by two marginal canals ($p, p$) at right angles with one another, one in the disc, the other in the crest. The canals were ciliated, and I could observe granules passing from one into the other.

The pneumatocyst shone through the disc, and did not extend into the crest at all. By carefully tearing away the fleshy substance with needles, I succeeded in isolating it (fig. 10). It then appeared as an almost hemispherical body, convex above, and flat below.

---

[1] Eschscholz's *Rataria*, rightly suspected by De Blainville to be young *Velellæ*, are said to have been a line long. Those observed by M. Vogt's friend (Vogt, l. c., p. 83) were five millimetres (one fifth of an inch) long, and were evidently much further advanced. The smallest *Velellæ* observed by Kölliker were three or four lines long, and differed in no essential respect from the adult except that they were more "*Rataria*-like," possessed no medusoid buds, and exhibited a smaller number of "small polypes," tentacles, and chambers in the pneumatocyst.

On two of its sides, in a plane perpendicular to that of the crest, there was a double crescentic mark, caused by a depression. The air did not completely distend the pneumatocyst, but appeared to be divided into seven or eight lobes below, so that, at first sight, the organ itself appeared to be lobed, but this was not really the case. It was, in fact, in the smallest specimens a simple vesicle, about one twentieth of an inch in diameter, with strong and thin walls, which, when it was burst and the air expelled, fell into sharp folds.

In the individual figured the commencement of the first chamber is indicated by a line, concentric with the outline of the pneumatocyst, which corresponds with the base of the first septum.

A *Velella* about twice the size of the foregoing (fig. 14) had a flatly campanulate disc, with a nearly circular outline. The crest was oblong, raised to an obtuse point in the middle, and somewhat narrowed at its attachment. The edges of the disc and crest had a blue fringe, internal to which were short, radial lines, of a yellowish-red colour, arising from an aggregation of corpuscles similar to those contained in the medusiform zöoids. The rest of the animal was colourless.

The pyramidal pneumatocyst inclosed a considerable quantity of air, and presented several concentric lines on its surface. The central polypite appeared somewhat four-lobed at its base, and contained the half-digested remains of small crustaceans. A single series of tentacles surrounded the polypite. Like those of the adult they were slightly enlarged at their extremities, which were covered with thread-cells, and presented a vacuolated axis marked by a dark line in its centre. They were attached in the re-entering angle between the limb and the central polypite. Apparently proceeding from the outermost margins of the latter were several small, ovate sacs, with two or more minute papillæ, containing thread-cells at their apex. The ectoderm and the ciliated endoderm could be plainly distinguished in the thin walls of the central polypite, and these small sacs, containing a cavity whose walls were likewise ciliated, and had precisely the same structure as those of the central polypite, were, I believe, simple processes of the latter.

The crest (fig. 12) was thin and membranous throughout, and divided by vertical septa into a number of canals. The innermost of these passed vertically upwards, but the outer were more or less curved in correspondence with the outline of the lateral margins of the crest. At the margin of the crest it was easy to see that the outer wall of the marginal canal was double, its ectoderm being lined by a distinct endoderm.

A small quantity of brown, hepatic matter had accumulated under the pneumatocyst in this individual. The disc was thicker and denser than the crest, but I did not work out its structure in this specimen.

In another of nearly the same size, or a little larger, the structure of the disc (fig. 11) was essentially the same as in the first-described specimen, but a number of reddish granules had accumulated in the marginal canal and in the peripheral extremities of the radial canals.

In a still larger individual the radial canals had become much narrower in proportion to their length (fig. 13). At their central ends their walls were simple and straight, and separated only by a thick, clear, transparent substance, but, externally, they were sharply folded, or drawn out into short, lateral sacculi; and, from the ends of these, ramified processes, as a sort of connective tissue, extended into the clear substance which separates the canals. At their peripheral ends, the canals, instead of being simply divided by a short septum, separated into two widely sacculated branches, full of brown granules. The canals were much nearer the inferior than the superior surface of the disc.

*Velellæ* one third of an inch long had the disc flat and oblong, and the crest oblique.

Incomplete as these observations are, they seem to me to prove sufficiently that, in its early stages, *Velella* departs in no respect from the typical structure of the *Physophoridæ*, and that the membranous limbs of both the crest and disc must be regarded as vertical and horizontal processes of that part of the hydrosoma which represents the pneumatophore of other *Physophoridæ*, and whose cavity has become subdivided by vertical partitions. The existence of these last, however, is nothing new, for if the pneumatophore of a *Physophora* or of an *Agalma* were flattened into a disc or pulled out into a crest, the septa which retain the pneumatocyst in its place would assume nearly the same position and relations as the partitions between the canals in the young *Velellæ*.

The hepatic mass does not at first exist, but appears to be developed in contiguity with the under surface of the pneumatocyst, like the cellular processes attached to this organ in *Rhizophysa;* and I imagine that the canals which eventually traverse it are mere subdivisions of the somatic cavity,[1] produced by the encroachment of the lobes of this organ, and their mutual anastomosis.

The pneumatic filaments remain as something peculiar to the Velellidan family.

The *Velellæ* on which my observations were made were taken on various occasions in the Pacific and Atlantic Oceans. Lesson's 'Acalèphes' was the only work which I could consult, and those who are acquainted with that singular though useful miscellany, will understand why I soon gave up the attempt to identify the *Velellæ* I met with, with any of the sixteen species which are enumerated therein. I can only say that some were right-handed, and some left-handed, and that Eschscholz's *Ratariæ* are obviously nothing more than such young *Velellæ* as I have described above.

M. Vogt describes a great peculiarity in the mode of growth of the *Velellæ*. He affirms that at a particular point of the circumference of the disc, the series of tentacles and of gonoblastidia always appear to be interrupted, overlapping one another as it were, like the ends of a broken ring. At this point, the young tentacles and the gonoblastidia are developed, and an aggregation of their buds is consequently always found here. The buds of the tentacles are, at first, cæca placed on the circular vessel of the limb, and " composed of two layers—an epidermal, blue layer, and another more transparent layer, in which the internal cavity of the bud is excavated." M. Vogt has obviously seen the ectoderm and endoderm. In the course of development the former becomes covered with thread-cells; the latter, increasing in thickness, "shows itself composed of muscular fibres." That is, as I believe, it becomes vacuolated, the intermediate substance between the vacuoles being the so-called muscular fibres.

Kölliker says nothing about the existence of a special "centre of gemmation," such as that described by Vogt; and Leuckart denies its existence, affirming that the development of the new organs takes place among the old ones in all parts indifferently. ('Z. N. K.,' p. 118.)

---

[1] The homology of these canals with the somatic cavity of other *Hydrozoa* is well pointed out by Vogt, p. 35.

## *Genus* PORPITA.

Pneumatocyst circular, produced into radiating lamellæ inferiorly, but unprovided with a crest. Tentacula branched.[1]

Forskål, whose powers of observation must have been of a very high order, not only left behind the very recognisable figures of *Velella* (which he calls *Holothuria denudata*), given in the 'Icones,' tab. xxvi, L, but his description ('Descriptiones,' p. 103) is admirable, and contains everything that was known about the genus up to within a very few years.

"Diameter latitudine digiti. Paginæ superioris discus vel nucleus, diameter dimidio minor ipsius animalis; paulum elatus ut umbo clypei depressi; albidus, striis concentricis et e centro radiantibus decussatus, rigidus, margine obscure cæruleus. Limbus disco dimidio angustior, cæruleus, immaculatus, pellucidus, flexilis, planus; linea circumcirca ad oram striis nigris centrum spectantibus composita. Paginæ inferioris tentacula omnia, disco jam descripto, nucleo scilicet, non limbo affixa. In medio apparet ventriculus limbi la itudine, basi globosus, superne terminatus ore cylindrico aperto; quod demitti et dilatari potest patulum ejusdem ambitus cum basi ventriculi; et conspectum dat intestinorum; quæ exserebantur gelatinosa, albida, longa. Reliquæ parti albæ nuclei adnectuntur tentacula parvula, lævia, basi ovata, adunata in stylum filiformem apice incrassatum; interiora tentacula alba; exteriora magis magisque cærulescentia et pellucida, exeuntia ad limbi oram, non vero excedentia. Nuclei margini cæruleo adnectuntur tentacula multorum ordinum, limbo longiora, inæqualia; exteriora seu superiora plerumque breviora; quorum longissima diametrum corporis parum superant; brevissima vix limbum excedunt; omnia filiformia, hyalino cærulescentia, linea media obscuriore; dimidia parte interiore nuda, dimidia exteriore triplici serie longitudinali ciliato glandulosa, ad utrumque enim latus et subtus in medio exeunt pedicelli hyalino cærulescentes, subverticillati, terminati glandula seu capitulo obscure cæruleo. Pedicelli atque capitula versus apicem gradatim increscunt; series infera terminat tentaculum capitulo medio fere sessili, inter glandulas laterales pedicellatas. Verticilli pedicellorum sæpe 5 vel 6 in quovis tentaculo. Varie incurvat animal et extendit tentacula glandifera; at nuda ista contrahit sæpe in cylindros crassiores, apice patulos. Limbus interdum margine læviter reflectitur. In fundo vasculi ubi Holothurias servavi vivas per horam unam alteramve, vidi ova an excrementa? dejecta; *subcubica, hyalina, circello fusco in medio baseos, et linea fusca subsinuata interiore, erecta ad singulos 4 angulos laterales. Oculo tantum armato apparuere.*"

From the last passage it is clear that Forskål observed, without knowing it, the detachment of the medusiform zöoids of *Porpita*.

Eschscholz ('System,' p. 176) calls the substance of the pneumatocyst of *Porpita* "kalkartig" (calcareous), while that of *Velella* is termed "knorplig" (p. 168), without

---

[1] At any rate, provided with more or less stalked knobs or capitula.

any particular reason being assigned for the distinction; the fact being that both have a cartilaginous consistence, while neither is calcareous. He describes the radiating perpendicular lamellæ of the distal surface, and says that the flatness or more rounded character of the body depends on the depth of these.

The capitula of the tentacles are called suckers (saugnäpfen), and are said to be provided with longer or shorter pedicles. Does the following passage refer to the pneumatic filaments or to the misunderstood peduncles of the gonoblastidia, or to both?

" Between the suckers one sees a great number of peculiar organs, which are probably receptacles for germs (keim-behälter). Mucous globules beset with white points are disposed in alternating series along a fine median tube " (l. c., p. 176).

I find no addition of any importance to our knowledge of the organization of *Porpita*, until the publication of Krohn's observations upon the pneumatic filaments cited above.

Subsequently to the promulgation of his discoveries, Kölliker's important investigations, which were first published in 1853 (' Bericht über einige im Herbste, 1852, angestellte Untersuchungen, Siebold and Kölliker's ' Zeitschrift,' 1853), have brought us much nearer to an exhaustive knowledge of the organization of this animal. I partly translate and partly condense his excellent memoir on *Porpita*, contained in ' Die Schwimmpolypen.'

"As in *Velella*, the pneumatocyst (knorpel-platte) of *Porpita* is thickest at the edge, thinnest in the middle, though, on the other, hand, each of the the air chambers, of which the outermost are the widest, is, on account of the circular form of the organ, of even diameter throughout. If they are filled with air, or in a fresh pneumatocyst (schale) still containing its air, it is observable that the inner contour of each air chamber is a simple circle, while the outer appears to be undulating; whence it follows that the septa have tolerably regular, small projections on their inner surfaces. From these septa, also, the elegant concentric striations, visible even with the naked eye, on the upper slightly convex face of the pneumatocyst (knorpel-scheibe), arise, whilst the radial striation visible on both faces, but especially on the under, results from linear elevations of the cartilaginous walls which, upon the under side, are so pronounced that they may rightly be termed ridges or lamellæ (Leisten oder Blätter).

" The relations of the air chambers of the pneumatocyst to the external parts are much more interesting in *Porpita* than in *Velella*. The pneumatic filaments (luftcanäle) discovered by Krohn, and already mentioned in describing *Velella*, are present, and in much greater numbers, as are also the pneumatic foramina, which have not as yet been noticed by any one. The pneumatic filaments arise from the inferior concave surface of the pneumatocyst, in as many series as there are radiating lamellæ, and in fact in such a manner that every air chamber, with the exception of the outermost, gives off one or many pneumatic filaments. Since the number of chambers in a middle-sized *Porpita* (four or five lines in diameter) is twenty-two or twenty-three, and that of the lamellæ of their concave surface (of which, however, many are very short, and only visible on the outer parts of the shell) is eighty or ninety, it results that the number of the pneumatic filaments is out of all proportion to that of the same organs in *Velella*. In other respects they are similar, only that they have thinner walls and are narrower (0·005—0·015‴), and are not only provided with internal projections, but also exhibit external prominences. After arising from the pneumatocyst, they at once enter the liver, and pass in a wavy but tolerably direct course through it, to end in the walls of the large central polypite, and of all the little ones which are disposed around it.

"Before this, however, they form a plexus on the lower face of the liver, in the membrane which carries the polypes, but, to all appearance, without divisions or anastomoses, of which no definite evidence was seen in *Porpita*, except that here and there a few canals arose from a common, very short stalk. In the central polypite these pneumatic filaments end, partly on the attached wall, partly on the lateral walls, in which latter position a strong magnifying glass even will show them as white wavy lines. In the smaller polypites four to six, also undulating canals, pass in their walls (*in* den Wänden derselben) as far as buds are attached, and then, so far as I could make out, end blindly.

"Though there may be no opening of the aeriferous apparatus of *Porpita* in this situation, it is very evident elsewhere, if a proper method of preparation be pursued. If all the soft parts be removed from the under surface of a *Porpita*, in fact, and if the convex surface be then observed with a low magnifying power, there is observable in it, besides the rich vascular network to be described immediately, whose trunks are arranged radially, many oval openings disposed serially between the vascular trunks, the outermost of which are largest, while the inner are smallest.[1]

"If the soft parts are now entirely removed, it becomes obvious that each of these apertures corresponds with a hole surrounded by a low, depressed wall on the upper lamella of the pneumatocyst, so that it leads directly into an air chamber. In a middle-sized *Porpita* I can count forty-five series of pneumatic foramina, and in each series nine to thirteen stigmata, so that, inasmuch as there are twenty-two to twenty-three air chambers, each series of stigmata cannot communicate with all the chambers.

"The most stigmata are possessed by the outermost chamber (which has sometimes one in every series) and the next to it. From thence their number rapidly diminishes, and the innermost chamber of all, which has the form of a round cell, has only a single central— sometimes smaller, sometimes larger—foramen, which lies, consequently, in the centre of the pneumatocyst. The size of the outer apertures, is 0·04—0·05‴; of the inner smallest ones, 0·015‴ — 0·024‴. . . . . . . The pneumatocyst of *Porpita* consists of the same homogeneous cartilage-like tissue that forms the skeleton of *Velella*, and there is no ground for the assumption of authors, from Eschscholz downwards, that it is calcareous" (l. c., pp. 57—59).

Professor Kölliker then goes on to show that the soft parts consist of a thin superior, and a thick inferior layer, united in the broad marginal limb. The upper layer is thin, and perforated by apertures which correspond with the pneumatic foramina. The lower layer, much thicker, incloses the liver and the renal organ, and gives attachment to the appendages. The upper surface of the lower layer exhibits radiating folds and grooves, which correspond with the elevations and interspaces of the lamellæ of the inferior surface of the pneumatocyst. The brown hepatic cells are lodged in this lower layer, and extend over nearly the whole area covered by the pneumatocyst.

The roof of the cavity of the great or central polypite exhibits, in the middle, eight radially disposed, cleft-like depressions, each with a round opening at the bottom, and many

---

[1] In fig. 3, pl. xii, however, the innermost foramina are the largest.

circumferential apertures, all of which communicate with the reticulated canals which traverse the hepatic mass, and then pass into the radiating, branched, and anastomosing canals, which traverse the inferior layer of the soft parts. Having reached the edge of the pneumatocyst, they divide into two sets of branches, some of which pass into the limb, while others ascend and ramify in the dorsal layer of the soft parts. All the larger canals were ciliated.

Kölliker alludes to the existence of peculiar gland-like organs, similar to those described by Vogt in *Velella*, in the limb of *Porpita*.

The canals of the peduncles of the smaller polypites or gonoblastidia open into the hepatic canals, and the buds resemble those of *Velella* in their general structure.

The canals of the tentacles are ciliated, at any rate in young specimens, and they communicate with the vessels which proceed from the hepatic canals.

Between the circumference of the central polypite and that of the liver there lies, on the under surface of the body, a white lamella, perforated by many foramina, which gives passage to the peduncles of the gonoblastidia and to the pneumatic filaments. It consists of a reticulated tissue, sharply defined, and invested by a thin, fibrous membrane inferiorly, while superiorly it runs into fine processes and trabeculæ, which pass between the hepatic canals.

The white colour of this plate arises from the presence of innumerable molecules, of which the smallest look like spheroidal dots, and appear quite dark, while the larger ones have the form of crystalline needles and rhombs, and are transparent, or are pale and rounded, and have a more fatty and albuminous appearance. The chemical reactions of the crystalline substance led Professor Kölliker to suppose it to be guanin, whence he concludes that this organ has a renal function.

With regard to the species of *Porpita*, Eschscholz admits the following:


1. PORPITA MEDITERRANEA.

The pneumatocyst is half as broad as the whole body, somewhat convex, and whitish on its proximal or upper surface. The limb is dark blue, as in all the other species. The central polypite and the inner gonoblastidia are whitish, the others becoming blue the nearer they are to the edge. Tentacula bluish, and provided in their outer half with three series of tolerably long-stalked capitula. The last capitulum of the lower series is sessile upon the point of the tentacle.

This is the *Holothuria denudata* of Forskål, and the *Porpita glandifera* of Lamarck. It is found in the Mediterranean, and attains a diameter of eight lines.


2. PORPITA RAMIFERA.

The pneumatocyst is convex at the sides, and flattened in the middle, and as convex distally (or on its under surface) as proximally (or on its upper surface). The middle part is dark brown ; the lateral parts are of a clear blue, and clear rays mark the whole. The blue limb is very narrow. The tentacles are blue, and not clavate, but thicker at their roots; and they have on their outer side only, usually four, and sometimes five, very long-stalked capitula.

This species, only half a line in diameter, was taken in the North Pacific. Is it an adult?

### 3. Porpita globosa.

The hydrosoma is almost globular. The flat upper part of the pneumatocyst is very small, has only a line in diameter, a dark-blue colour, and about thirty-two radiating striæ. The broad limb is dark blue ; the rest of the body, which consists of the proper globular part, is supported by the distal lamellæ of the pneumatocyst, which are greatly elongated and expanded downwards and laterally. The pneumatocyst, in fact, extends even beyond the limb, its sides here inclining downwards and outwards. This part is coloured bright blue, and is marked with a great number of radiating brown lines. The tentacles spring from the broadest part of the body ; they are filiform, and in their larger outer moiety are covered with almost sessile capitula. From the line of their attachment the body contracts again, presenting a convex contour.

In the only specimen which Eschscholz took he observed a tentacle which, very thick and coloured in the middle, allowed a yellowish juice to be seen through its walls. The stomach and the gonoblastidia were yellowish—the latter surrounded by a brownish villous ring, out of which fine white filaments hung. This last Eschscholz regards as a germ-receptacle. This species attains three lines in diameter, and was taken near the Cape de Verde Islands.

It would be very desirable to re-examine this remarkable species. The "brownish villous ring" and the "fine white filaments" seem clearly to be the gonophores and the pneumatic filaments.

### 4. Porpita umbella.

The proximal surface of the pneumatocyst is flat, colourless, or whitish ; the limb broad and dark blue. The tentacles have short stalked capitula on their outer thicker half. The central polypite and the inner gonoblastidia are white, the outer gonoblastidia are bluish.

Eschscholz considers this to be the *Porpita gigantea* of Peron and Lesueur. It was taken in the equatorial and the temperate parts of the Atlantic, and attains an inch in diameter.

### 5. Porpita cœrulea.

The pneumatocyst is quite flat, and has a blackish-blue colour.[1] Forty-two radiating

---

[1] For brevity's sake I have used the term pneumatocyst in these definitions in a broad sense, so as to include the layer of the hydrosoma which overlies it.

striæ were counted, and these had little tubercles (zacken) disposed along their length. The blue limb is a line and a half broad.

With a strong magnifying power it may be observed that the outer edge of the limb (equal to one fifth of the whole) is marked by fine excentric darker striæ, which may be regarded as muscular fibres, by whose aid the marginal limb may be bent upwards or downwards. The rest of the limb appears dotted. The bluish tentacles gradually thicken towards the ends, where they are trihedral, and their outer half is beset with three series of almost stalked capitula. The tentacles vary in length, the largest surpassing the diameter of the body, the shortest not projecting further beyond the limb than its breadth. In a large and uninjured specimen there were seven series of tentacles of different lengths.

The gonoblastidia are whitish and bluish, as in the preceding species. The bodies, which appear to be germ-receptacles, have the appearance of yellowish-brown (hellhornfär-bigen) racemes. The largest specimens attain the diameter of an inch.

It chanced that I fell in with *Porpita* only once during the cruise of the "Rattlesnake," and the observations I made are of no moment. But some very large *Porpitæ*, which, though they have long been preserved in spirit, are in very good preservation, having recently come under my notice, I am enabled to add some particulars of interest to what is already known.

The proximal or superior face of the disc in this species is quite flat, and measures, including the limb, about one inch and a half in diameter, but its thickness does not exceed one thirteenth of an inch. The limb, one eighth of an inch wide, is thin and flexible. The base of the large central polypite measures not more than one quarter of an inch in diameter, so that it occupies but a very small portion of the distal or inferior face of the disc. The small, or gonoblastidial, polypites are exceedingly numerous, occupy an area half an inch wide on each side, and, when distended with food, as many of them are, they acquire a transverse diameter of one eighth, and a length of one fourth, of an inch. The space between the zone occupied by these polypites, or the gonoblastidial zone, and the limb, is occupied by a narrow area, rather less than one eighth of an inch wide, which presents a reticulated appearance, and to which the numerous rows of tentacles, almost all of which were detached in my specimens, were attached.

This tentacular zone, as I will call it, is somewhat convex downwards and outwards, while the rest of the inferior surface of the disc is flat.

It is impossible to say what may have been the original coloration of this species. At present, all my specimens have a uniform pale-yellowish hue, which inclines to brown over the gonoblastidial area. The proximal surface of the disc is covered with numerous small tubercles, set at irregular intervals, and remarkably large and prominent in the central region, while they become smaller and less conspicuous peripherally.

The presence of these tubercles leads me to think that this species may be the *Porpita cærulea* of Eschscholz, which is, perhaps, identical with the *Porpita Atlantica* of Lesson ('Acalèphes,' p. 590).[1]

With respect to the general character of the polypites, the gonoblastidia, and their buds, I have nothing of importance to add to the account given by Kölliker, except that the roof of

---

[1] There is no means of ascertaining whence the specimens were obtained.

the central polypite does not present that arrangement of eight radially disposed, cleft-like depressions described and figured in *P. Mediterranea*. On the contrary, it exhibits a great number (some forty) of septiform membranous bands, which radiate between the centre and the periphery of the roof of the polypite, becoming deeper as they go, until, at the circumference, their height is equal to the thickness of the distal layer of the hydrosoma.

Similar but very much smaller bands, not exceeding seven or eight in number, appeared to me to be developed in the roof of the gonoblastidial polypites, but it was not easy to assure oneself of the fact.

The hydrosoma exhibits, as in *Porpita Mediterranea*, a thin proximal, and a thick distal, layer, between which the pneumatocyst is inclosed. As the other parts are all disposed in relation to the structure of the last-named organ, it will be convenient to consider its structure first.

The proximal or upper surface exhibits a beautifully regular, radiating striation, each stria terminating in a little projection at the periphery of the disc, which thus acquires somewhat the appearance of a toothed wheel. In the circumferential half, or thereabouts, of the surface of the disc, these striæ are the expression of ridges, with intermediate valleys, which attain a height and depth nearly equal to half the total thickness of the disc; but, towards the centre, the inequalities gradually diminish, the valleys becoming filled up and the ridges covered over, until, in the central half of the proximal surface of the disc, the general surface is even, and would be quite flat and smooth, if it were not for the numerous conical tubercles scattered over it.

These tubercles attain a diameter of one sixtieth of an inch at their base, and one fortieth of an inch in height, and they are disposed without reference to the direction of the radiating ridges. The apparent radiating striation of the central region of the pneumatocyst is due only to the shining through of the deeper structures.

A radial section of the pneumatocyst (woodcut *A*, p. 126) shows that its proximal or upper wall (*f*), which is not more than $\frac{1}{360}$th of an inch thick at the periphery, gradually increases in thickness towards the centre, until, in the middle, it attains a diameter of one twenty-eighth of an inch, or, in other words, has twelve times the thickness it possesses at the circumference.

On the other hand, as it passes into the distal or inferior wall, the substance of the pneumatocyst becomes thinner and thinner, until, over the whole distal surface, it has a thickness of less than $\frac{1}{1000}$th of an inch. Where thin, it appears structureless; but where thick, it is obviously composed of a great number of superimposed lamellæ.

I conclude from this structure that the pneumatocyst has originally very thin walls, to which very little, if any, addition is made on the distal surface; while, as the animal grows and becomes older, new layers are constantly added to the whole of the proximal wall of the pneumatocyst.

The concentric chambers of the pneumatocyst are more than fifty in number, and the septa which divide them from one another are thicker where they join the proximal layer of the pneumatocyst.

The central chamber is octagonal, and has a diameter of one thirty-sixth of an inch. Viewed with a low power, it seems to be divided into eight compartments by as many ribs, which unite in a circular disc in its centre, and radiate thence to its angles. In the centre of this disc there appears to be a small circular foramen, $\frac{1}{1200}$th of an inch in diameter, and each compartment appears to have a similar but rather smaller foramen terminating a conical prolongation of the compartment. These foramina look so clear and plain that it is difficult to persuade oneself they do not open on the surface. But they do not. They are, in fact, covered over by a considerable thickness of the laminated pneumatocystic substance, which is wholly imperforate.

Each of the eight radiating ribs probably indicates the position of one of the valleys of the pneumatocyst when it was not larger than the central chamber. Filled up in the adult state by the additions which have been made to the proximal wall, each valley would become more opaque than the intermediate ridge, which must necessarily have less deposit over it, and hence must look like a more solid rib.

Of the fifty or sixty concentric chambers which surround the central one, those midway between the centre and the circumference are, on the whole, larger than the central or the peripheral ones.

The pneumatic foramina ($f^8$) have an average diameter of about $\frac{1}{900}$th of an inch. Each is situated at the extremity of an urn-shaped process of the pneumatocyst, which has very delicate walls, and is always seated upon one of the ridges—never in a valley. The urn-shaped process (woodcut $B$, p. 126) is about $\frac{1}{400}$th of an inch high, and has nearly the same width in the middle, but it narrows to its peduncle below and to its mouth above. The mouth is surrounded by an everted and deflected lip, about $\frac{1}{2400}$th of an inch wide, whose margins are slightly denticulated.

Every ridge exhibited a pneumatic foramen for each of the ten or twelve outer chambers of the pneumatocyst, except in the case of those ridges which were too short to extend over so many chambers; and all their foramina were, so far as I could observe, open. Beyond this point, however, the foramina occurred far less frequently, and while they were continued nearly to the centre along some radii, stopped far short of it along others, so that in no case have I found more than twenty-four foramina in one radial line; and more than this, so far as I have been able to ascertain, all the foramina on the central side of the twelfth or thirteenth are closed by the extension of new layers of the substance of the pneumatocyst over them.

The thin distal wall of the pneumatocyst is somewhat arched and concave under the central chamber, but is otherwise smooth. Eight groups of pneumatic filaments (of which there are four or five in each group) arise from this wall opposite the pneumatic foramina in the proximal wall.

The pneumatic filaments are simply tubular prolongations of the thin distal wall, which have an average diameter of $\frac{1}{1000}$th of an inch, and exhibit annular constrictions at intervals. They arise close together, but can hardly be said to have a common stem.

In the succeeding chambers the distal wall is produced into lamellar folds, which radiate like the ridges of the proximal wall, though they are two or three times more numerous, and become deeper towards the periphery, where they end in margins which are convex downwards and outwards. At their deepest they make up about half the total vertical diameter of the pneumatocyst (woodcut $C$, p. 126).

The concentric septa, which divide the chambers ($f^{10}$) of the pneumatocyst from one another, present, in a vertical radial section, a contour which is convex peripherally, and slopes away more towards the centre distally than proximally. They send prolongations down into the lamellar folds or diverticula, which are directed still more obliquely, so that each diverticulum is divided into a series of primary compartments ($f^{11}$), whose axes are directed very obliquely upwards and outwards when the animal is in its natural position. These primary compartments are divided and subdivided into secondary and tertiary compartments, which become smaller and more numerous towards the free edge of the lamella, from which alone the little groups of pneumatic filaments are given off. These filaments, similar to those which arise from the central chamber, pass directly into the distal layer of the hydrosoma, and sometimes at once go straight through it. The majority run obliquely, so as to traverse the hydrosoma in all directions. Whether they anastomose or not, I cannot say; but I have never seen any clear instance of such an occurrence. Eventually, they seem to pass out on to the distal surface of the hydrosoma, and there terminate in free ends, those which are in the neighbourhood of the gonoblastidia at first twining about among the gonocalyces.

No pneumatic filament ever ends *in* the walls of the polypites, they are all *on* their walls, and, so far as I have seen, no pneumatic filaments enter the tentacular area.

The hydrosoma, or proper body of the *Porpita*, which incloses the pneumatocyst, is composed of a thin proximal, or dorsal layer, and a thick distal or ventral layer. In the former, the anastomosing canals described by Kölliker are very beautifully displayed. It in addition exhibits a number of comparatively large apertures, through which the tubercles ($f^9$) of the pneumatocyst pass. The hydrosoma, gradually thinning, rises for a short distance upon the bases of these tubercles, and then can be traced no further, so that I have no doubt the tubercles are naturally bare. Besides these apertures, there are a number of very much smaller ones, not more than $\frac{1}{300}$th — $\frac{1}{400}$th of an inch in diameter, which correspond with those urn-shaped tubercles which bear the pneumatic foramina.

With regard to the inferior or distal layer of the hydrosoma, the only points I find worth noting are the structure of the "tentacular area" and the distribution of the somatic canals. As I have said, I find no pneumatic filaments traversing this region, or, at least, passing out through it; nor does the hepatic mass extend into it. The reticulated appearance which it presents is due to the meshwork formed by a peculiar tissue, which consists of bands running perpendicularly from one face of the distal layer of the hydrosoma to the other, and then spreading out and passing into the superficial substance. They resemble very much, in fact, those fibrous bands which pass vertically through the substance of the dermis in many fishes and *Reptilia*, and tie together the successive layers of bundles of connective tissue.

The lamellæ of the proximal surface of the distal layer correspond with, and accurately fit into, the intervals between the lamellar diverticula of the pneumatocyst. Their proximal edges are thin and sinuous, presenting shallow excavations, separated by sharp points. They rise in height towards the circumference, and close to it, slope rapidly, so as to present a convexity the opposite of that of the diverticula of the pneumatocyst.

Each lamella has a wide sinus running along its proximal or dorsal edge, and communicating, by a series of more or less vertical channels, with the sinuses which lie in the hepatic substance.

These last appear to be disposed in several tiers, but the opacity of the mass renders it difficult to come to any clear conclusion on this head. Apparently from the discoloration of the specimens, there is no distinguishable white renal organ, but I have met with many minute crystals and granules similar to those considered to be Guanin by Professor Kölliker. Not having had any opportunity of examining *Porpita mediterranea*, I will not enter upon the consideration of the apparent differences in structure between that species and the one which I have studied.

It would be very interesting to trace out the development of *Porpita*, but, from the observations I have detailed respecting *Velella*, I have little doubt that the early state of the two forms is very similar; and that, in *Porpita* as in *Velella*, the sinuses must be regarded as the somatic cavity cut up and subdivided by the union of the opposed layers of the endoderm.

The most remarkable feature in the organization of both genera, however, is the penetration of the hydrosoma by the pneumatic and other tubercles on the proximal, and by the pneumatic filaments on the distal side.

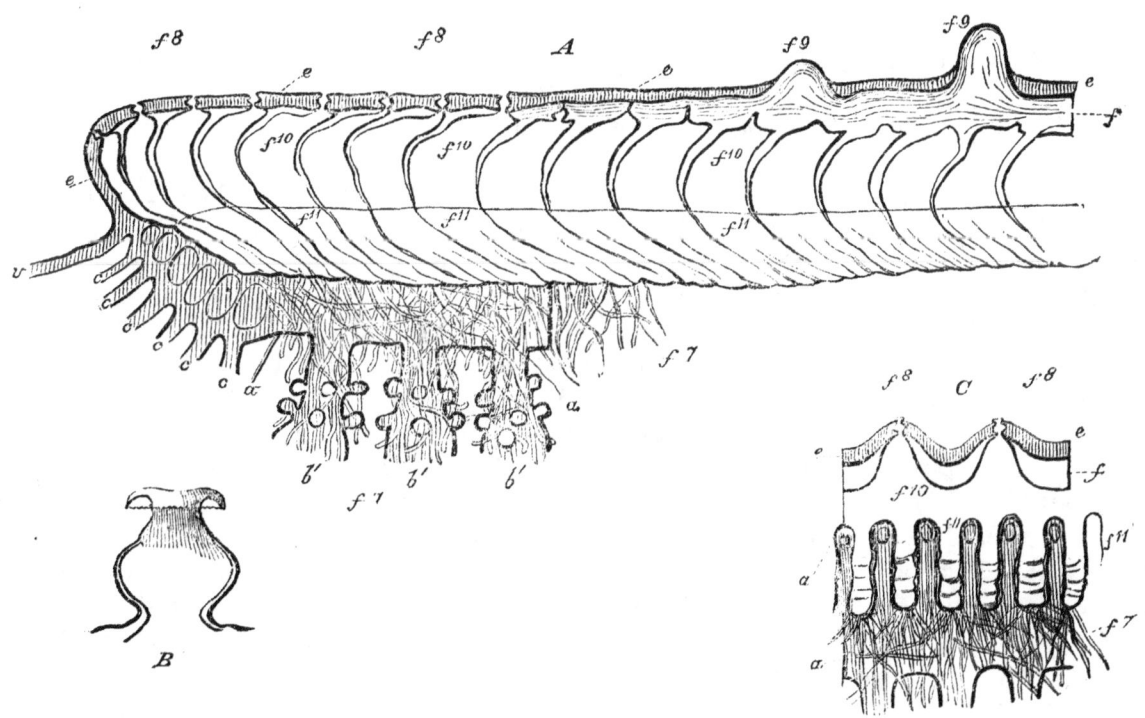

DESCRIPTION OF THE WOODCUTS.—*A.* Diagram of a radial section of the large *Porpita.* *a.* The distal or inferior layer of the hydrosoma. *b′.* The gonoblastidial polypites with their gonophoric buds, among which the pneumatic filaments, $f^7$, are seen twining. *c.* The tentacles. *d.* The limb. *e.* The proximal or superior layer of the hydrosoma. $f^8$. The pneumatic apertures. $f^9$. The tubercles of the proximal layer of the pneumatocyst. $f^{10}$. The air-chambers. $f^{11}$. Their prolongations into the lamellæ. *B.* One of the urn-shaped pneumatic apertures. *C.* Diagram of a transverse, or tangential, vertical section of *Porpita.*

Of the family of *Apolemiadæ*, and of the genera *Halistemma* and *Forskalia*, I have seen no specimens, but to render this work more useful to future observers I add figures and descriptions of them, borrowed from the works of Gegenbaur, Kölliker, and Leuckart.

## *Fam.* APOLEMIADÆ.

### *Genus* APOLEMIA. (*Eschscholz.*)

The pneumatophore is small; the hydrophyllia lanceolate in outline and curved, so that their proximal sides are convex.

APOLEMIA UVARIA (*Eschscholz*).   Pl. XII, fig. 8.

*Stephanomia uvaria*, Peron and Lesueur, 1807.

Gegenbaur, whose figure of this species I have copied, gives so excellent an account of its structure (Beiträge, p. 37), that I cannot do better than transfer it (with a little condensation and borrowing here and there from Leuckart) to my own pages.

The nectocalyces are disposed in two lateral series of three or four in each, and constitute an oval mass, measuring altogether about an inch and a half in length. They have the form of a truncated cone whose basal edges are rounded off. The aperture of the nectosac, which resembles a broad-bodied bottle, and occupies the greater part of the nectocalyx, is situated at the apex of the cone.

The pyriform pneumatophore is wholly devoid of pigment.

Scattered, filiform, and very contractile hydrocysts are attached to the cœnosarc between the nectocalyces, beyond which the cœnosarc is cylindrical, a line to a line and a half in thickness, and carries at regular intervals (of about two inches) the plume-like groups of polypites and other appendages; so that the whole colony, approximating towards the type of the *Calycophoridæ*, consists of similar segments. Attached to the cœnosarc, immediately behind the nectocalyces, is a compact bundle of young undeveloped organs, which, by the subsequent outgrowth of particular parts of the cœnosarc to which they are attached, become separated into distinct bundles.

Each group of organs is, according to Leuckart ('Z. N. K.,' p. 67), attached by a distinct peduncle, and consists proximally of a number of *hydrophyllia*, succeeded by two or three polypites and a great number of vermiform hydrocysts, at the base of each of which is a simple tentacle. The hydrophyllia are ovate or clavate bodies, a few lines in length, which are attached to the cœnosarc by short peduncles. The larger ones are slightly curved, so as to have a proximal convex and a distal concave surface.   They present many dots and specks, which are for the most part aggregations of thread-cells.   The hydrophyllia are capable of independent motion, and in the undisturbed condition of the animal they are constantly elevated and depressed.   On irritating the creature they are all closely adducted, so as to protect the organs over which they lie.   The hydrocysts are from six to twelve lines long, and almost cylindrical, and from the base of each springs a long tentacle.

The polypites are six or seven lines long, even in the contracted condition.   They have six villous or hepatic ridges.

The structure of the simple tentacles has been referred to above (p. 11).   The gonophores have not yet been found attached to an entire hydrosoma, but Leuckart ('Z. N. K.,' p. 71) describes them in the detached groups of appendages.

They appear to be developed in bunches among the hydrocysts, and sometimes in connexion with their peduncles, and the gynophores, at any rate, exhibit distinct calyces and manubria ; the latter containing a single ovum.

Leuckart observed a specimen of *Apolemia* a foot long.   Its pneumatophore measured two lines, its nectocalyces from six to eight lines in length.

*Fam.* STEPHANOMIADÆ.

*Genus* HALISTEMMA (*mihi*).

Tentacular sacculi, without involucra, and ending in a single filament. The nectocalyces in a double parallel series.

HALISTEMMA RUBRUM. Pl. XII, fig. 9.

> *Agalma rubra,* Vogt.
> *Agalmopsis punctata,* Kölliker.
> *Agalma (Agalmopsis) rubrum,* Leuckart.

This species was discovered by Vogt, and was subsequently described by Kölliker, whose figure (the distal end of the hydrosoma being omitted for want of room) I have copied. As Leuckart ('Z. N. K.,' p. 73), however, has, with the works of Vogt and Kölliker before him, studied this species, I prefer to give an abstract of his description of it. Professor Leuckart considers this form (the type of his *Agalmopsis*) to belong to a sub-genus of *Agalma*, so that the general characterisation of this genus, which he gives at page 72, is applicable to *Halistemma*.

The pneumatophore is of moderate size, and is without a pigment spot. The nectocalyces, of which there are sometimes as many as thirty pairs, are cubical, compressed from above downwards, and provided at their proximal ends with two pairs of processes, an upper and a lower, the latter having a very considerable size and a wedge-like form, and projecting much more than the upper ones. These processes serve to embrace the cœnosarc, and to interlock with the opposite nectocalyces. Cf the nectocalycine canals, there are not only the ordinary four radiating and the circular, but in addition curved cæcal processes (mantelge-fässe), as in *Hippopodius* and *Praya*. The lateral radial canals form a double loop. The cœnosarc is spirally coiled. The polypites are exceedingly large, and the hepatic ridges have a reddish colour.

The branches of the tentacles are very large, having a length of as much as a line in the coiled condition, and of four lines when extended.

The hydrocysts are slender, and without projecting villous ridges, but otherwise resemble young and undeveloped polypites. Their tentacles are slender, and without sacculi. Four to eight hydrocysts in various stages of development are interposed between every pair of polypites.

The hydrophyllia are about eight lines long, and three and a half lines broad, thicker in the middle than at the sides, and somewhat concave on their inner faces. They are frequently devoid of lateral processes or teeth. They are not fixed by their upper ends to the cœnosarc, but by a proper peduncle, which is inserted a little behind their proximal ends, which are free and solid.

The reproductive organs are like those of *Stephanomia*, and they are attached directly to the cœnosarc.

*Halistemma rubrum* attains a length of three feet, and appears to be not uncommon in the Mediterranean, especially in winter.

## Genus FORSKALIA. (*Kölliker*.)

The tentacular sacculi are without involucra, and end in a single filament. The necto-calyces are arranged in many series around the cœnosarc.

FORSKALIA EDWARDSII (*Kölliker*). Pl. XII, fig. 10.

The chief points of interest in Kölliker's description of this species ('Schwimmpolypen,' p. 2, et seq.) are the following :

The pneumatophore has a brownish-rose colour. The nectocalyces are arranged so as to form a cylinder containing eight or nine longitudinal, and twelve to sixteen transverse, rows, and each has a yellow spot upon its mouth.

The polypites have brownish-red hepatic striæ. The sacculi are red. The hydrophyllia are flat, broad, and terminated by three rounded points ; the hydrocysts are colourless, but occasionally of a lively red at their apices. The manubria of the androphores are yellowish-white, but orange internally. The animal, which was very common at Messina, attained a length of from six to twelve inches or more.

The cœnosarc is a straight or slightly undulating tube, with relatively thick walls, in which longitudinal and transverse muscular fibres are clearly visible. It is exceedingly contractile, and, in shortening, takes on the form of a close spiral.

The pneumatophore is ovate or pyriform, and a third of a line in length, and the air contained in the pneumatocyst is divided into a large superior, and a smaller, inferior, bubble.

The nectocalyces have the form of a cone, whose apex is turned towards the cœnosarc, its base outwards. To speak more exactly, the basal surface, which has a rounded quadri-lateral circumference, presents in the centre a mammillary elevation, truncated at the end, which exhibits a circular aperture leading into the nectosac. According to the greater or less projection of this mammillary elevation, the nectocalyx, viewed from above, has a rhomboidal form, or more that of a simple cone. In a lateral view the nectocalyces appear to be oval or rectangular, with rounded edges ; the oral region not unfrequently projecting a little. Many of the nectocalyces are also quite irregularly rounded cuboids, so that their form can hardly be defined in words.

At the upper end of the cylinder formed by the regularly arranged perfect nectocalyces, numerous undeveloped nectocalyces may always be discovered.

The nectosac has the form of a short gourd, and the four radiating nectocalycine canals take a straight course to the circular canal.

The hydrocysts are fixed directly to that portion of the cœnosarc which lies beyond the nectocalycine cylinder, whilst the polypites, with their hydrophyllia and tentacles, are attached to the ends of special stalks.    In this region the somatic cavity, which has the form of a wide canal, is excentric, being situated nearer the convex side of the cœnosarc.    In many places it gives off cæcal diverticula, which pass at right angles into the substance of the thicker wall.

The hepatic striæ are eight to twelve or more in number, and are situated in the proximal third of the digestive cavity of the polypite.

The stems of the tentacles give off, on one side, branches to which the sacculi are attached.

The hydrophyllia have a triangular form, their prolonged proximal ends or apices being attached to the peduncles of the polypites, while the basal or distal ends are divided into three points.    They are slightly concave on the inner side, slightly convex externally, where they present a slight median ridge.

The hydrocysts are of two kinds—simple, attached immediately to the cœnosarc; and double, one large and one small, attached by a long common peduncle to the cœnosarc.    A single and double hydrocyst are commonly associated in pairs.    Each hydrocyst has a slender simple tentacle.

The androphores and gynophores are usually, if not always, attached to the base of the double hydrocyst.[1]

Two to four androphores and a larger number of gynophores are usually associated together.    In structure they appear, from Kölliker's description, very closely to resemble those of *Stephanomia amphitridis*.

---

[1] Whence these should probably be regarded as gonoblastidia.

## REMARKS ON DOUBTFUL GENERA AND SPECIES OF *CALYCOPHORIDÆ* AND *PHYSOPHORIDÆ*.

---

Besides those which have been incidentally referred to in the text, the following genera and species of *Calycophoridæ* and *Physophoridæ* appear to me not to be sufficiently well established, or to be otherwise open to criticism.

*Genus* ACIES.

> *A. palpebrans,* Lesson. 'Voyage de la Coquille,' Zoologie, ii, 2, 1830.

Lesson himself seems to regard this as a mere sub-genus of *Porpita*. No figure is given, and the description is wholly insufficient.

*Genus* ANGELA.

> *A. cytherea,* Lesson. 'Acalèphes,' 1843, p. 496, pl. ix, fig. 1.

All the author of this genus really knows of it is, he says, derived from a drawing, "communiqué par M. Rang sans nom et sans renseignements." Under such circumstances, it is hardly worth while quoting his definition.

*Genus* ANTHOPHYSA.

*A. rosea,* Brandt, 'Prodromus,' cited in Lesson's 'Acalèphes,' appears to be an *Athorybia*.

*Genus* APOLEMIOPSIS.

> *A. dubia,* Brandt. 'Prodromus.'

"Canalis reproductorius filiformis, tenuis, elongatus, cui vesiculæ parvæ, biseriatæ, porro tentacula simplicia verrucis parvis quadriseriatis obsessa ; nec non tubuli nutritorii adnexi et ut e figura apparet, partes cartilagineæ fere semilunares adhærent."

*Genus* BRACHYSOMA.

> *B. erythrophysa*, Brandt. 'Prodromus.'

Probably a mutilated and contracted Physophorid.

*Genus* CUNEOLARIA.

> *C. incisa*, Eysenhardt. 'Nova Acta,' x, 1821.

A detached nectocalyx of a Physophorid.

*Genus* CUPULITA.

> *C. Boodwich*, Quoy and Gaimard. 'Voy. de l'Uranie,' Zoologie, p. 580, 1824.

An imperfect description and figure of what appears to be one of the *Stephanomiadæ*. The authors give up the genus in the 'Zoology of the Astrolabe,' t. iv, p. 53.

*Genus* DIPHYSA.

> *D. singularis*, De Blainville. 'Manuel,' p. 117, 1830.

De Blainville founded this genus upon a specimen collected by Quoy and Gaimard; but his account of its structure is brief and insufficient to enable one to form an idea of the real nature of the object.

*Genus* DISCOLABE.

> *Rhizophyza discoidea*, Quoy and Gaimard.
> *Discolabe Mediterranea*, Eschscholz.

Thus described by Quoy and Gaimard in the 'Annales des Sciences Naturelles,' t. x, 1827 : A little flattened disk, from whose circumference depend about a dozen slightly rose-coloured appendages, consisting of little orbicular bodies connected with one another. In the middle of the disc below there is a bundle of transversely striated suckers, whose base is surrounded by little yellowish bodies. The middle of the upper part of the disc gives off a very long tube, containing an air-bubble at its extremity, which is reddish. Length, an inch and a half; diameter of the disc, five lines. Taken in the Straits of Gibraltar. Figured in Pl. V. B. Eschscholz, who based the genus *Discolabe* on this form, did not observe any specimen of it himself.

*Genus* PYRAMIS.

*Pyramis tetragona*, Otto.   'Nova Acta,' t. xi, 1823.
*Eudoxia pyramis*, Eschscholz.

Apparently the distal nectocalyx of an *Abyla*.


*Genus* PHYSOPHORA.

*P. alba* and *P. intermedia* of Quoy and Gaimard ('Voy. de l'Astrolabe,' Zoologie, t. iv) both belong to the genus *Agalma*.


*Genus* PLETHOSOMA.

*P. cristalloides*, Lesson.   'Voy. de la Coquille,' Zool., ii, 2, 64, 1830.

This is a combination of a contracted piece of one of the *Stephanomiadæ* with an *Abyla*, apparently *A. pentagona!*


*Genus* POLYTOMUS.

*P. cruciata*, Lesson.   'Voy. de la Coquille,' Zool., ii, 2, p. 45, 1830.

A detached nectocalyx of one of the *Physophoridæ*.


*Genus* RACEMIS.

*R. ovalis*, Delle Chiaje.   'Memorie,' t. iv, p. 4, and p. 30.  1829.

The account of this genus, given at p. 4 of the fourth volume of the 'Memorie,' is but a dilution of the following 'Descrizione technica,' at p. 30: "*Racemis*—Vesiculæ globosæ celerrimo mota præditæ et in formam ovatam dispositæ.  *R. ovalis*—Corpore ovali vesiculis globosis."  The figures given, Tab. L, figs. 11 and 12, are quite unintelligible to me.


*Genus* RATIS.

*R. Medusæ*, Lesson.   'Voyage de la Coquille,' 1830, Zool., ii, 2, p. 60.

Apparently a young *Porpita*, but there is no figure, and the description is very imperfect.

*Genus* SARCOCONUS.

A genus built up by Lesson ('Acaléphes,' p. 477), out of the odds and ends of fragments of *Stephanomiadæ*, observed by Chamisso and Eysenhardt, and by Quoy and Gaimard.

*Genus* STEPHANOMIA.

*S. lævigata*, described by Quoy and Gaimard in the 'Zoology of the Voyage of the 'Uranie,'' p. 585, and figured in pl. lxxxvi, fig. 2, looks like a fragment of *Stephanomia amphitridis*. Of the species described as *Stephanomiæ* in the 'Zoology of the Voyage of the Astrolabe,' *S. helianthus* and *S. melo* are *Athorybiæ; S. hippopoda* is a *Hippopodius; S. triangularis* is an *Agalma; S. imbricata, S. heptacantha,* and *S. tectum* apparently belong to the same genus; *S. foliacea* is very like a true *Stephanomia (mihi); S. alveolata* is pretty clearly a *Forskalia;* and *S. cirrhosa* would seem to be part either of a *Halistemma* or of a *Stephanomia*.

*Genus* TETRAGONUM.

*T. Belzoni*, Quoy and Gaimard. 'Voy. de l'Uranie,' Zoologie, p. 579.

Probably the detached distal nectocalyx of an *Abyla*.

# NOTE ON THE TERMINOLOGY OF THE ORGANS OF THE HYDROZOA.

Since I have strongly acknowledged the value of Professor Allman's contributions to our knowledge of the *Hydrozoa*, and since I have gladly made use of certain of the terms which he has invented (e. g. *gonophore*), I feel bound to assign my reasons for not adopting the whole of his terminology.

The transition between what Professor Allman terms sporosacs and his "*Medusæ*" is so gradual, that I know not where the line of demarcation is to be drawn between the two. If the title of *sporosac*, however, could be applied to such reproductive organs as those of *Hydractinia*, which are simple sacs without a trace of medusoid structure, I think the term would be useful.

"Ectotheca" and "blastostyle" appear to me to be very good terms when applied to the central axis and the capsule of such "compound gonophores" as those of *Laomedea;* but I think that when the stalk of the gonophores of *Tubularia* (with which the stem of similar organs in the *Physophoridæ* is homologous) is also called blastostyle, the same name is applied to different things. The stem of the "gonoblastidium" of the *Physophorid* contains, I apprehend, the representatives of both the blastostyle and the ectotheca of *Laomedea*.

Again, the "generative polypes" of *Hydractinia* are surely homologous with the stalks of the gonophores in *Tubularia;* but to these, and, as I think, with justice, Professor Allman does not apply the term "blastostyle."

When we know a medusiform body to be simply the detached reproductive organ of a hydrozoon, it seems to be better to avoid all chance of confounding it with a truly independent organism. I have, therefore, abstained from using the word "*Medusa*," except in the sense defined at p. 21; and for me Professor Allman's *Medusæ* are medusiform gonophores.

Finally, the term manubrium should, I think, be restricted to the central polype-like sac of a medusiform gonophore, which is surely the homologue of the whole sporosac of *Hydractinia*, and not of its central cavity only.

# BIBLIOGRAPHY.

The following are the full titles of the books and detached papers cited in the foregoing work, arranged alphabetically according to the names of the authors:

ALLMAN. 'On the Anatomy and Physiology of *Cordylophora*;' 'Philosophical Transactions;' 1853 (with plates).

'On the Structure of the Reproductive Organs of certain Hydroid Polypes;' 'Proceedings of the Royal Society of Edinburgh,' Session 1857-8.

'Additional Observations on the Morphology of the Reproductive Organs in the Hydroid Polypes;' Ibid., 1858.

DE BLAINVILLE. 'Manuel d'Actinologie ou de Zoophytologie' (with an Atlas of plates); 1834.

BORY DE ST. VINCENT. 'Voyage dans les quatre principales Iles des Mers d'Afrique;' 1804 (with a 'Collection de Planches').

BOSC. 'Histoire naturelle des Vers' (with figures); 1802.

BUSCH. 'Beobachtungen über Anatomie und Entwickelung einiger worbelloser Seethiere' (with plates); 1851.

CHAMISSO and EYSENHARDT. 'De Animalibus quibusdam e Classe Vermium Linneana' (cum tabulis xi, æneæ pictis); 'Nova Acta physico-medica Academiæ Cæsareæ Leopoldino Carolinæ Naturæ Curiosorum,' tomi decimi, pars secunda; 1821.

CHIAJ, DELLE. 'Memorie su la storia et notomia degli animali senza vertebre del Regno di Napoli;' 1823—1829; 4 vols. (with plates).

'Descrizione e Notomia degli Animali invertebrati della Sicilia citeriore osservati vivi negli anni 1822—1830;' 1841—1844.

(Six volumes of text, and two of plates.)

COSTA. 'Note sur l'appareil vasculaire de la Velelle (*Armenistarium Velella*);' 'Annales des Sciences Naturelles,' serie deuxième, Zoologie, tom. xvi; 1841.

CUVIER. 'Le Regne Animal;' 1817.

EDWARDS, MILNE. 'Observations sur la Structure et les Fonctions de quelques Zoophytes, Mollusques, et Crustacés des Côtes de la France' (Lues à l'Acad. des Sciences, Aôut 16, 1841); 'Annales des Sciences Naturelles,' deuxième serie, Zoologie, tome xvi, 1841.

EICHWALD. 'Observationes nonnullæ circa fabricam *Physaliæ*;' 'Mémoires de l'Académie Impériale des Sciences de St. Petersbourg,' t. ix; 1824.

ESCHSCHOLZ. 'System der Acalephen, eine ausführliche Beschreibung aller Medusenartigen Strahl-thiere,' mit 16 Kupfertapeln; 1829.

EYSENHARDT. 'Zur Anatomie und Naturgeschichte der Quallen:' 1, Von dem *Rhizostoma Cuvierii* (Lam.); 2, Ueber die Seeblasen; 'Nova Acta physico-medica Academiæ Cæsareæ Leopoldino Carolinæ Naturæ Curiosorum,' tom. x, pars secunda; 1821.

FORSKAL. 'Descriptiones Animalium, Avium, Amphibiorum, Piscium, Insectorium, Vermium, quæ in itinere orientali, observavit Petrus Forskål,' post-mortem auctoris edidit Carsten Niebuhr; 1775.

'Icones rerum Naturalium;' 1776.

GEGENBAUR. 'Zur Lehre vom Generations-wechsel,' (with a plate); 1854.

'Beiträge zur naheren Kenntniss der Schwimmpolypen, (with plates);' Siebold and Kölliker's 'Zeitschrift für Wiss. Zoologie;' 1854.

HOLLARD. 'Recherches sur l'Organisation des Velelles,' (présentées à l'Académie des Sciences, le 2e Octobre, 1843); 'Annales des Sciences Naturelles,' troisième serie, Zoologie, tome iii; 1845, (with figures).

HUXLEY. 'On the Anatomy of *Physalia*;' 'Proceedings of the Linnean Society;' 1848.

'Observations upon the Anatomy of the *Diphydæ* and the Unity of Organization of the *Diphydæ* and *Physophoridæ*;' 'Proceedings of the Linnean Society;' 1849.

'On the Anatomy and Affinities of the Medusæ,' (with plates); 'Philosophical Transactions;' 1849.

'Report on the Structure of the *Acalephæ*;' 'Reports of the British Association;' 1851.

'Ueber die Sexual Organe der Diphyden und Physophoriden,' (with figures); 'Müller's Archiv;' 1851.

HYNDMAN. 'Note on the Occurrence of the Genus *Diphya* on the Coast of Ireland,' (with figures); 'Annals of Natural History,' vii; 1841.

KÖLLIKER. 'Die Schwimmpolypen oder Siphonophoren von Messina,' (with plates); 1853.

KROHN. 'Notiz über die anwesenheit eigenthümlichen Luftkanäle bei *Velella* und *Porpita*;' Wiegmann's 'Archiv für Naturgeschichte,' 14r Jahrgung, B. i; 1848.

LAMARCK. 'Histoire Naturelle des Animaux sans Vertèbres,' 2d ed.; 1835—1845.

LEACH. 'Tuckey, Narrative of an Expedition to Explore the River Zaire;' 1818.

LESSON. 'Duperrey, Voyage autour du Monde sur la corvette La Coquille executé pendant les années 1822—1825,' Zoologie, (with plates).

'Centurie Zoologique,' (with plates); 1830.

'Histoire Naturelle des Zoophytes Acalèphes,' (with plates); 1843.

LESUEUR. 'Mémoire sur quelques nouvelles espèces d'Animaux Mollusques et Radiaires, recueillies dans le Méditerranée près de Nice;' 'Journal de Physique,' t. lxxvi; 1813.

LEUCKART. 'Ueber den Bau der Physalien und Siphonophoren;' Siebold and Kölliker's 'Zeitschrift für Wiss. Zoologie,' Bd. iii; 1851.

'Zoologische Untersuchungen,' 1st Heft, (with plates); 1853.

(Quoted under 'Leuckart, Z. U.')

'Zur näheren Kenntniss der Siphonophoren von Nizza,' (with plates); 1854.

(Quoted under 'Leuckart, Z. N. K.')

MEYEN. 'Beiträge zur Zoologie;' 'Nova Acta physico-medica Academiæ Cæsareæ Leopoldino Carolinæ Naturæ Curiosorum,' tom. xvi, Supp. I; 1834.

MÜLLER, JOHANNES. 'Ueber eine eigenthümliche Meduse des Mittelmeeres und ihren Jugendzustand;' Müller's 'Archiv;' 1851.

OLFERS, VON. 'Ueber die grosse Seeblase (*Physalia Arethusa*) und die Gattung der Seeblasen im Allgemeinen;' 'Abhandlungen der Königlichen Akademie der Wissenschaften zu Berlin;' 1831.

OTTO. 'Beschreibung einiger neuen Mollusken und Zoophyten,' (with plates); 'Nova Acta Akad. Leopol. Cæs. Nat. Cur.,' t. xi; 1823.

PERON. 'Voyage de découvertes aux Terres Australes;' 1807.

PHILIPPI. 'Ueber den Bau der Physophoren und eine neue Art derselben, *Physophora tetrasticha;*' Müller's 'Archiv für Anatomie, Physiologie, &c.;' 1843.

QUATREFAGES, DE. 'Mémoire sur l'organisation des Physalies;' 'Annales des Sciences Naturelles;' 1853.

QUOY and GAIMARD. 'Freycinet, Voyage autour du Monde sur les corvettes L'Uranie et La Physicienne, fait pendant les années 1817 à 1820,' Zoologie, (with plates); 1824.

'Observations Zoologiques faits à bord de L'Astrolabe dans le Détroit de Gibraltar,' (with figures); 'Annales des Sciences Naturelles;' 1827.

'Dumont D'Urville, Voyage de la corvette L'Astrolabe, executé pendant les années 1826—1829,' Zoologie, (with plates); 1830—1834.

SARS. 'Fauna littoralis Norvegiæ,' (with plates); 1846.

VOGT. 'Recherches sur quelques Animaux inférieurs de la Méditerranée;' 'Mémoires de l'Institut National Genevois,' tome 1er, (with plates); 1853.

WILL. 'Horæ Tergestinæ, oder Beschreibung und Anatomie der im Herbste 1843, bei Triest beobachteten Akalephen,' (with plates); 1844.

# DESCRIPTION OF THE PLATES.

---

The letters have the same signification in Plates I to XI. The short ruled lines indicate the natural sizes of the objects.

    *a.* Cœnosarc (κοινὸς, common; σάρξ, flesh).

    *b.* Polypite; $b^1$, villi; $b^2$, pyloric valve.

    *c.* Tentacle; $c^1$, pedicle of the sacculus (reniform body in *Physalia*); $c^2$, involucrum; $c^3$, sacculus; $c^4$, filament; $c^5$, median lobe; $c^6$, basal sac; $c^7$, muscular band.

    *d.* Somatocyst (σῶμα, body; κυστις, a vesicle).

    *e.* Pneumatophore (πνεῦμα, air; φορέω, I bear).

    *f.* Pneumatocyst (πνεῦμα, κυστις); $f^1$, the endoderm reflected over it; $f^2$, the cellular processes of this layer of the endoderm; $f^5$, the mesentery-like lamellæ connecting the pneumatocyst with the pneumatophore; $f^6$, the air contained in the pneumatocyst.

    *g.* Nectocalyx (νηκτὸς, having the power to swim; καλύξ, a cup); $g^1$, the proximal nectocalyx of a Calycophoridan; $g^2$, the distal nectocalyx; $g^3$, the nectocalycine duct and canals, both radiating and circular, and in gonocalyces as well as in nectocalyces; $g^4$, the nectosac; $g^5$, its aperture, surrounded by its membranous valve; $g^6$, the hydrœcium (οικος, a house) of the proximal and the hydrœcial canal of the distal nectocalyx.

    *h.* Hydrocysts.

    *k.* Hydrophyllium; $k^1$, phyllocyst (φυλλον, a leaf).

    *l.* Gonocalyx (γόνος, progeny).

    *m.* Gonoblastidium (βλάστη, a bud).

    *n.* Androphore; $n^1$, its calyx; $n^2$, its manubrium; $n^3$, spermatozoa.

    *o.* Gynophore; $o^1$, calyx; $o^2$, manubrium; $o^3$, ova.

    *x.* Endoderm.

    *y.* Ectoderm.

# PLATE I.

Fig.

1. *Diphyes dispar*, complete.

1 *a*. An anterior view of the distal end of its proximal nectocalyx.

1 *b*. A lateral view of the distal nectocalyx.

1 *c*. A posterior view of the same object.

1 *d*. A young proximal nectocalyx.

1 *e*. A polypite, with its hydrophyllium and tentacles, much magnified.

2. *Diphyes appendiculata*, complete.

2 *a*. A front view of the distal end of its proximal nectocalyx.

2 *b*. A posterior view of its distal nectocalyx; the bristle ($g^6 g^6$) is supposed to be passed through the hydrœcial canal.

2 *c*. The hydrophyllium of the same species.

3. *Diphyes Chamissonis*? a lateral view of the proximal nectocalyx.

3 *a*. An enlarged view of the distal end of this nectocalyx.

3 *b*. The hydrophyllium.

4. *Diphyes mitra*? a lateral view of the proximal nectocalyx.

4 *a*. A front view of the same.

4 *b*. A polypite, with a gonophore, and a possibly imperfect hydrophyllium.

PLATE I.

Fig 1

DIPHYES.

# PLATE II.

Fig.

1. *Abyla bassensis,* complete ; a lateral view.

1 *a.* The same, so placed as to show the posterior side of the distal nectocalyx.

1 *b.* The proximal nectocalyx from in front and above.

1 *c.* The polypite, with its hydrophyllium.

2. *Abyla pentagona,* complete ; a lateral view.

2 *a.* The distal nectocalyx from behind.

2 *b.* The proximal nectocalyx enlarged, from one side.

2 *c.* A young distal nectocalyx of the same.

2 *d.* A polypite, with its hydrophyllium and a gonophore.

2 *e.* The hydrophyllium detached.

3. *Abyla Vogtii,* the proximal nectocalyx ; an antero-lateral view.

3 *a.* The same ; a postero-lateral view.

3 *b.* A polypite, with its hydrophyllium and gonocalyx.

3 *c.* A young gonophore magnified.

PLATE II

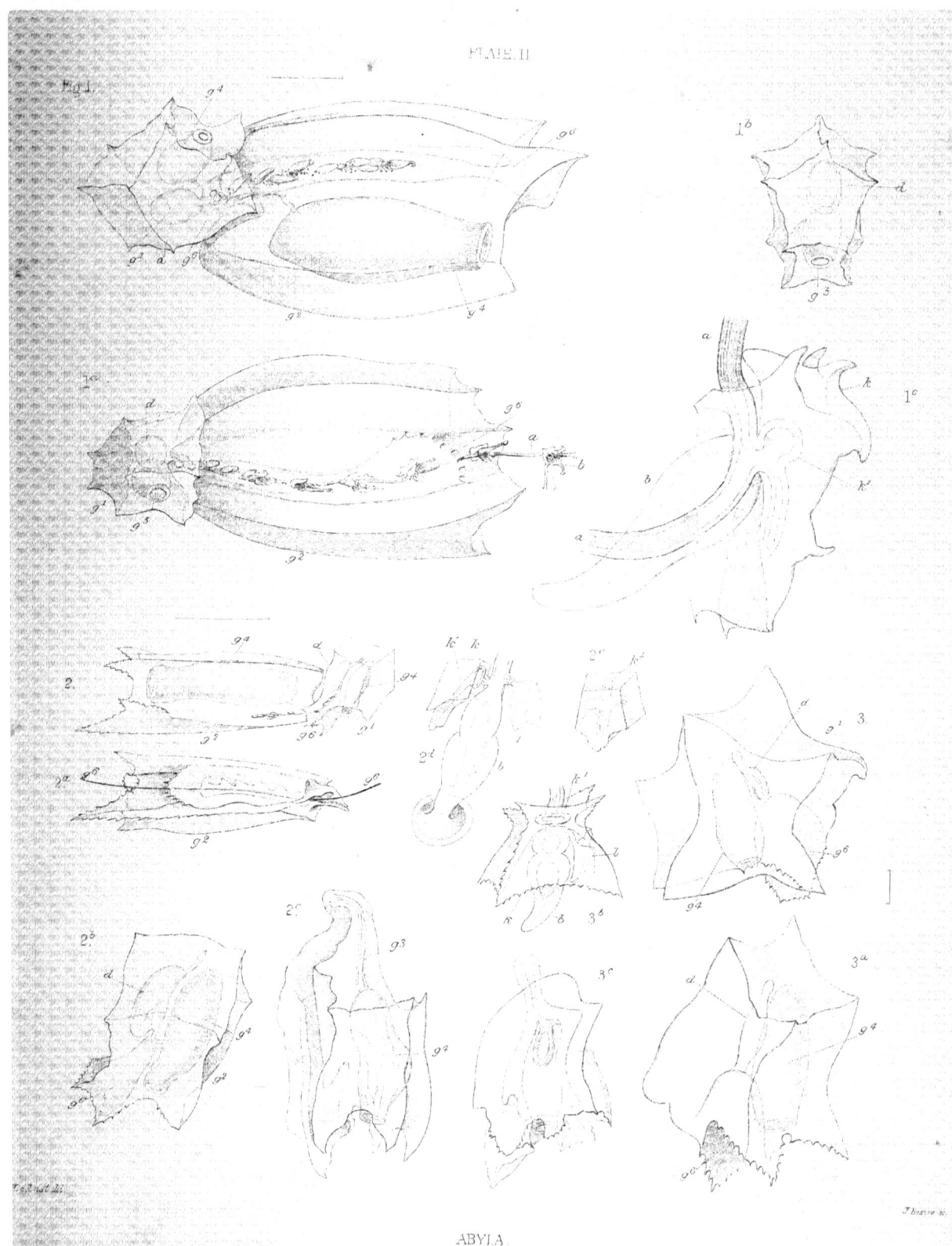

ABYLA.

# PLATE III.

Fig.

1. *Abyla trigona,* complete ; a lateral view.

1 *a.* The proximal nectocalyx from in front.

1 *b.* The same, viewed laterally.

1 *c.* The distal nectocalyx from the left side.

1 *d.* The distal end of the same.

1 *e.* A polypite, with its hydrophyllium.

2. *Abyla Leuckartii;* a lateral view of the proximal nectocalyx.

2 *a.* The same, viewed from behind.

2 *b.* The same, viewed from in front.

3. *Praya Diphyes?*   (Compare Pl. XII, fig. 2.)   A lateral view of a nectocalyx.

3 *a.* An anterior view of the same.

4. *Sphæronectes Köllikeri,* complete ; a lateral view.

5. *Galeolaria filiformis.*   (Compare Pl. XII, fig. 1.)   A lateral view of the distal nectocalyx.

5 *a.* A posterior view of the same.

6. *Eudoxia Lessonii,* complete ; a lateral view.

6 *a.* The distal end of the gonocalyx.

7. *Eudoxia Bojani,* complete.

7 *a.* The hydrophyllium detached.

PLATE III.

Fig 1

ABYLA _ PRAYA _ SPHÆRONECTES _ GALEOLARIA _ EUDOXIA.

# PLATE IV.

Fig.

1. *Eudoxoides sagittata,* two views.

2, 2 *a,* 2 *b. Aglaismoides Eschscholzii,* in different positions.

3. *Aglaismoides elongata,* complete ; but with only a small gonophore.

3 *a.* The hydrophyllium alone.

3 *b.* A complete specimen, with two large androphores and a small gynophore.

4, 4 *a. Sphenoides australis.*

4 *b.* One of its detached free swimming gynophores.

4*. Possibly young specimens of this species.

5, 5 *a. Cuboides vitreus.*

5 *b.* One of its gynophores.

6, 6 *a,* 6 *b.* Different views of *Enneagonoides Quoyi.*

PLATE IV.

EUDOXOIDES_ AGLAISMOIDES_ SPHENOIDES_ CUBOIDES_ ENNEAGONOIDES.

PLATE VI.

Fig.I.N.S.

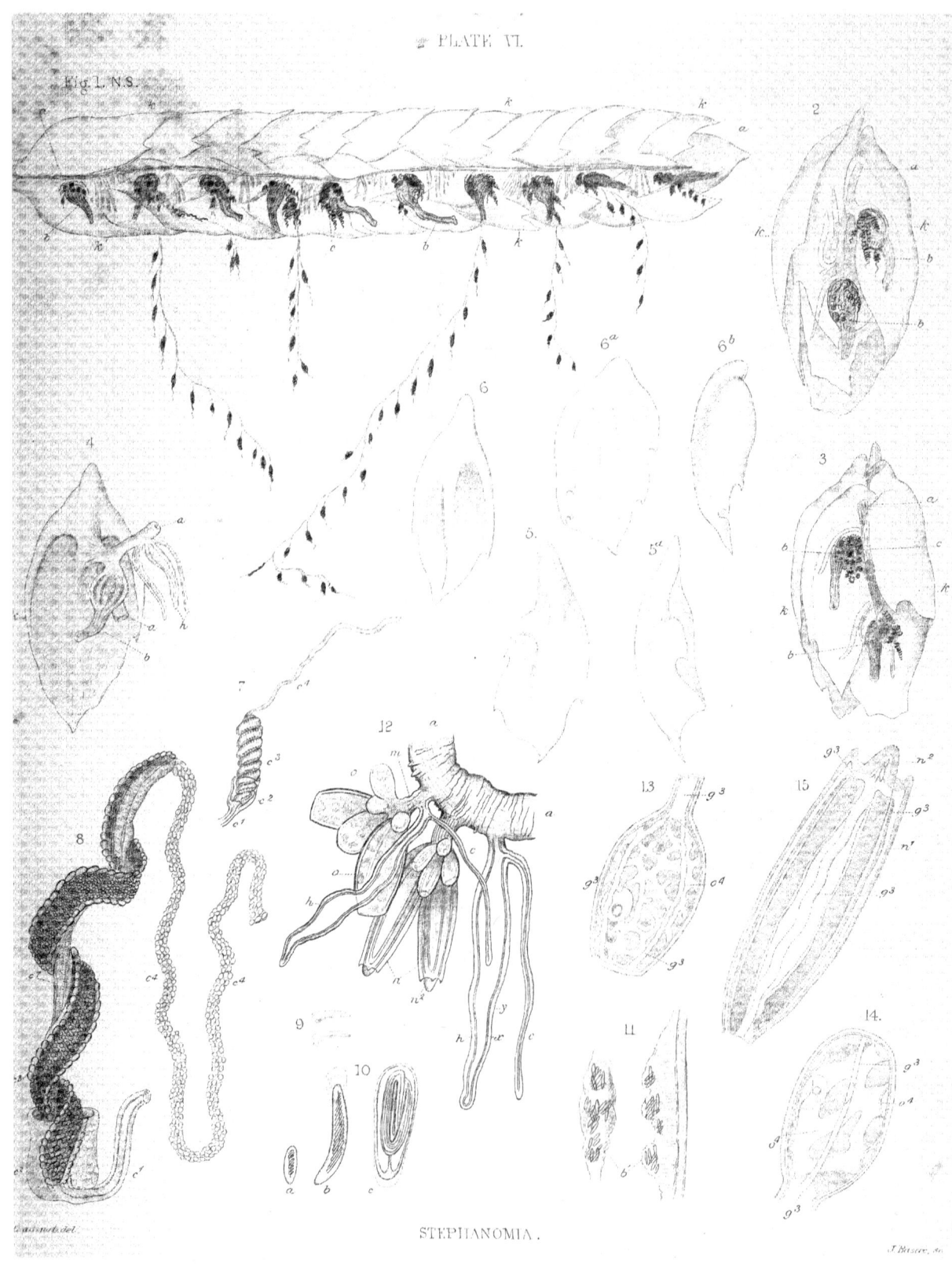

STEPHANOMIA.

# PLATE VI.

Fig.

1. *Stephanomia Amphitridis.* A fragment taken on the east coast of Australia.

2, 3. A portion of this slightly enlarged, and viewed in different aspects.

4. A single hydrophyllium, with a polypite, hydrocysts, and part of the cœnosarc.

5, 5 *a*, 6 *a*, 6 *b*. Two views of other hydrophyllia.

6. Another hydrophyllium.

7. The end of one of the tentacular branches, magnified.

8. The same more highly magnified.

9. The " peculiar bodies" mentioned at p. 73.

10. Thread-cells.

11. Villi.

12. Part of the cœnosarc, with hydrocysts and gonoblastidia.

13, 14. Gynophores with their single ova.

15. An androphore.

PLATE VI.

STEPHANOMIA.

# PLATE VII.

Fig.

1. *Agalma breve*, complete; magnified.    Taken on the east coast of Australia.

2. Its pneumatophore.

3. A fully formed and (figs. 4 and 5) young nectocalyces.

6. A young hydrophyllium.

7. The end of a tentacular branch.

8. Part of the cœnosarc, with hydrocysts and gonoblastidia.

9, 10. Young and fully formed gynophores.

11. An androphore.

12. A young *Agalma*.

PLATE. VII.

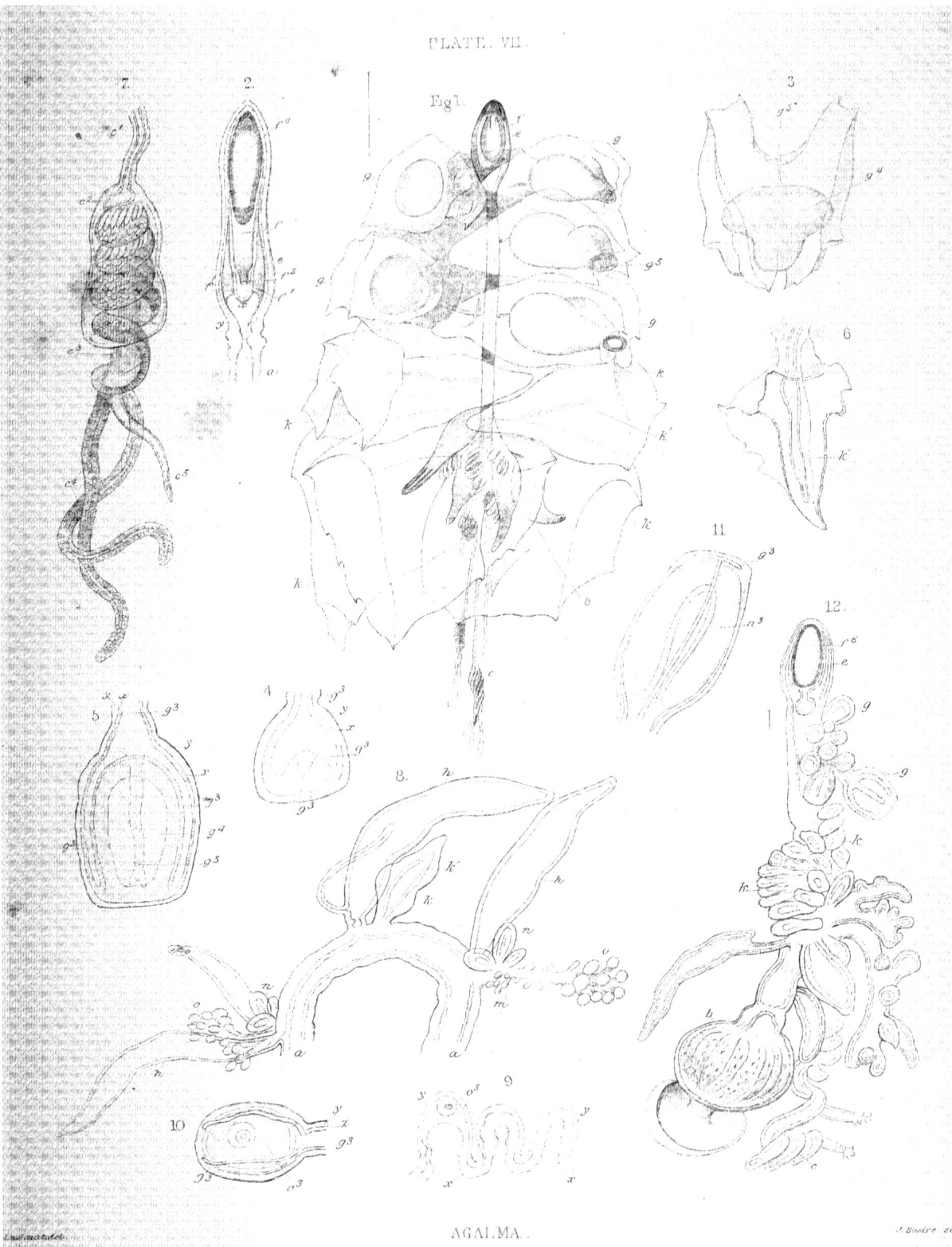

AGALMA.

## PLATE VIII.

Fig.

1. A sketch of *Physophora* — ?

2. A young *Physophora* — ?

3 exhibits the mode of connexion of a hydrocyst with the dilated distal end of the cœnosarc.

4. The pneumatophore.

5—8. Successive stages of the tentacular branches.

9. A thread-cell.

10 *a*—12. Successive stages and various views of the nectocalyces.

13. *Rhizophysa filiformis.*

14. Its pneumatophore.

15. One of the cellular processes developed from the reflected layer of the endoderm.

16. A polypite, with its tentacle.

17. Part of a tentacle, with its lateral branches.

18. Part of the proximal end of such a tentacle, with its budding branches.

19. A villus.

20. Part of a tentacular branch.

PLATE VIII.

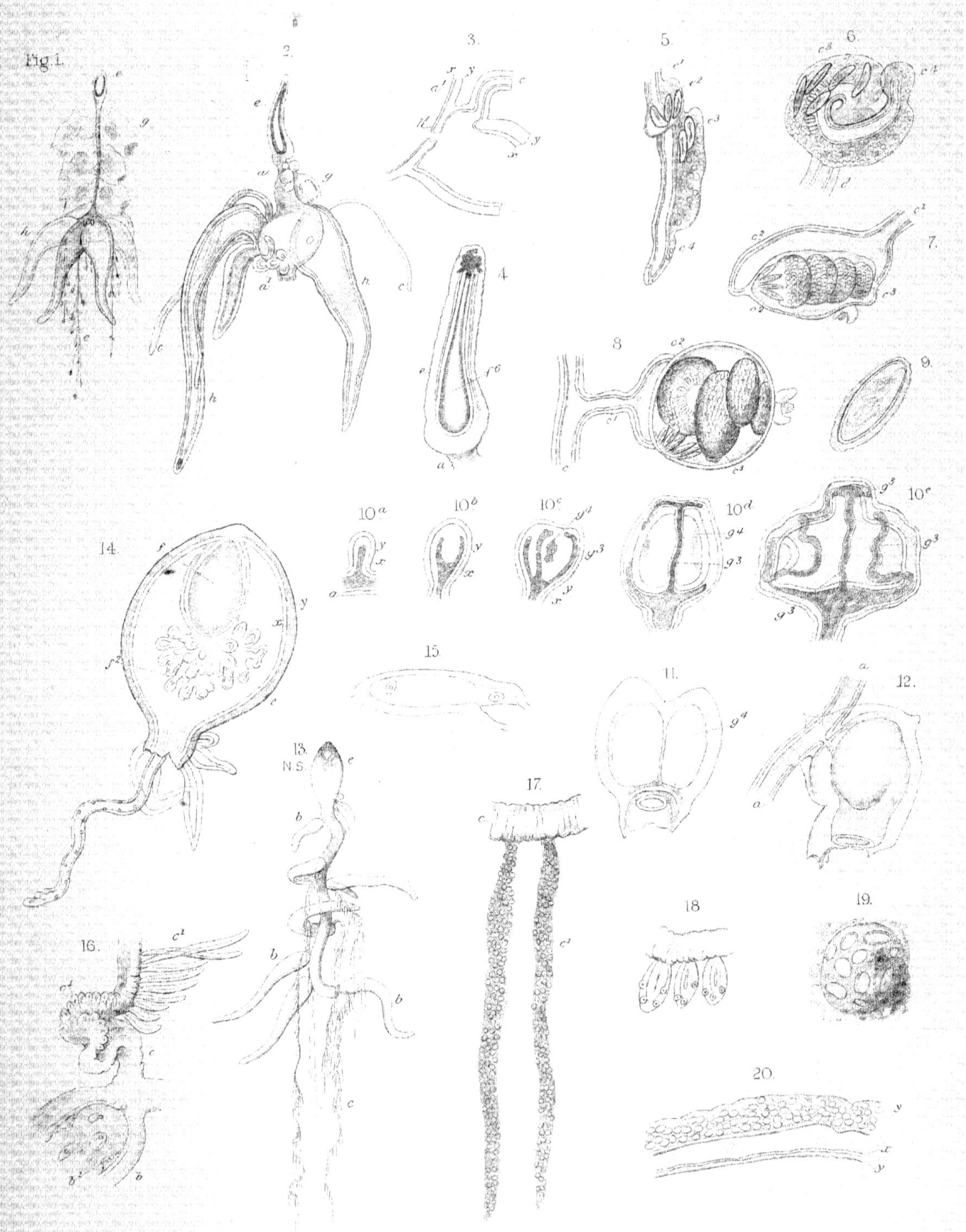


PHYSOPHORA. RHIZOPHYSA.

T.H.H. ad nat del.

J. Basire sc.

# PLATE IX.

Fig.

1. *Athorybia rosacea* ; a lateral view.

2. The same magnified, and viewed from above.

3. The same deprived of most of its hydrophyllia, and viewed from above.

4, 5. Hydrophyllia.

6. A polypite.

7, 8. Some of its villi.

9 *a—f*. The ends of the tentacular branches in various stages of development.

10, 11. Large and small thread-cells.

12. A gonoblastidium, with androphores, gynophores, and hydrocysts.

13. Gynophores attached to their common stem.

14, 15. Similar bodies enlarged, and viewed separately.

PLATE IX.

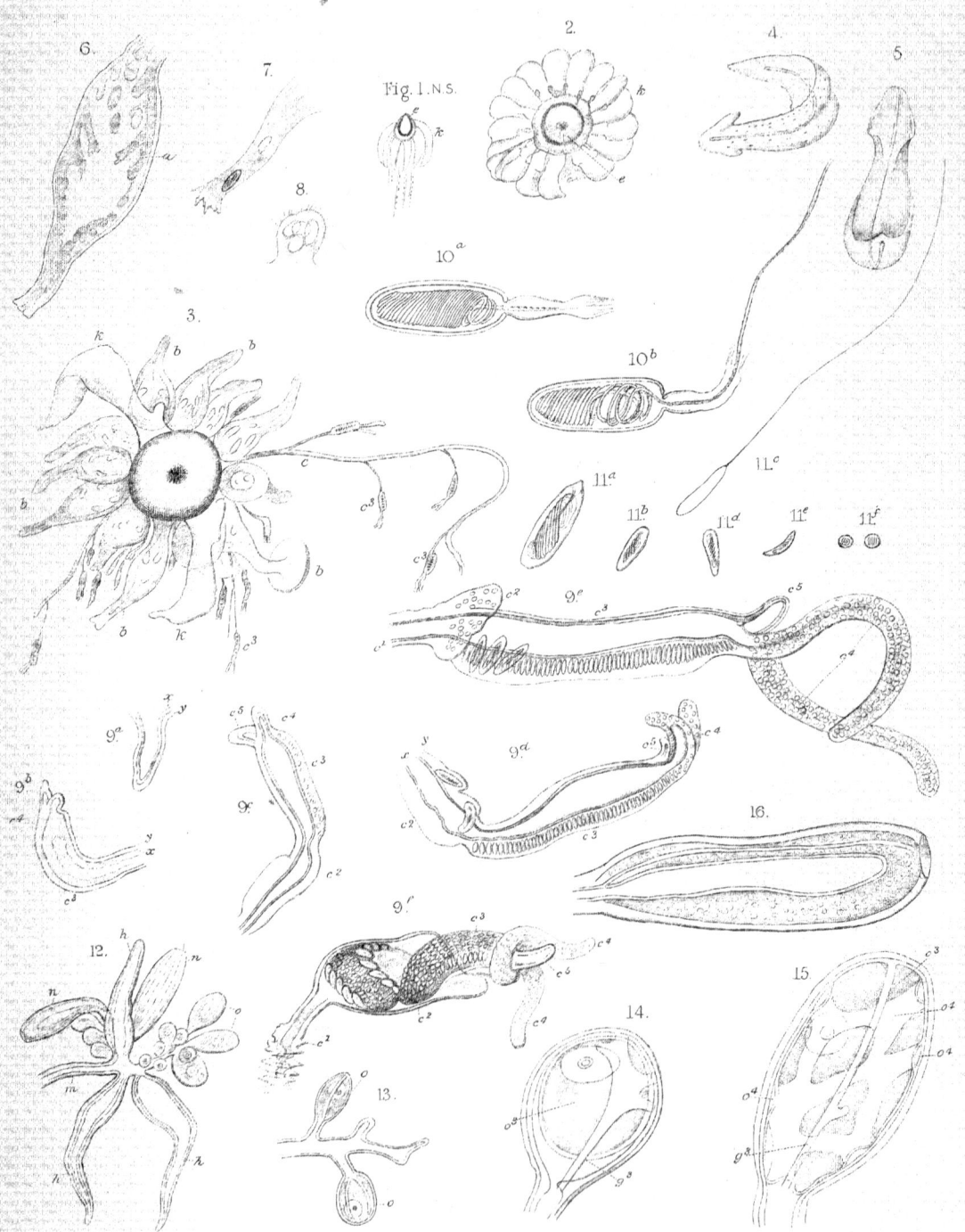

ATHORYBIA.

# PLATE X.

Fig.

1. A very young *Physalia*, with only a single polypite and tentacle.

2. A somewhat older specimen.

3. Opening of the pneumatocyst in a young specimen.

4. A polypite.

5—7. Various views of villi.

8. Some of the elevations which cover the outer surface of the lip of the polypite.

9, 10. Young polypites.

11. A tentacle, with its basal sac.

11 *a*. Part of the proximal end of that tentacle ; 11 *b*, a young tentacle.

12. A portion of the distal moiety of this tentacle, exhibiting the reniform enlargements ; 12 *a*, 12 *b*, the thread-cells contained in them.

13. One of the " velvety processes" magnified.

13 *a*. A similar process of the natural size ; and 13 *b*, somewhat magnified.

14 *a—d*. Successive stages of the androphore ; 14 *e*, young spermatic elements.

15 *a—e*. Successive stages of the gynophores.

PLATE X.

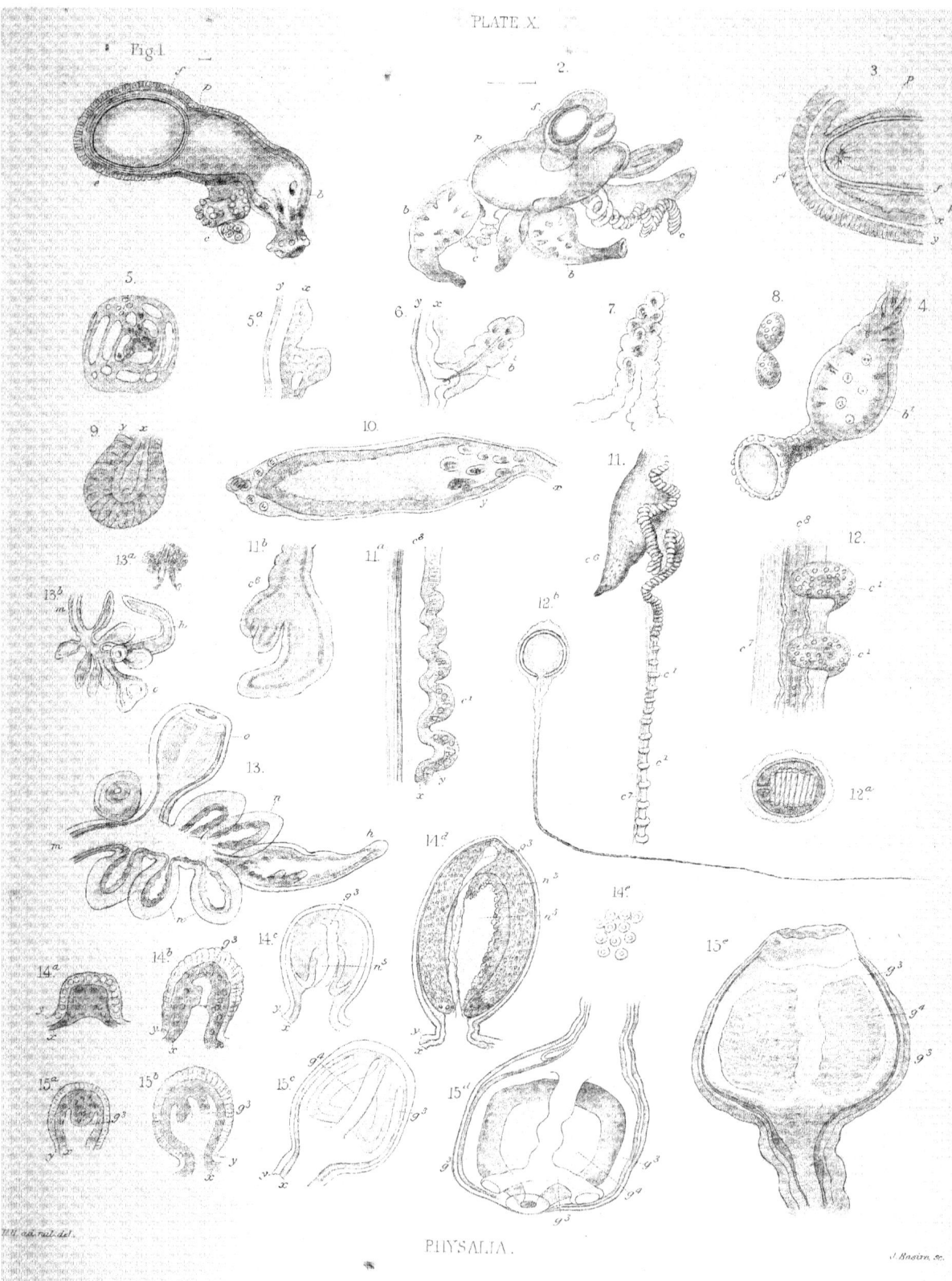

PHYSALIA.

# PLATE XI.

Fig.

1. Disc of a *Velella* viewed from above, and having the crest cut off.
2. A vertical section of the pneumatocyst.   It has been accidently inverted.
3. A tentacle.
3 *a*. A part of the crest, much magnified.
4. A small or gonoblastidial polypite.
5. A lateral view of a young gonophore.
6. A terminal view of the same.
7. A more advanced gonophore.
8, 8 *a*. Detached gonophores.   (See Pl. XII, fig. 13.)
9. A very young *Velella* (*Rataria*).
10. Its pneumatocyst.
11. Part of its disc.
12. A portion of its crest.
13. A portion of the disc of a larger specimen.
14. A still more advanced specimen.

PLATE XI.

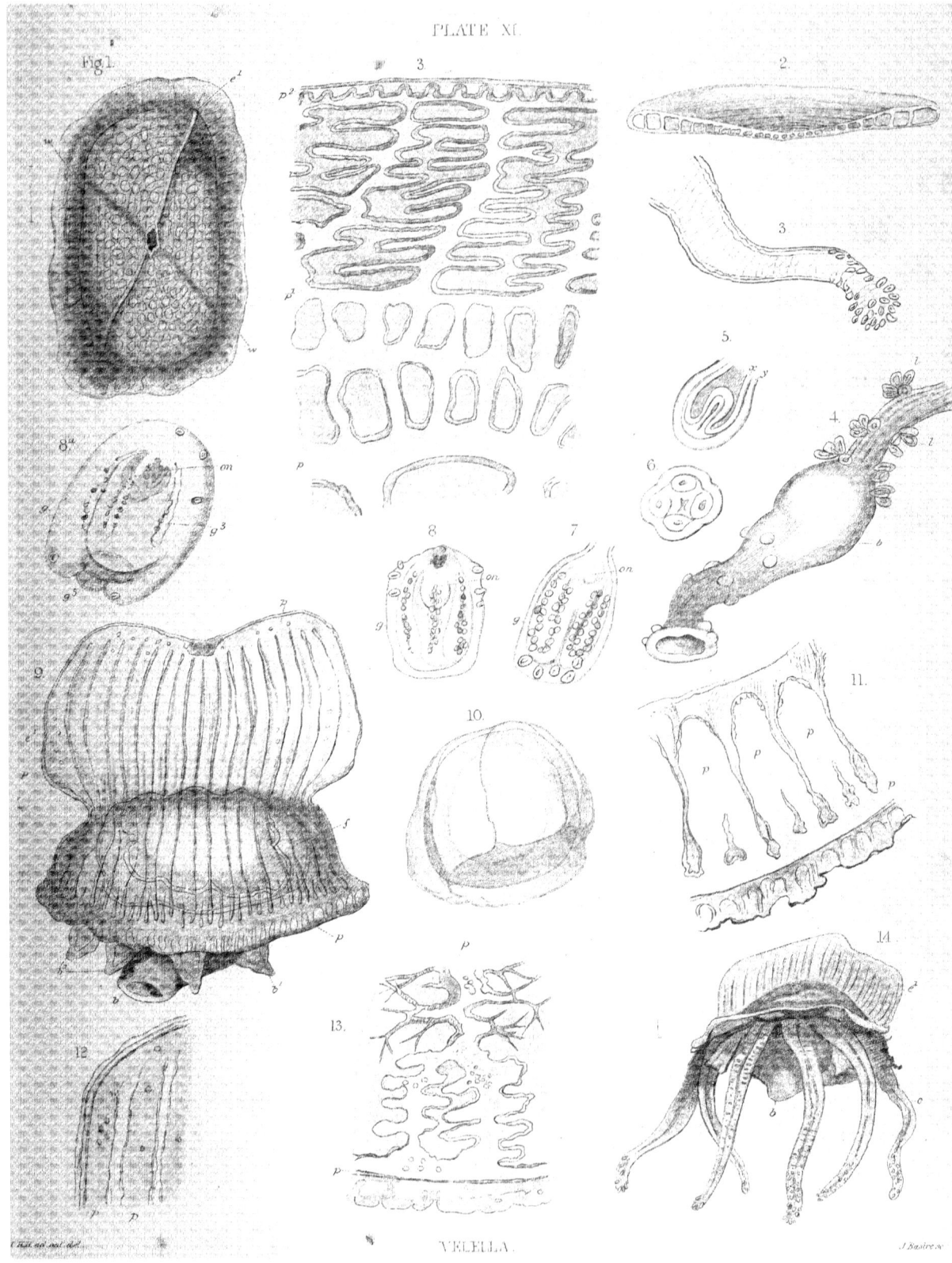

Fig 1.

VELELLA.

PLATE XII.

Fig.

1. *Galeolaria filiformis*, magnified (after Gegenbaur). *A*, proximal, *B*, distal nectocalyx; *a*, somatocyst; *b*, nectocalycine canals; *c*, aperture of the proximal, *d*, of the distal nectosac; *e*, valvular projection at the aperture of the distal nectosac; *f*, cœnosarc, with the polypites; *h*, nectosac of the proximal, *i*, of the distal nectocalyx.

2. *Praya maxima*, slightly enlarged (after Gegenbaur). *A, B*, the nectocalyces; *a, a*, their nectosacs; *b*, origin of the cœnosarc, *d*; *c′, c′*, nectocalycine canals; *e*, polypites, with their hydrophyllia and tentacles.

3. A single zöoid viewed laterally (after Gegenbaur). *a*, hydrophyllium; *b*, gonocalyx and manubrium; *c*, polypite; *d*, tentacle.

4. *Hippopodius neapolitanus* (after Kölliker). *a*, perfect, *b*, undeveloped, nectocalyces; *c*, nectosacs; *d*, cœnosarc, with six undeveloped polypites; *e*, fully developed polypites, near which gonophores, which are omitted, were seated; *f*, tentacles.

5. The proximal end of the cœnosarc, with some nectocalyces still attached (after Leuckart).

6. *Vogtia pentacantha* (after Kölliker). *a*, nectocalyces; *b*, polypites; *c*, androphore; *d*, gynophore; *e*, tentacles.

7. Different views of the nectocalyces. *a*, aperture of the nectosac.

8. *Apolemia uvaria* (after Gegenbaur). The proximal end of the hydrosoma, about three fifths of the natural size. *a*, pneumatophore; *b*, hydrocysts among the nectocalyces; *c*, cœnosarc; *d*, hydrophyllia; *e*, hydrocyst; *f*, tentacles; *g*, polypites.

9. *Halistemma rubrum* (after Kölliker); less than the natural size. *a*, pneumatophore; *b*, young nectocalyces; *c*, fully formed nectocalyces; *d, e*, cœnosarc; *f*, hydrophyllia; *g*, polypites; *h*, hydrocysts; *i*, tentacles of the polypites; *k*, tentacles of the hydrocysts.

9 *a*. The end of a tentacular branch. *a*, the pedicle; *b*, the sacculus; *c*, the filament.

10. *Forskalia Edwardsii* (after Kölliker). *a*, pneumatophore; *a′*, young nectocalyces; *b, b′, c*, cylinder formed by the nectocalyces, and traversed by the cœnosarc, *i*; *d*, polypites; *e*, hydrophyllia; *g*, hydrocysts; *h*, tentacles.

11. The end of one of the full-grown tentacular branches of *Physophora Philippii*, much magnified (after Kölliker). *a*, the pedicle; *b*, the outer layer of the involucrum; *c*, its middle, and *d*, its inner layer; *e*, its cavity, in which the sacculus lies, and which opens at *h*; *f*, the free end of the sacculus; *g*, a muscular band fastened to its other end.

12. *Physalia* (*utriculus*)? Natural size (original). *a*, crest; *b, c*, pneumatophore and cœnosarc; *d*, its processes; *e*, the polypites; *f*, velvetty masses; *g*, tentacles; *h*, tentacular sacs.

13. *Chrysomitra striata;* about twice the natural size (after Gegenbaur). *a*, gelatinous substance of the nectocalyx.

14. *Porpita mediterranea*, seen from below (after Kölliker). *a*, the central polypite; *b, b, b*, small or gonoblastidial polypites; *c, c*, small tentacles; *d, d*, large tentacles; *e*, marginal limb.

15. A perpendicular section through the same (after Kölliker). *a*, pneumatocyst, with its chambers; *a′*, central chamber; *b*, proximal layer of the hydrosoma; *c*, limb; *d*, small, *e*, large, tentacles; *f*, liver; *g*, central polypite; *h*, gonoblastidial polypites, with the gonophores, *h′*; *i*, renal organ, or white plate.

PLATE XII.

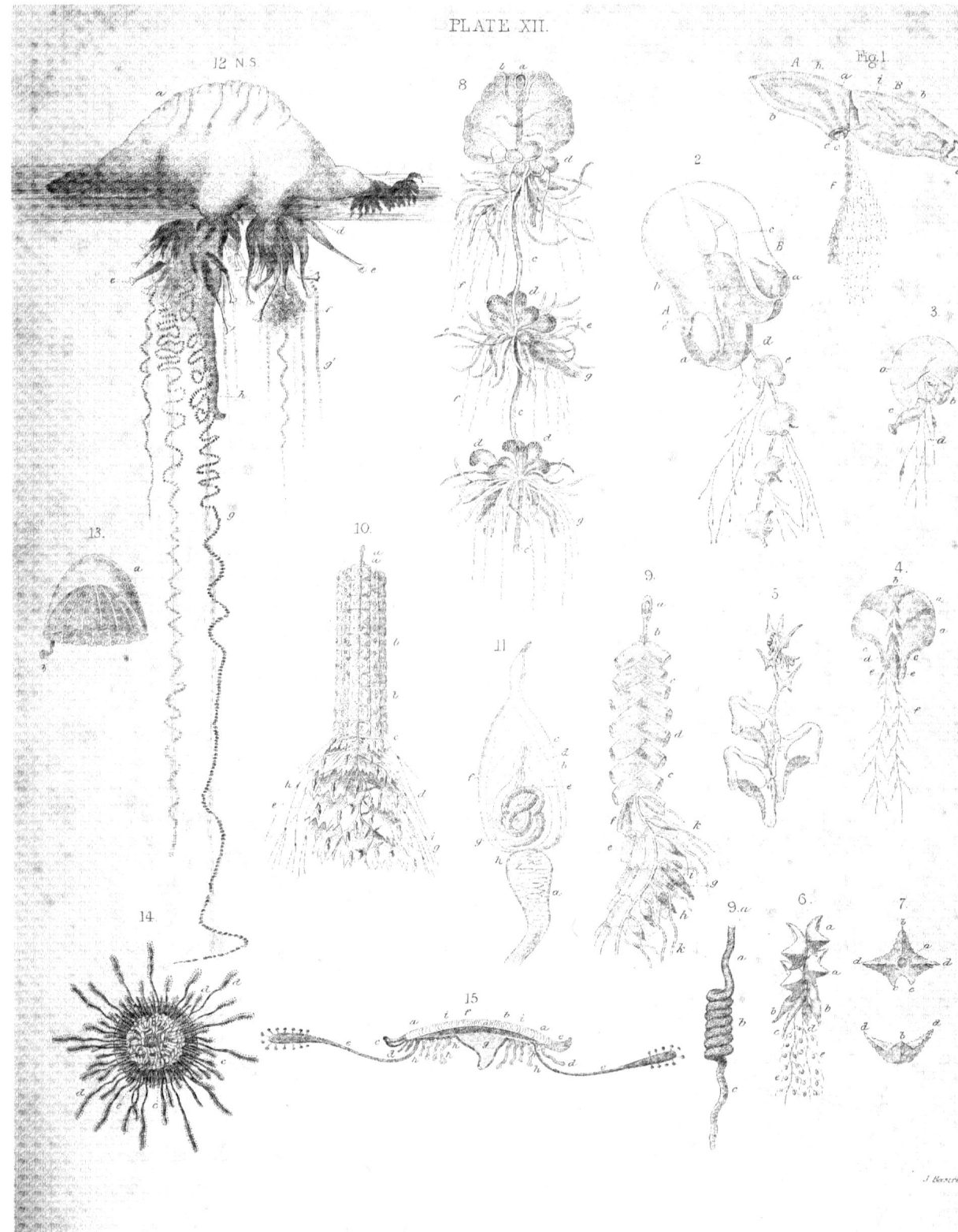

J. Basire

www.ingramcontent.com/pod-product-compliance
Lightning Source LLC
Chambersburg PA
CBHW080412290526
45791CB00008BA/2241